the
HOMEMADE
KITCHEN

the
HOMEMADE KITCHEN

RECIPES FOR COOKING WITH PLEASURE

ALANA CHERNILA

PHOTOGRAPHY BY JENNIFER MAY

CLARKSON POTTER/PUBLISHERS
New York

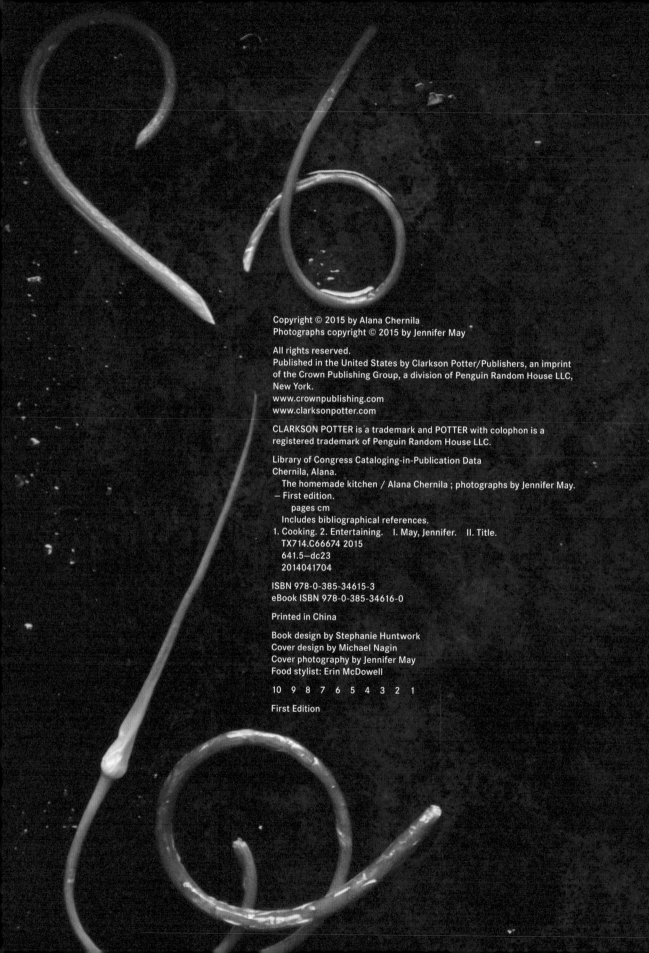

Published in the United States by Clarkson Potter/Publishers, an imprint
of the Crown Publishing Group, a division of Penguin Random House LLC,
New York.
www.crownpublishing.com
www.clarksonpotter.com

CLARKSON POTTER is a trademark and POTTER with colophon is a
registered trademark of Penguin Random House LLC.

Library of Congress Cataloging-in-Publication Data
Chernila, Alana.
  The homemade kitchen / Alana Chernila ; photographs by Jennifer May.
— First edition.
    pages cm
  Includes bibliographical references.
1. Cooking. 2. Entertaining.   I. May, Jennifer.   II. Title.
  TX714.C66674 2015
  641.5—dc23
  2014041704

ISBN 978-0-385-34615-3
eBook ISBN 978-0-385-34616-0

Printed in China

Book design by Stephanie Huntwork
Cover design by Michael Nagin
Cover photography by Jennifer May
Food stylist: Erin McDowell

10   9   8   7   6   5   4   3   2   1

First Edition

FOR JAMIE

›››››››››

'Tis the gift to be simple, 'tis the gift to be free
'Tis the gift to come down where we ought to be,
And when we find ourselves in the place just right,
'Twill be in the valley of love and delight.

—Joseph Brackett, *Shaker Dance Song*

CONTENTS

START
∵• where you are •∴

Let us speak honestly about why we cook, and who we are.

The world of home cooking can be a challenge to navigate. On one side, we're encouraged to eat real food—hopefully organic, GMO-free, local, non-toxic, and photo-worthy food, cooked at home, and blissfully enjoyed at a table with our family while we have device-free conversation. In the wake of current problems with our food system and their effect on our general health, these aren't new issues, they're just more urgent. On the other hand, all this focus on the redemptive power of home cooking can feel oppressive and judgmental. Even now as I'm finishing this book, a new wave of responses to cheerleaders of home cooking has appeared—essays like "Let's Stop Idealizing the Family Dinner," "Cooking Sucks," and "What If You Just Hate Making Dinner?"

I wouldn't say I live on one side of the discussion or the other; in fact, you'll find me in both camps, depending on the moment. Talk to me on a Saturday morning when I'm working at the farmers' market, and I'll convince you that a locally grown kohlrabi (cut into fries, roasted with olive oil and salt) can change your life. Walk into my kitchen when the whole family is grumpy with hunger and I can't figure out what's for dinner, and I'll pour you a glass of wine and admit that I, too, just hate making dinner. One perspective doesn't negate the other.

But the reality is that we all have to eat, and in my house, cooking is how we get there. Sometimes my husband, Joey, cooks, and sometimes my older daughter, Sadie, takes a dinner night, but because I tend to do it well and happily, and I'm usually home to put the chicken in the oven, the cooking often falls to me.

So why do I cook? To eat, of course. But there's more to it. And that's where this book comes in.

I cook because feeding myself is the one basic, essential, daily requirement that I can do entirely in my own way. Even more, when I come into the kitchen to figure out how to make a great loaf of bread or a creamy batch of yogurt and then *I actually do it*, the benefits go far beyond the buttered toast or yogurt for that week's lunches. Not only do I get to eat what I've made, I also get to delight in my ability to create it. Small as the act might be, having the power to feed myself and my family makes me feel optimistic about my own resources to create what I want in life. This optimism isn't limited to the kitchen; with practice I can extend my optimism beyond the kitchen into my community and even my government. I can choose, day by day, to pay attention to the small moments, to love the work of life, and ultimately, to love the days I get to live it. When I create what I want to eat, the simple task becomes the seed that empowers me to live the life I want, and to create that, too. And when I cook and eat in a way that reflects how I want to live, it means I have the opportunity three (or more!) times a day to make decisions that help me live that life.

That's why I cook.

I am a brave home cook. However, I am not the kind who will always reliably feed you the most delicious meal you've had in ages, because if you are coming over, I have taken the opportunity to try something new. This courage leads to risk, and when the end result isn't looking quite right, this risk leads to panic, which I temper with wine. I love most of all to have crowds of people over for dinner, but especially in those moments, I am a slow chopper, a messy cook, and I can't stop talking. I relish high-quality ingredients, but sometimes just for the way their bottles line up on my counter, so I save the fancy containers and refill them with cheap supermarket olive oil and kosher salt. I am mildly disorganized, generally spontaneous, and prone to embarrass my two kids by breaking into a dance in the supermarket aisle. I'll state my opinions with great certainty, and just as easily change my mind. I have a garden I share with the groundhogs under the porch and the deer in the field beyond the yard, and I love it most in those few moments after dinner when all I want to do is to have my hands in the dirt. My garden grows as many weeds as vegetables, but toward the end of every summer it never fails to feed us lots of one thing or another.

As much as I love to read and hear about all the wild and expensive food experiences out there, it's the basic foods I love the most. Warm bowls of

> Why do I cook?
> To eat, of course.
> But there's more to it.
> And that's where this
> book comes in.

porridge with maple syrup and cream in the early morning before everyone's off to school. Homemade jam on toast, with a perfect balance of sweet and tang tailored to my taste. Onion soup that smells so good the neighbors ask, What is that amazing scent wafting down the block? Simple salads of greens, hard won and fresh picked from the planter on the back porch, tossed with creamy feta dressing. Chicken potpie on a night when we really need it. These are the foods that fuel us through our lives, and I love them most when I make them here, in my kitchen.

Homemade food is the opposite of perfection. It holds the stamp of its maker. It's salty because you wanted it that way, or it's made with the kind of tomato you chose to grow when poring over seed catalogs last January. This process of cooking at home is my window into what I want to create in life as a whole. I want to make it better, unique, delicious, stamped with my own love and work. It's going to be imperfect, and I'm good with that. I have a friend whose mother slips a lemon seed or two into everything she makes, "so they know it's homemade."

This book is a map for how, day in and day out, food shapes my life for the better, in the kitchen and beyond it. I hope it makes you hungry. I hope this book inspires you to feel more adventurous and optimistic in your own kitchen. But most of all, I hope this map leads you to where it's gotten me: the recognition that you can create the life you want out of all of the small, ordinary moments of every day.

I've never been one for rules, but I've built this book around a collection of phrases I've taped up on the fridge over the years, just to help me remember that I really can create the life I want. Within each chapter, you'll find a mix of recipes for homemade staples and dishes to create with those staples. At the heart of it all is the desire to live well, to enjoy my days, and to do what I can to support the well-being of my family and friends, my community, and, if I'm lucky, the world beyond it. Together, meal by meal, day by day, we can make it better.

START
where you are

BE
a
BEGINNER

FEED
YOURSELF

Put your Hands
in the Earth

~ BE ~
ACTIVE

USE
·YOUR·
SCRAPS

DO YOUR BEST, AND THEN LET GO.

Be
Helpful

DO THE
WORK

slow
down

Eat
Outside

INVITE PEOPLE
OVER

DON'T
BE afraid
OF FOOD

My daughter Sadie is learning how to create a meal.

Sadie is eleven, and as she starts to figure out who she will become, she seeks new skills that pique her curiosity or pull her in ways she can't yet describe. Trumpet, Shakespeare, writing, cooking. The list shifts as inspiration strikes, but cooking holds firmly to its place in the lineup, and I think it will stick with her. This is my clue: when it's been a hard day, she puts both hands firmly on the counter (usually as I'm scrambling to get dinner ready) and says, "I need to bake cookies."

It's not just that she wants to *eat* cookies. I know the urge started that way. But she also needs to find the perfect recipe, set up the ingredients, and feel the dough as it comes together. She craves the smell of those cookies in the oven as much as the cookie itself. She wants the thing she craves, and she's hungry for the act of making it. But most of all, she hasn't bungled the idea of the end result with fear and expectation, which can be so easy to do. She'll try something new if it sounds delicious to her, and she's up for the risk.

I've been a beginner many times, and I think my willingness to try anything new has helped me in the kitchen. Since graduating from college, I've taught everything from dance to calculus. I've written book contracts and studied wood finishes and been a personal assistant to a film director. I've cooked for movie crews, served in public office, sold vegetables at the farmers' market, and birthed and parented children. My only qualification for any of these jobs was that I was willing to try. And each time, I had no idea how to begin. Like Sadie, standing alone at the counter with a craving and a cookbook, I looked for a recipe. I asked for help. But most of all, I would take a deep breath and remember that we're all beginners. It only gets harder when we try to prove otherwise, whether to ourselves or to the table we're feeding. When we enter the kitchen, we must be ready and willing to fail, but not expecting to do so.

> That space between what we want to do and what we know we can do—that's where creativity and resourcefulness live.

That space between what we want to do and what we know we can do—that's where creativity and resourcefulness live. That space is a good place to begin. Start there, and then see what you're hungry for.

HOW TO COOK AN EGG

The first time I cooked for Joey, I fried him an egg with a crispy white and a runny center. I'm sure I'm not the first one to woo with a well-made egg, as it's perfectly suited to the task and worth your while to perfect. If you can make a good egg, you can make breakfast, lunch, or dinner. You can spiff up leftovers, turn a salad into a meal, or make everyone happy with a carbonara (see page 169). An egg is both junk food and health food, pleases most picky kids, and can be found anywhere. A regular old grocery store egg is delicious, healthy, and good enough. But if you can afford the extra few bucks for eggs from chickens that have seen the sun and eaten grass, the yolk will be brighter, far more flavorful, and packed with more nutrition. The better the chickens eat, the better the eggs they produce. If you do get eggs from a farm, a neighbor, or (lucky you!) your own chickens, and they haven't been washed or refrigerated, you can leave eggs out at room temperature for a week. Otherwise, store them in the refrigerator.

FRIED EGG

Heat just enough butter, ghee, olive oil, or coconut oil over medium heat to cover the bottom of your pan. Crack an egg into the pan, cover the pan, lower the heat to medium low, and let the egg sit undisturbed until the edges are crispy and a faint layer of white surrounds the circumference of the yolk, about 3 minutes. Add salt and pepper while the egg fries so they incorporate right into the cooked egg. For a firmer yolk, cook for 4 to 5 minutes. Fried eggs should be eaten right away.

POACHED EGG

Crack an egg into a ramekin or teacup and drain off the bit of watery white that will come off first. Bring a small pot of water to a high simmer, then swirl the water with a spoon to create a gentle whirlpool. Slide the egg into the water and let it cook, undisturbed, for about 3 minutes. Use a slotted spoon to remove the egg. Salt and pepper just before serving. Poached eggs can be stored in cold water in the refrigerator for up to 12 hours. If you intend to store them, just slightly undercook them; then finish them off for 30 to 45 seconds in simmering water when you're ready to serve.

SOFT-BOILED EGG

Bring a pot of water to a boil. Gently lower an egg into the water and reduce the heat to medium low. Cook for 5 minutes, then use a slotted spoon to remove the egg. Run it under cold water. Serve right in the shell, in an egg cup. (Note: If you're starting with a room-temperature egg, reduce the cooking time to 4 minutes.) Soft-boiled eggs should be eaten right away. Serve with salt and pepper on the table, and salt and pepper as you eat your egg.

HARDISH-BOILED EGG
(FIRM BUT BRIGHT YELLOW YOLK)

Follow the directions for soft-boiled, but increase the cooking time to 9 minutes (8 minutes for a room-temperature egg). Store unpeeled in a covered container in the refrigerator for up to 5 days or peeled for up to 3 days.

HARD-BOILED EGG

Follow the directions for soft-boiled, but increase the cooking time to 12 minutes (11 minutes for a room-temperature egg). Store unpeeled in a covered container in the refrigerator for up to 5 days or peeled for up to 3 days.

SCRAMBLED EGGS (2)

Crack 2 eggs into a bowl and add a splash of milk or cream, a pinch of salt, several grinds of pepper, and, for extra credit, 1 tablespoon mayonnaise. Set a small pan over medium-low heat and melt enough butter or ghee to cover the bottom of the pan. Whisk the eggs until slightly foamy and pour them into the pan. Let them sit undisturbed for about 20 seconds, until there's a soft crust around the perimeter of the pan. Use a silicone spatula or wooden spoon to gently push the eggs around the pan as they cook. When the eggs are scrambled and still slightly wet, raise the heat to high for about 5 seconds. Remove from heat and serve immediately.

HOW TO COOK A VEGETABLE

When I was in high school, my friend Cea and I used to frequent Paul and Elizabeth's restaurant in Northampton, Massachusetts. We'd have ten bucks between us, and we'd order one of their oversized whole-wheat rolls, fish chowder, and a side of steamed broccoli drizzled with olive oil.

I loved Cea in the way I loved many people then: all at once, like my heart was divided into a jigsaw puzzle, each piece holding the face of someone, and that part of my heart pulsed when I was with them. All this love made me an extreme kind of teenager, and every behavior was led by my desire to share pleasure with people. This was true for all my pursuits of the common hedonistic activities of teens (you fill in the blank), but for me, these shared bowls of steamed broccoli held just as much, if not more, pleasure than any late-night forbidden beer by the lake or joint passed behind the railroad tracks. We'd eat the broccoli with our fingers, each picking up a gently contoured trunk and devouring the dense crown before crunching through the tender stalk. I remember feeling so grown-up and fed by those dates, but most of all I remember the satisfaction I took in the perfectly steamed broccoli, especially in comparison to the broccoli served in our school dining hall, which was either boiled to the point of dissolution, or withered and smelling of old refrigerators at the salad bar.

There might not be anything so pleasing to eat as a well-cooked vegetable. Why? Because it can go so terribly wrong. There are many ways to cook a vegetable well, but I'm going to focus on my two favorite methods: steaming and roasting.

> **STEAMING.** Track down a pot with a removable steamer insert. Bring a few inches of water to a boil—no higher than the bottom of the insert—and fill the steamer insert with vegetables before covering tightly. If you don't have a steamer, you can combine the vegetables with about an inch of water in a covered pot. Steam until just tender, then transfer to a bowl and toss with simple dressings like olive oil, lemon, tamari, or some combination of the three.

> **ROASTING.** Most vegetables do well at 425°F, cooked until they have little blackened bits. Toss the vegetable in a bit of olive oil and salt and lay out on a greased or parchment-lined baking sheet in a single layer. Nearly every vegetable can be roasted with great success, but some are clear winners.

ASPARAGUS

STEAM: Steam until tender, 3 to 5 minutes.
ROAST: Toss with olive oil, sprinkle with salt, and roast in a 425°F oven on a baking sheet until tender and just beginning to brown, 10 to 12 minutes.

GREEN BEANS

STEAM: Steam until tender, 3 to 5 minutes.
ROAST: Toss with olive oil and salt and roast in a 425°F oven until crispy, 15 to 20 minutes.

BEETS

STEAM: Peel, slice, and steam until tender, 25 to 30 minutes.
ROAST: Scrub beets, leaving skin and tail intact. Put into a roasting pan with ½ inch water and cover tightly with foil. Roast in a 375°F oven until tender when pricked with a fork, 40 to 60 minutes, depending on the size of the beets. Let the beets cool, then slide them out of their skins before cutting.

BROCCOLI

STEAM: Steam stems, leaves, and florets until tender but still bright green, 4 to 6 minutes.
ROAST: Toss with lemon and olive oil and roast in a 425°F oven until brown and crispy, about 20 minutes.

BRUSSELS SPROUTS

STEAM: Steam whole Brussels sprouts until tender, 15 to 20 minutes.
ROAST: Halve or leave whole. Toss with olive oil and salt and roast in a 425°F oven until tender but not mushy, 35 to 45 minutes.

CABBAGE

STEAM: Steam until tender, 3 to 4 minutes for sliced Napa cabbage, 7 to 9 minutes for other varieties.
ROAST: No

CARROTS

STEAM: Peel and cut carrots uniformly to your desired size. Steam until tender, 5 to 10 minutes, depending on the size.
ROAST: Toss with olive oil and salt and roast in a 425°F oven whole or in pieces, until lightly browned on the outside and tender on the inside, 15 to 20 minutes.

CAULIFLOWER

STEAM: Cut into florets and steam for 5 to 7 minutes.
ROAST: Cut into florets and toss with salt, olive oil, and a pinch of fennel or cumin seed. Roast in a 425°F oven until browned, 25 to 30 minutes.

Hearty greens include kale, watercress, Swiss chard, turnip greens, kohlrabi greens.

STEAM: Steam until tender, 5 to 7 minutes.
ROAST: No

⟨⟨⟨ SWEET POTATOES ⟩⟩⟩

STEAM: Steam whole sweet potatoes for 30 to 35 minutes, then cut in half to serve.
ROAST: Cut into 1½-inch slices and arrange in a roasting pan. Drizzle with olive oil and sprinkle with salt, and cover tightly with aluminum foil. Roast in a 375°F oven until tender all the way through, 40 to 55 minutes.

⟨⟨⟨ WHITE POTATOES ⟩⟩⟩

STEAM: Cut potatoes to your desired size, or leave small potatoes whole (peeled or unpeeled). Sprinkle with salt and steam until tender when pricked with a fork, 15 to 25 minutes.
ROAST: Cut potatoes to your desired size, or leave small potatoes whole (peeled or unpeeled). Toss with olive oil and salt and roast in a 425°F oven until crispy, 30 to 45 minutes.

⟨⟨⟨ SUMMER SQUASH ⟩⟩⟩

STEAM: No
ROAST: Slice, toss with olive oil and salt, and roast in a 400°F oven until golden, about 10 minutes.

⟨⟨⟨ WINTER SQUASH ⟩⟩⟩

STEAM: Cut into slices with or without skin and steam until fork tender, about 10 minutes for more delicate squash and up to 25 minutes for tougher-skinned squashes.
ROAST: Cut into slices, or simply in half. Rub with olive oil and roast flesh side down on a baking sheet in a 375°F oven until tender, 35 to 55 minutes, depending on the size of the squash. You can also peel the squash and cut it into cubes. Toss with olive oil and salt and bake until cooked through and crispy, about 30 minutes.

ROASTED TOMATOES FOR THE FREEZER ✦ This is a major staple in my kitchen, and during tomato season I often have a few trays of tomatoes roasting away in the oven. Core and halve or quarter full-size tomatoes. Cherry tomatoes can be halved or left whole. Line a rimmed baking sheet with parchment and lay the tomatoes on it flesh side up. Scatter with any combination of basil, oregano, and thyme. Add salt, pepper, and a drizzle of olive oil. Roast in a 250°F oven until the tomatoes release their juice and start to dry out at the edges, from 1 to 2 hours for cherry and paste (plum) tomatoes to 4 to 5 hours for big, juicy heirlooms. If you're in a time crunch, you can up the heat to 325°F and shorten the time—just keep an eye on them. Let the tomatoes cool and then tip the whole tray into a freezer bag, lay flat, and freeze to use in place of canned tomatoes.

HOW TO TURN FRUIT INTO JAM

MAKES 1 ½ TO 2 CUPS

The secret that jam makers keep is that making jam is easy, and it can be done with whatever and however much fruit you have. A jar of jam can last two to three weeks in the fridge, so you can make one jar at a time with just a few minutes of stirring at the stove, no canning required. Thicken it with a little sugar, pour it into a jar, and you have jam. If you're not canning your jam, you don't have to pay attention to pH or acidity, so if you like to experiment, play around with sweetness, herbs, and other flavors with your fruit. Sugar is a preservative, so take note that if you use less sugar, you'll need to eat your jam faster. This formula works well with berries, rhubarb, stone fruit, pears, and cantaloupe. Just adjust the water and sweetener according to the water and sugar content of the fruit you're using. This is a quick jam that's great for all sorts of uses in the kitchen. In the interest of ease and versatility, this recipe creates a loose jam, and there's no need to worry about temperature or getting it to "set."

1 pound fruit, fresh or frozen (weighed after pitting, peeling, or cutting if appropriate—see chart on pages 26–27)	2 to 4 tablespoons water ¼ to ½ cup sugar or honey ½ teaspoon fresh lemon juice, or more to taste	Optional: herbs, spices, other flavor additions (see chart)

1 Combine the fruit and water in a heavy-bottomed pot and set over medium heat. Bring to a low boil, cover the pot, and reduce the heat to medium low. Cook, stirring every few minutes, until the fruit breaks up into sauce, 10 to 15 minutes.

2 Uncover the pot and stir in the sugar or honey. Raise the heat to medium and continue to cook, uncovered, stirring often to prevent the jam from burning on the bottom of the pot, until the sauce thickens, 15 to 20 minutes. Stir in the lemon juice. Taste, and adjust for sweetness if necessary. Allow to cool and transfer to a jar. If you've added whole spices (see chart for ideas), you can either remove them now or leave them in the jar to continue to infuse the jam for a stronger flavor.

This recipe can be a base for any fruit/flavor combination you dream up. Here are some of my favorites.

❧ BLACKBERRIES ❧

PREPARATION: None
FLAVOR IDEAS:
✦ Add the seeds of a vanilla bean with the sugar.
✦ Add 1 teaspoon rose water instead of the lemon juice.

❧ BLUEBERRIES OR HUCKLEBERRIES ❧

PREPARATION: None
FLAVOR IDEAS:
✦ Add a cinnamon stick with the sugar.
✦ Add 1 teaspoon grated lemon zest with the lemon juice.
✦ Add 1 teaspoon finely chopped mint to the berries.

❧ CANTALOUPE ❧

PREPARATION: Peel, remove seeds, and cut into chunks.
FLAVOR IDEAS:
✦ Add the seeds of a vanilla bean with the sugar.

❧ CHERRIES ❧

PREPARATION: Pit and halve.
FLAVOR IDEAS:
✦ Add the seeds of a vanilla bean with the sugar.
✦ Add ½ teaspoon almond extract with the lemon juice.

❧ GOOSEBERRIES ❧

PREPARATION: Remove tops and tails.
FLAVOR IDEAS:
✦ Lay whole elderflowers over the jam for the last few minutes of cooking. Cover the pot to let the scent infuse the jam. Remove the elderflowers.

❧ NECTARINES ❧

PREPARATION: Pit and slice or chop.
FLAVOR IDEAS:
✦ Peel and mince a 2-inch piece of ginger. Add it to the fruit.
✦ Use lime in place of the lemon juice.

❧ PEACHES ❧

PREPARATION: Peel, pit, and slice or chop.
FLAVOR IDEAS:
✦ Add a splash of bourbon with the fruit.
✦ Add a cinnamon stick to the fruit as it cooks.
✦ Sweeten with honey.

❧ PEARS ❧

PREPARATION: Peel, core, and chop.
FLAVOR IDEAS:
✦ Add the seeds of a vanilla bean with the sugar.
✦ Sweeten with caramel in place of the sugar.

 **PLUMS**

PREPARATION: Pit and halve or slice.

FLAVOR IDEAS:

✦ Peel and mince a 2-inch piece of ginger. Add it to the fruit.

✦ Add star anise, a cinnamon stick, and nutmeg to the fruit as it cooks.

 **RASPBERRIES**

PREPARATION: None

FLAVOR IDEAS:

✦ Add a splash of kirsch or Grand Marnier with the lemon juice.

RHUBARB

PREPARATION: Chop

FLAVOR IDEAS:

✦ Peel and mince a 2-inch piece of ginger. Add it to the fruit.

✦ Replace ¼ of the water with rose water.

STRAWBERRIES

PREPARATION: Hull (save the hulls; see page 132) and halve or slice larger berries.

FLAVOR IDEAS:

✦ Add the seeds of a vanilla bean with the sugar.

✦ Add 2 to 3 tablespoons Pinot Noir with the sugar.

✦ Add 2 tablespoons mint simple syrup (see page 233) with the lemon juice.

STORAGE NOTES: This keeps well in the refrigerator for 2 to 3 weeks. Or you can freeze your jam in freezer-safe containers for up to a year. Thaw in the refrigerator.

STORAGE NOTES ✦ Fridge pickles keep
in the refrigerator for 4 to 6 months.

HOW TO MAKE A PICKLE

MAKES JUST UNDER A QUART OF BRINE

Joey is the pickle maker in our house, and when the summer hands us twenty pounds of cucumbers, they're his. Those pickles sit in the basement through the winter, and we pull out a jar every so often to eat with sandwiches or slice onto burgers. But "pickle" has become more useful to me as a verb than a noun, and whenever I have a few too many vegetables in the fridge, I make refrigerator pickles. Nearly every vegetable pickles well: green beans, snap peas, or gingered carrots can slip into salads or Ploughman's Snacks (page 241). Most vegetables will keep in the fridge for six months. As you eat up the pickles, use the brine to make Rye Bread (page 211). My favorite brine is adapted from Mary Karlin's book *Mastering Fermentation*. I like to make the brine and keep it in the fridge; then I can make a little jar of pickles whenever I have extra vegetables. The more flavor-packed your ingredients, the tastier the whole jar will be, so garlic cloves or scapes, onions, and hot peppers are all great additions to your mix.

2 cups warm water	2 tablespoons honey	1 teaspoon whole-grain mustard
1½ tablespoons sea salt	1½ cups cider vinegar (raw or pasteurized)	

To make the brine, combine the water, sea salt, and honey in a quart jar. Stir to dissolve the salt and honey. Add the vinegar and mustard. Cover, shake to combine, and refrigerate indefinitely.

To make pickles, stuff a clean jar with vegetables, herbs, and spices. Top with brine so that it covers the produce. Fasten a piece of cheesecloth or thin fabric to the top with a rubber band. Leave the jar out on the counter for about 8 hours. Then replace the cloth with the jar lid and refrigerate. The pickles will be ready to eat the next day, but they'll get even better with age.

SOME OF MY FAVORITE FRIDGE PICKLES

- Carrot sticks, radishes, and chunks of fresh ginger
- Green beans, dill, and a few garlic cloves
- Sugar snap peas
- Asparagus with tarragon

HOW TO MAKE A SALAD

For me, the kitchen is the place where I get to have problems with easy solutions. There are enough problems with hard or no solutions elsewhere in the house and beyond, so I take the easy ones where I can get them.

Take washing lettuce, for example. I'm not sure why I so dislike washing lettuce. I have a nice salad spinner, so I'm perfectly equipped. I've tried to step out of the box and dry it Alice Waters style with a dish towel, or to swing the whole towel around over my head like someone told me the French do. But the truth is, I am always making salad either at lunch, when I am hungry *now* and have no patience for the process, or when the rest of dinner is already on the table and I think, "No! The salad!" before pulling down the spinner with a deep sigh.

The section of the grocery store produce aisle with washed greens in bags or plastic boxes overwhelms the tiny selection of actual heads of lettuce, and I'm guessing there's a collective hatred of washing lettuce. Most people will shell out two or three times what they'd spend on a much fresher and greener one-pound head of lettuce for a measly eight ounces of slimy, triple-washed mesclun at the grocery store—at least I often would. But that problem, like the best of them, was one with an easy solution.

Steer on over to the little section of lettuce heads and pick your way through them until you find a few of the brightest and freshest. Grab something bitter to mix in if that's your thing—radicchio, endive, frisée, arugula—it's all fair game. Bring it all home and—here's the important part—separate the leaves and wash them all at once *right away*. If you have more than one head, you can fill your sink with water and do it there, drying in the salad spinner or a dish towel as you go. Otherwise, the salad spinner should do the trick from start to finish. Next, find a large container or bag. I use a big reusable glass or plastic container, but anything will do. Dump in the lettuce. Add a dry paper towel to the container. Put it in the fridge. Done.

It's the simplest thing in the world, but it changes "No! The salad!" to "Yes! The salad!" forever. You'll be more likely to put lettuce on sandwiches when making them early in the morning before work or school, and I predict you'll be more likely to reach for the lettuce in general. That initial time investment pays off all week with every leaf. And you can spend the extra money you save on good olive oil, which takes us to the next step.

BASIC VINAIGRETTE

MAKES ABOUT ¾ CUP

This recipe makes enough for about two large salads. Leftovers will keep on the counter for a week or so. You can also refrigerate the dressing, but the olive oil will solidify when cold. Just take the jar out a little before you want to use it and give it a good shake.

1 tablespoon finely minced garlic or shallot (from 2 to 3 garlic cloves or ½ shallot)	2 tablespoons wine vinegar (red, white, or champagne) ½ teaspoon kosher salt	Freshly ground pepper ½ cup extra-virgin olive oil

1 Combine the garlic, vinegar, salt, and several grinds of pepper in a 1-cup jar. Let it sit for about 10 minutes so the garlic can pickle.

2 Add the olive oil, screw the lid on the jar, and shake well. Taste, and adjust the seasoning if needed. To dress your salad, add the dressing a bit at a time, tossing it in and tasting as you go.

VARIATIONS

• Mustard vinaigrette: Add 1 tablespoon Dijon or whole-grain mustard with the vinegar.

• Add a small handful of finely chopped fresh basil, parsley, thyme, or oregano.

• Substitute lemon juice for half or all of the vinegar.

STORAGE NOTES ✦ This dressing keeps at room temperature for about a week, or in the refrigerator for up to 3 weeks.

HOW TO ROAST A CHICKEN

I feel about "perfect" roast chicken as I do about God: everyone has a different way of getting there, and I'm pretty sure that everyone is mostly right. Nigel Slater started me out with his hot oven, his bird irreverently stuffed with whole heads of garlic, half lemons, and herbs strewn this way and that. Then Laurie Colwin convinced me that the only way to do it right was in a low oven for hours. Ina Garten taught me to roast on a bed of vegetables, and then Judy Rodgers came in with her hot cast-iron pan and her demand that I must salt days and days ahead of dinnertime. Thomas Keller insisted that I *must* truss . . . And then there was the spatchcocking. I made them all in search of the one definitive method. There were minutely different degrees of dryness, varying tastes depending on the source or happiness-while-living of my chicken. But really, roast chicken is perfect. And even if it's not, there's nothing that a little extra gravy won't fix.

I count roast chicken among the easy dinners that will never fail me, and my recipe here is the simplest that works for me. Don't rinse your chicken but if the skin is wet, pat it dry with paper towels. Nestle it into a roasting pan or cast-iron skillet. Rub 2 teaspoons of salt into the skin and inside the cavity. Rub (patiently and messily) a few tablespoons of softened butter or ghee over the skin. Squeeze half a lemon over the whole bird and put the spent rind inside the body cavity. Roast in a 425°F oven until the skin is crispy, the leg wiggles freely in the socket, and, if you need extra assurance, the temperature in the thickest part of the thigh is 160°F. I find this takes about 70 minutes for a 3-pound bird, and closer to 90 minutes for a 5-pound bird. You can absolutely cook 2 chickens at the same time, but take care not to press them together.

When your chicken is done, transfer it to a cutting board and let it sit for at least 10 minutes before carving. Set the roasting pan over low heat on the stovetop and whisk in ½ cup wine, stock, cream, or in lean times, water. Let the whole mixture boil away for a minute as you scrape any brown bits off the bottom of the pan so they can melt into the sauce. Taste the sauce and add a bit of salt if you think it needs it.

Carve the chicken any which way it pleases you. You can follow the lines of the joints, and carve it into eight pieces or chop it right down the center into two. Or you can pick off your favorite bits, wrap up the rest and put it in the fridge for the week's meals. Remember to save your bones for stock (page 132).

HOW TO TRANSFORM MILK

If you have milk or cream in the refrigerator, you have most of what you need to make many of the simple dairy products you usually buy. Even the cultures are often already in your refrigerator! When it comes to simple cultured dairy like yogurt, crème fraîche, or sour cream, nearly every product follows a similar pattern:

1 Bring milk or cream to a certain temperature.
2 Pour into a clean container.
3 Add culture.
4 Let it sit in a warm place until set.

Yogurt: Heat 2 quarts whole milk over medium-low heat to 180°F. Let the milk cool to 110°F. (At this point, you can transfer the milk to clean jars or continue on to culture the milk in your pot.) Add either 1½ teaspoons powdered yogurt starter or ½ cup plain, unsweetened, full-fat yogurt (dividing equally between the jars if you've divided the milk). If using powdered starter, whisk gently to combine, but if using yogurt, do not stir. Keep the culturing milk warm until thickened by wrapping it in a warm blanket in the warmest part of your house, leaving it by a wood stove, or tucking it into a cooler filled with warm water. Culture for 10 to 24 hours, until the yogurt is as sour as you like it. Transfer to the refrigerator. Stores well for 2 to 3 weeks. Makes 2 quarts.

Crème Fraîche: Combine 1 pint heavy cream and 3 tablespoons cultured buttermilk or ½ teaspoon powdered crème fraîche culture in a clean jar. Stir to combine, cover with cheesecloth secured with a rubber band, and leave at room temperature until thickened, 16 to 24 hours. Cover and refrigerate. Stores well for 7 to 10 days. Makes 2 cups.

Sour Cream: Follow the directions for crème fraîche, but use 3 tablespoons sour cream or ½ teaspoon powdered sour cream culture in place of the crème fraîche culture.

Buttermilk: Heat 1 quart whole milk over medium heat to 72°F. Whisk in ½ teaspoon buttermilk culture, transfer to a clean jar, cover with cheesecloth secured with a rubber band, and leave at room temperature until thickened, 12 to 16 hours. Stores well for 7 to 10 days. Makes 1 quart.

For simple cheese, there is an added step of separating the curds and whey. Homemade ricotta, which is technically just fresh cheese, demonstrates this process.

> **Ricotta:** Combine ½ gallon whole milk, ⅓ cup fresh lemon juice, and ½ cup heavy cream in a large pot over medium-low heat, stirring occasionally until the mixture reaches 180°F, about 45 minutes. Increase the heat to medium high and cook, watching closely, until the surface of the milk starts to erupt but does not boil, about 5 minutes. It will register between 195°F and 205°F on a thermometer. Remove from heat and let the pot sit for 10 minutes. Set up a cheesecloth-lined strainer over a large bowl to catch the whey. Spoon the curds into the strainer and let the cheese drain for 30 minutes. Pour the whey into a jar and use in soups, smoothies, and bread recipes. The cheese stores well for 3 to 4 days. Makes ¾ to 1 pound of cheese.

For more simple home dairy, see Feta Cheese (page 113), Chèvre (page 99), Cultured Butter (page 115), and Kefir (page 104).

> **WHAT TO DO WITH WHEY** ✦ The cloudy yellow liquid that drains from your cheese curd, yogurt, or soy curd is whey, and it's a great ingredient in itself, packed with nutrition and flavor. Save the whey to use in place of the liquid in bread recipes or soups. I especially love it in Dal (page 186) and Roasted Red Pepper Corn Chowder (page 81). Use whey to give a boost to the brine of your sauerkraut or Kimchi (page 107), or simply as a liquid in smoothies. Yogurt whey is delicious on its own—I love to stir in a little lime, maple syrup, and cardamom and drink it like lemonade. Whey keeps in the refrigerator for about 2 weeks, or in the freezer for up to 6 months.

HOW TO COOK GRAINS

We all have our grains of childhood. For some, it's Uncle Ben's white rice, quick-boiled with that mysterious flavor packet. For me, it was short-grain brown rice, which my mother cooked perfectly in her pressure cooker. These days, there are so many wonderful grains that are widely available, so there's no excuse to stick to only one. The recipe for most grains is to combine with water and cook until done, but it's the subtleties of toasting, timing, and adding fat and salt that eliminates the risk of crunchy undercooked rice (totally inedible) or mushy, bitter quinoa (blech). If you buy grains in large quantities or don't go through them quickly, store them uncooked in the freezer to keep them fresh. I make many of my grains in the rice cooker, so I've included instructions for that as well. Keep in mind that all grains vary from batch to batch, and there are several varieties of each grain, so these times and ratios are just guidelines.

LONG-GRAIN BROWN RICE

START WITH: 1 cup
ADD LIQUID: 1¾ cups water or stock (can replace up to half the total amount with coconut milk)
SALT AND FAT: ¼ teaspoon salt; optional: 2 teaspoons butter or olive oil
HOW TO COOK IT: Rinse rice in several changes of water. Combine rice, liquid, salt, and fat, if using, in a pot and let sit for 30 minutes. Cover, bring to a boil, reduce the heat to medium low, and cook until tender, 30 to 40 minutes.
MAKES: 3 cups
TO MULTIPLY: Add 1½ cups liquid for each additional cup of rice.
RICE COOKER: 1 cup dry + 2 cups liquid + ¼ teaspoon salt
Cook on regular cycle.

SHORT-GRAIN BROWN RICE

START WITH: 1 cup
ADD LIQUID: 2 cups water or stock (can replace up to half the total amount with coconut milk)
SALT AND FAT: ¼ teaspoon salt; optional: 2 teaspoons butter or olive oil
HOW TO COOK IT: Rinse rice in several changes of water. Bring the liquid to a boil; add rice, salt, and fat, if using. Cover, return to a boil, then reduce

the heat to medium low. Cook until the rice is tender and liquid is absorbed, 35 to 40 minutes.

MAKES: 3 cups

TO MULTIPLY: Add 1½ cups liquid for each additional cup of rice.

RICE COOKER: 1 cup dry + 2 cups water + ¼ teaspoon salt

Cook on regular cycle.

WHITE RICE

START WITH: 1 cup

ADD LIQUID: 1½ cups water or stock (can replace up to half the total amount with coconut milk)

SALT AND FAT: ¼ teaspoon salt; optional: 2 teaspoons butter or olive oil

HOW TO COOK IT: Rinse rice in several changes of water. Bring the liquid to a boil; add rice, salt, and fat, if using. Cover, return to a boil, then reduce the heat to medium low. Cook until the rice is tender and liquid is absorbed, 20 to 25 minutes.

MAKES: 3 cups

TO MULTIPLY: Add 1½ cups liquid for each additional cup of rice.

RICE COOKER: 1 cup dry + 1½ cups liquid or stock + ¼ teaspoon salt + 1 tablespoon butter

Cook on regular cycle.

SUSHI RICE

START WITH: 1 cup

ADD LIQUID: 1½ cups water

SALT AND FAT: None

HOW TO COOK IT: Rinse rice in several changes of water, squeezing the grains as the water runs over the bowl. Bring the water and rice to a boil, then reduce the heat to medium low. Cook until the rice is soft and water is absorbed, 25 to 30 minutes. Dump into a wooden bowl. Add 1 tablespoon brown rice syrup or maple syrup, 1 tablespoon rice vinegar, and ½ teaspoon salt. Stir frequently with a wooden spoon until the rice is cool to the touch. Cover with a damp towel until serving.

MAKES: 3 cups

TO MULTIPLY: Add 1¼ cups water for each additional cup of rice.

RICE COOKER: Combine 1 cup rice + 1½ cups water. Soak in the rice cooker for 30 minutes before cooking.

Cook on regular or sushi cycle. Cool and use the same additions as in the stovetop method.

MILLET

START WITH: 1 cup

ADD LIQUID: 1¾ cups water or stock

SALT AND FAT: ½ teaspoon salt, 1 tablespoon butter or olive oil

HOW TO COOK IT: Toast millet in a hot, dry saucepan until it smells good and starts to pop. Add 1¾ cups boiling liquid, the salt, and butter and bring to a boil. Cover, reduce the heat to medium low, and cook until the liquid is absorbed, about 25 minutes. Remove from heat, fluff with a fork, and cover for 10 minutes.

MAKES: 3½ cups

TO MULTIPLY: Add 1¾ cups liquid for each additional cup of millet.

RICE COOKER: 1 cup dry + 1¾ cups water or stock + ½ teaspoon salt + 1 tablespoon butter or olive oil

Toast the millet as in the stovetop method. Transfer the millet to the rice cooker and combine with the liquid, salt, and butter. Cook on regular cycle.

QUINOA

START WITH: 1 cup

ADD LIQUID: 1½ cups water or stock

SALT AND FAT: ½ teaspoon salt, 1 teaspoon olive oil

HOW TO COOK IT: Rinse thoroughly in a fine-meshed sieve. Toast, stirring often, in a hot, dry saucepan until the grains dry out and smell nutty. Add 1½ cups boiling liquid, the salt, and the olive oil and bring to a boil. Cover, reduce the heat to medium low, and cook undisturbed for 20 minutes. Remove from heat, fluff with a fork, and cover for 5 minutes.

MAKES: 3 cups

TO MULTIPLY: Add 1½ cups liquid for each additional 1 cup of quinoa.

RICE COOKER: 1½ cups washed quinoa + 2 cups water or stock + ¼ teaspoon salt. Cook on regular cycle, then let quinoa steam for 10 minutes in the cooker before serving.

POLENTA

START WITH: 1 cup

ADD LIQUID: 4 cups water, or 2 cups water and 2 cups milk

SALT AND FAT: 1 teaspoon salt, 1 tablespoon butter

HOW TO COOK IT: Bring liquid and salt to a boil. Whisk in the polenta and lower the heat. Cook, covered, over medium-low heat, stirring often, until the polenta is smooth and not gritty, about 45 minutes. Add more liquid in the final 10 minutes if it gets too thick. Stir in the butter before serving.

MAKES: 4 cups

TO MULTIPLY: Add 4 cups liquid for each additional cup of polenta.

RICE COOKER: No

BARLEY

START WITH: 1 cup

ADD LIQUID: 3 cups water or stock

SALT AND FAT: ¼ teaspoon salt; optional: 1 teaspoon butter or olive oil

HOW TO COOK IT: Bring the liquid and salt to a boil. Add the barley and bring back to a boil. Reduce the heat to medium low, cover, and simmer until tender, 30 to 40 minutes. Drain off any residual liquid, remove from heat, stir in the fat, if using, and cover for 10 minutes.

MAKES: 3 cups

TO MULTIPLY: Add 3 cups liquid for each additional cup of barley.

RICE COOKER: 1 cup barley + 2 cups liquid + ¼ teaspoon salt
Cook on regular cycle, then let barley steam in the cooker for 10 minutes.

FARRO

START WITH: 1 cup

ADD LIQUID: 1¾ cups water or stock

SALT AND FAT: ¼ teaspoon salt; optional: 1 teaspoon olive oil

HOW TO COOK IT: Toast in a hot, dry saucepan for about 3 minutes. Add boiling liquid, salt, and olive oil, if using. Bring to a boil, cover, then reduce the heat to medium low. Cook until tender, about 25 minutes. Drain off any residual liquid.

MAKES: 2½ cups

TO MULTIPLY: Add 1¼ cups liquid for each additional cup of farro.

RICE COOKER: 1 cup farro + 1½ cups liquid + 1 tablespoon olive oil + ¼ teaspoon salt
Toast the farro as in the stovetop method. Transfer the farro to the rice cooker, add the liquid, and soak for 1 hour. Add the oil and salt and cook on regular cycle.

STORAGE NOTES ✦ You can freeze cooked grains! Just store in single or meal-sized portions, and thaw in the refrigerator.

HOW TO MAKE PIECRUST

MAKES TWO 9-INCH CRUSTS

Whenever I make piecrust, I always make double what I need. If I have a spare crust in the fridge, there are vast possibilities. Quiche! Pie! Tarts! This is the basic method from my first book, *The Homemade Pantry*. The recipe was originally inspired by one from Shirley Corriher's *Bakewise*. Her stand-mixer method transformed me into a confident pie maker, and I've heard from countless others that it's done the same for them.

2 sticks (230 g) cold unsalted butter, cut into ½-inch squares, plus additional for greasing the dish	2¼ cups (270 g) all-purpose flour ⅓ cup (75 ml) cold water	2 teaspoons cider vinegar ½ teaspoon kosher salt

1 Combine the butter and flour in the bowl of a stand mixer, using your hands to coat the butter in the flour. Put the bowl in the refrigerator.

2 Combine the water, vinegar, and the salt in a measuring cup, stirring to dissolve the salt. Put the mixture in the freezer for 10 minutes.

3 Remove the mixtures from the refrigerator and freezer. Using the paddle attachment, blend the flour mixture on low speed until it has the texture of crumbly meal. With the mixer still running, slowly pour the water mixture into the bowl. The dough will be crumbly at first, then after 10 or 20 seconds, it will come together in a ball. Stop the mixer.

4 Turn the dough out onto the counter and press it together into a large disk. Cut the dough in half; wrap each piece in plastic and press each into a disk. Refrigerate for at least 1 hour and up to 3 days.

VARIATIONS

• Single crust: Use 1 stick (115 g) unsalted butter + 1¼ cups (150 g) flour + 1 teaspoon cider vinegar + ¼ teaspoon salt. Reduce the water to 3 tablespoons (45 ml).

• Whole-grain crust: Replace half the all-purpose flour with whole-wheat pastry or spelt flour.

NOW MAKE PIE

Take the dough out of the refrigerator 15 minutes before you're ready to roll. Grease a 9- or 10-inch pie dish with butter and give it a light dusting of flour. Lightly flour the counter. Unwrap one of the disks, place it on the counter, and, starting from the center, roll the dough into a circle about 12 to 14 inches in diameter and ⅛ inch thick. To transfer the crust, fold it in half, then fold that semicircle in half again so that you have a quarter of a circle. Line up the corner of the quarter with the center of your pie dish and unfold the quarter back into a semicircle, then into the full circle.

Once you have your crust, you can make any kind of pie or tart you want.

BERRY PIE

METHOD: Combine about 3 pints (1.1 kg) berries, ½ to ⅔ cup (100 g to 130 g) sugar (depending on the tartness of your berries), the zest and juice of 1 lemon, a pinch of salt, and ¼ cup (30 g) cornstarch or arrowroot powder in a mixing bowl. Let the mixture sit for a few minutes, then scrape it into the bottom crust. Roll out the second crust, transfer it to the pan so it covers the filling, and trim so it hangs about an inch over the sides. Crimp the edges together and cut 4 steam vents in the center of the crust. Put the pie in the freezer while you preheat the oven to 375°F. Transfer the pie to a baking sheet and bake until the crust is golden and the juices bubble through the vents, about 1 hour. Cool before serving. Depending on the water content of your berries, the pie might be a bit runny, so have lots of ice cream ready.

APPLE OR PEAR PIE

METHOD: Peel, core, and slice 3 pounds (1.4 kg) fruit into ½-inch slices. Toss the fruit with ¼ cup (60 ml) maple syrup, ¼ cup (30 g) all-purpose flour, the zest and juice of 1 lemon, 2 teaspoons cinnamon, and a pinch of salt. Let the mixture sit for a few minutes, then scrape it into the bottom crust. Roll out the second crust, transfer it to the pan so it covers the filling, and trim so it hangs about an inch over the sides. Crimp the edges together and cut 4 steam vents in the center of the crust. Put the pie in the freezer while you preheat the oven to 425°F. Transfer the pie to a baking sheet and bake until the crust is golden and the juices bubble through the vents, about 1 hour. Cool before serving.

⟨⟨⟨ CUSTARD PIE ⟩⟩⟩

METHOD: Freeze a single rolled-out unbaked crust for at least an hour. Fill the crust with 2 cups berries or sliced fruit. Combine 4 eggs, ⅓ cup (75 ml) maple syrup, 1 cup (225 g) plain whole-milk yogurt (for homemade, see page 34), 1 teaspoon vanilla extract, and ¼ teaspoon kosher salt in a blender and blend until smooth. Pour the custard over the fruit and bake in a 375°F oven until firm, 45 minutes to an hour. Cool to room temperature before serving.

⟨⟨⟨ SAVORY GALETTE ⟩⟩⟩

METHOD: Don't put your crust in a pie pan; roll a single crust into a rough circle and transfer to a parchment-lined baking sheet. Brush the crust with olive oil. Arrange thinly sliced fresh or roasted vegetables on it, leaving about 2 inches empty along the perimeter. Top with fresh herbs, grated Parmesan or a soft cheese such as Chèvre (page 99) or Feta Cheese (page 113), and salt. Fold the edge of the crust over the filling, brush a bit more olive oil on the outside of the crust, and sprinkle with coarse salt. Bake in a 400°F oven until golden, 45 to 55 minutes. Carefully transfer to a cooling rack and cool slightly before serving. For quiche, see page 196.

⟨⟨⟨ SWEET GALETTE ⟩⟩⟩

METHOD: Follow the directions for a savory tart, but use jam, crème fraîche, or mascarpone instead of the olive oil. Toss sliced fruit with 1 to 2 tablespoons sugar, then arrange on the crust. Brush the outside rim of the crust with melted butter, milk, or a beaten egg, and scatter coarse sugar over the crust.

STORAGE NOTES: Unbaked dough: Refrigerator, 2 to 3 days; freezer (wrapped in disks or rolled out), 4 months
FRUIT PIES: Room temperature (wrapped), 2 days; refrigerator (wrapped) 3 to 4 days; freezer, unbaked pie (tightly wrapped), 4 months (thaw overnight in the refrigerator and bake as if just made)
CUSTARD PIES: Refrigerator (wrapped), 4 to 5 days
GALETTES: Room temperature (wrapped), 1 day; refrigerator (wrapped), 4 days; freezer (bake and cool the galette, freeze on a baking sheet, then tightly wrap), up to 4 months (thaw overnight in the refrigerator and warm in a 350°F oven for 10 to 15 minutes)

HOW TO USE FRESH HERBS

Whether you buy them at the store or the farmers' market or grow them yourself, fresh herbs will take whatever you create in the kitchen and make it better. When I have herbs in the garden, I pick them in fragrant, green handfuls, and I throw them into anything I'm about to eat.

Here are some of my favorite ways to use fresh herbs:

Salad dressings: Chop up a little parsley, tarragon, sage, thyme, or basil and add it to a vinaigrette.

Water: Tap water gets fancy and delicious with herbs. Shove a few stems of mint, basil, parsley, or lemon balm in a pitcher of water.

Gremolata: Chop together 1 small garlic clove, the zest of 1 lemon, and 1 cup flat-leaf parsley. This is especially wonderful on beef stew or long-braised meats.

Smoothies: Try basil, mint, or parsley in a smoothie. One of my favorite combinations is blueberries, buttermilk or kefir, and a small handful of mint leaves.

Pesto: Finely chop a cup of herbs and stir in ¼ cup olive oil. Salt to taste. You can also add garlic and chopped nuts or Parmesan cheese before adding the oil. Serve on pasta, in Minestrone (page 140), or as a dip.

Salsa verde: Chop together 1 cup flat-leaf parsley, 1 tablespoon capers, 10 anchovies, a minced garlic clove, and about ½ cup olive oil. Eat with roasted chicken and potatoes. You can also add some tarragon into the mix.

Vinegar: To infuse vinegar, fill a clean bottle with tarragon, sage, thyme, or nasturtium flowers. Add a peeled garlic clove for extra credit. Heat red or white wine vinegar until hot but not boiling, and pour it over the herbs. Let it cool, top with the lid, and store it in the back of your pantry for a month.

to preserve herbs:

Most herbs will dry on a wire rack or hung out of the light for ten days. Herbs with a higher moisture content, like mint and basil, do better in a dehydrator or very low oven. Dry herbs with the stem; then once dry, remove the leaves from the stem and store in an airtight jar or double bagged in the freezer for up to 6 months.

You can also freeze herbs by chopping them finely, loosely filling the cubes of an ice cube tray, and topping off each cube with olive oil. Freeze the tray, then remove the cubes and store them in a freezer bag for up to 6 months. Throw a cube right into the pan when you want to use that herb.

HOW TO MAKE PASTA

Fresh pasta is nearly as easy to prepare as dried pasta, especially if you have the right tools. I have both a hand crank roller and a rolling attachment for my KitchenAid mixer, and I love them both. The hand crank machine takes a little more time and work but makes me feel like an Italian grandmother, and the KitchenAid attachment does the job so quickly, it really does make fresh pasta a weeknight meal option. It all depends on your preference. Of course, if you want to go entirely rustic, a rolling pin does the trick, too.

To make fresh pasta, shape 2 cups (240 g) all-purpose flour into a wide volcano on the counter. Break 3 large eggs into a bowl, and slowly tilt the eggs into the center of the volcano, using a fork to incorporate the eggs into the flour from the center out. Don't be afraid of an errant egg skidding across the counter—just gently shoo it back to the flour. If you have a bench knife, switch over to that, and use it to keep chopping and folding the egg into the flour. (Otherwise, a fork will work.) Once you have a loose dough, use your hands to knead it vigorously until it comes together, about 5 minutes. It will seem like it won't happen and then—there it is! You have a smooth dough. Alternatively, you can combine the flour and eggs in the bowl of a stand mixer, and knead it with the dough hook.

Cut the dough into 6 pieces, shaping each into a ball. Cover the balls of dough with plastic wrap or a damp dish towel and let them rest on the counter out of the sunlight for 30 minutes. To create strips of pasta, put one ball of dough through your roller at its thickest setting. Fold the strip in thirds, then put it through the roller again at the next thinnest setting. Repeat until the pasta is as thin as possible. Cut the pasta to your preferred shape, either using your roller to cut tagliatelle or spaghetti, or going more freeform to cut bowties or orecchiette. Hang the pasta on a rack to dry or lay it out on a floured counter for at least 5 minutes and up to 2 hours.

Of course, if your time and energy has gone elsewhere, dried pasta will save the day. The key to cooking dried pasta is to boil it in lots of water, and to stir often to keep it from sticking. Salt the water generously, add a clove of garlic if you like, and always save a cup of cooking water before draining to add to whatever sauce you make with the pasta. The starchy, salty water adds flavor and silkiness to every pasta dish.

STORAGE NOTES ✦ Store rolled
fresh pasta or unrolled dough in the
refrigerator for up to 2 days. Or freeze
balls of unrolled dough or rolled pasta in
well-floured nests for up to 3 months.

FEED
YOURSELF

When you are accustomed to shaping your meals around the people who eat them, it can be easy to forget that cooking for yourself is a worthy endeavor.

Most days I work at home, and I am often guilty of neglecting my own lunch, rifling through the fridge at 2:00 p.m. only to emerge with a hunk of cheese and a few crackers that I bring back to my desk.

Cooking, sitting, and eating alone is a habit that, like many others, can start with a feeling of resistance that is quickly overcome once we actually do it a few times. Then, it turns into something quite wonderful. When it comes to lunch or those rare dinners when I'm by myself, each chop of the knife and sizzle in the pan is its own affirmation that I am worth it. And so is the folded napkin and well-placed fork just for me.

There is a dish that I often eat for lunch when I'm by myself because no one in my family will eat it with me: I call it Dandelion Greens with a Perfect Fried Egg. The bliss of cooking for myself is that no one will whine that they don't like dandelion greens or that they want their egg soft-boiled and separate from the rest (that's the girls). No one will add bacon or turn it into a sand-wich because it's too girly to be a real lunch (that's Joey). The day I discovered this combination, I had one hand in the cheese drawer and the other going for

> Each chop of the knife and sizzle in the pan is its own affirmation that I am worth it.

crackers, with only a few minutes before I had to go pick up the girls from school. A bunch of dande-lion greens, sadly neglected, peeked at me from the crisper drawer, and before I knew it, I was creating a real lunch. And although the crackers and cheese certainly make an appearance now and then, the joy of cooking for myself has taken over. The perfect egg is only mine, and I have only myself to please.

DANDELION GREENS *with* A PERFECT FRIED EGG

If it's spring and you have young dandelion leaves popping up in your yard, you can use them for this recipe. Just taste one of the leaves to make sure it's not too bitter. Cultivated dandelion greens that you find at the supermarket or farmers' market tend to be a bit milder, and there are a few wonderful varieties out there, each with its own color and flavor. If you can't find dandelion greens, feel free to use arugula or spinach.

2 tablespoons extra-virgin olive oil, plus additional for drizzling

Hefty pinch of dried red pepper flakes

½ bunch dandelion greens (about 8 stems), lower tough part of the stems removed, greens roughly chopped

1 large egg

2 tablespoons chopped fresh dill

Finishing salt and freshly ground pepper

1 Heat the oil in a frying pan or cast-iron skillet over medium-high heat. Add the red pepper flakes to the oil and let them sizzle for about 10 seconds. Add the dandelion greens and toss in the hot oil until they just begin to wilt, about 1 minute. Transfer the greens to a bowl.

2 If the pan seems dry, add a bit more olive oil. Lower the heat to medium low, crack the egg into the pan, and cover the pan. Cook until crispy around the edges and runny in the center, 3 to 4 minutes. Gently place the egg over the greens. Top with an additional drizzle of olive oil as well as the dill, salt, and pepper.

SPECIAL SALT ✦ I mostly use two kinds of salt in my kitchen: a fine salt for cooking and a large-flake salt for finishing a dish. The fine salt can be sea salt, kosher salt, or table salt, but I prefer Diamond Crystal kosher salt. When it comes to the crunchy "finishing" salt, Maldon is my go-to.

BUTTER LETTUCE *with* DATES *and* RICOTTA

SERVES 1

This inspired salad is a recipe from my friend Jess Fechtor, from her blog *Sweet Amandine*. It was my first introduction to dates cooked in butter, and those, along with the ricotta and butter lettuce, make a wonderful trio of sweet, creamy, and crunchy—there's really nothing like it.

1 tablespoon unsalted butter	⅓ to ½ small head of butter lettuce, torn into large pieces	¼ cup walnuts or pecans, toasted and roughly chopped
4 or 5 dates, pitted and quartered (any will work, but I like Medjool or Deglet)	1 tablespoon Mustard Vinaigrette (page 31)	Finishing salt and freshly ground pepper
	⅓ cup ricotta (for homemade, see page 35)	

1 Melt the butter in a heavy skillet over medium-high heat. Add the dates and cook without stirring until their skins harden and caramelize, about a minute. Shuffle the dates and cook for another 2 minutes, stirring occasionally.

2 Meanwhile, toss the lettuce in the vinaigrette. Arrange it on one side of a large plate, and spoon the ricotta alongside the lettuce. When the dates are done, tip them and their sweet brown butter over the ricotta. Scatter the nuts and finishing salt over the plate, focusing especially on the dates and ricotta. Give the whole plate a few grinds of pepper.

TOAST THOSE NUTS ✦ A toasted nut is infinitely more delicious than a raw one. You can toast a handful of nuts quickly in a dry skillet on the stovetop or roast your nuts and seeds in the oven. I toast most nuts at 350°F on an ungreased baking sheet just until they start to brown, 6 to 9 minutes. Seeds roast faster, in 4 to 6 minutes.

BREAD *with* RADISH BUTTER

SERVES 1, WITH LOTS OF BUTTER LEFT OVER FOR SNACKS AND HORS D'OEUVRES LATER

When I work at the very first farmers' markets in May, usually the only kinds of produce we have for sale are radishes. But those radishes! There's nothing so beautiful as a spring radish. The French Breakfasts with their dainty white tips, the perfectly round Amethysts with their magenta skin, and the classic red Cherry Bells—they all inspire frenzy, and I always swipe a bunch for myself. Radishes start out milder in the spring, and as the sun infuses them deeper into the summer, they get spicier. I like this best with mild early radishes.

4 tablespoons (½ stick) unsalted butter, at room temperature

2 or 3 small radishes, finely minced

2 chives, finely snipped with scissors

1 teaspoon fresh lemon juice

1 teaspoon finishing salt

2 slices bread (sourdough with a thick, crunchy crust is best for this)

Stir together the butter, radishes, chives, lemon juice, and salt in a small bowl. Spread generously on bread, reserving the rest of the radish butter for a snack later.

STORAGE NOTES ✦ Refrigerate the butter in a tightly covered container for 4 to 5 days, or freeze it in an airtight container for up to 3 months.

SHAKSHUKA

If you have a frying pan built for single egg, this is the time to pull it out. Shakshuka is also a great use for that little bit of leftover tomato sauce. Just brighten it up with fresh herbs if you have them, and heat the sauce before cooking the egg in it. And if you have ricotta or plain whole-milk yogurt, try this with a dollop of either on the side.

1 tablespoon unsalted butter	1 cup chopped fresh tomato (1 large tomato) or 1 cup chopped canned tomatoes	1 large egg
2 tablespoons chopped onion		Extra-virgin olive oil
⅓ cup diced sweet red pepper	2 tablespoons chopped fresh herbs (any combination of parsley, oregano, dill, basil, thyme)	Freshly ground pepper
½ teaspoon kosher salt		Thickly sliced bread, for serving
1 tablespoon minced garlic (2 to 3 cloves)		

1 Melt the butter in a small frying pan over medium heat. Add the onion and red pepper and cook, stirring often, until softened, 3 to 5 minutes. Add the salt, garlic, and tomato, stir, and continue to cook until the mixture thickens, another 3 to 5 minutes.

2 Stir in the herbs. Crack the egg directly into the sauce, lower the heat to medium low, and cover the pan. When the egg has a faint shadow of white over the yolk, 2 to 3 minutes, remove from heat. Transfer gently to a bowl, drizzle with olive oil, and give the dish a few grinds of pepper. Eat with a hunk of bread for dipping.

THE NEW BITTER

I once spent a year as a governess for a family that included three girls who were eleven, thirteen, and fifteen. Each had a beautiful first and second name that blended together, and not one of them looked like the other two, although they all had hair halfway down their backs, one white-blond, one nearly black, and the eldest, red. Three days a week I'd teach them math, science, literature, philosophy, and whatever else they requested.

Their mother, Meredith, a stunning woman then in her mid-thirties, also had hair halfway down her back, dark, like the middle child's. They had all spent time romping in India, and maybe as a result, she was a woman who could pull off a shawl like I've never seen. She was often barefoot with black jeans that matched her hair and never a bit of makeup.

There was always a new dietary theme in the house. Raw milk, homemade French pastry, nutritive bone broths, a mint tea bag ripped open for the salad dressing—I encountered all of these things for the first time over the course of that year. At the time I had no interest in food beyond just eating it, but a year later, I'd be writing recipes in my own kitchen, many of which would be inspired by those first bites in between lessons. I couldn't help but try to re-create them, as I'd always walk away from our days together with the taste of a new flavor in my mouth.

And so it went with broccoli raab. One day as we were finishing up our lessons, I watched Meredith roughly chop a whole bunch of broccoli raab and throw it into a pan with a bit of water and a hunk of butter. A few minutes later it was on a plate, served alone with nothing but a rough slice of Cheddar cheese. It seemed so unorthodox to eat only a pile of steaming bitter greens for lunch. On any other table, it would have been a side dish. But I asked what it was, and then I was able to re-create this simple lunch with this new, strange vegetable.

BROCCOLI RAAB *with* CHEDDAR POLENTA

I love broccoli raab beyond all other vegetables. I often eat it as Meredith taught me, just plain with a slice of Cheddar cheese. But for something a bit more traditional, I've worked it into a real, proper lunch.

1 teaspoon olive oil or ghee (for homemade, see page 139)	1 tablespoon unsalted butter	¼ cup water
	2 cups coarsely chopped broccoli raab (leaves, flowers, and all but the end of the stems), from ½ medium bunch	¼ teaspoon finishing salt
2 slices cooked polenta (see page 138), about the size and thickness of ½ slice of bread		Optional: ¼ teaspoon dried red pepper flakes
1 ounce sharp Cheddar, cut into two ¼-inch slices		

1 Heat the olive oil in a skillet over medium heat. Fry the polenta slices in the oil until warmed through and crispy on both sides, 7 to 10 minutes. Lay a slice of Cheddar on each slice of polenta, lower the heat, and cover until the cheese melts, about 1 minute. Transfer the polenta slices to a deep bowl.

2 Meanwhile, combine the butter, broccoli raab, and water in a medium saucepan over medium-high heat. Bring to a boil, cover, and reduce the heat to medium low. Cook, stirring occasionally, until the broccoli raab is tender and bright green, 4 to 5 minutes. Scoop the broccoli raab over the polenta and top with salt and red pepper flakes, if using.

ENDIVE *with* SARDINES *and* LEMON

SERVES 1

I never would have known what to do with my first can of sardines were it not for a kind aunt who insisted I just hadn't lived until I'd had a real, perfectly salted sardine sandwich. She picked up fancy white bread at the bakery, slathered it with softened butter, and deftly pulled open the greasy can without splattering one drop of oil. Then she smashed the tiny oily fish into a rich and salty hash.

"Tuna, shmuna," she said to me, as we each ate half of the sandwich that was, in fact, one of the most delicious things I could remember eating.

I find that people often confuse sardines with anchovies, another oily and misunderstood fish, and in both cases, one wrong preparation can turn the eater away forever. Americans just haven't discovered the canned sardine like the French (mashed on grilled bread), the British (the delicious sandwich of my aunt), or the Italians (pasta, of course). But those single-serve cans are perfect for lunch. Taste your sardine mash as you go, and when it tastes so good you want to just eat the whole bowl, scoop it onto your endive. This is also a great hors d'oeuvre for a party if you want to make it on a larger scale. Just triple the recipe and it will fill a platter beautifully.

1 3½- to 4½-ounce can sardines in olive oil, lightly drained (if you have sardines in water, just add 1 teaspoon olive oil after draining)	2½ tablespoons coarsely chopped fresh flat-leaf parsley Grated zest of ½ lemon	1 hefty squeeze of lemon juice ¼ teaspoon finishing salt 1 endive, separated into single leaves

1 Combine the sardines with most of the parsley, lemon zest, lemon juice, and salt in a bowl. Mash with a fork and taste. Add more lemon juice or salt if needed.

2 Divide the mixture evenly among the endive leaves. Sprinkle the remaining lemon zest and parsley over the plate for garnish.

THE ARLESIENNE, *or* A FRENCH SALAD

There is a French grocery and cafe, Bizalion's, about a mile from where I live. The owners, Jean-François and Helen, are French and Irish, respectively, and the combination of these tastes and sensibilities lands exactly where I want to eat. The menu is mostly French, with two boards behind the counter, one for sandwiches and one for salads. For a year or two, I worked a few shifts a week there. I learned so much, as I have in every service job, just by serving the food that's been imagined by someone who loves to eat.

The most popular dishes are the simplest. There's an avocado, halved, the hollows filled with mustardy vinaigrette, less a recipe than a reminder that the perfect partner for an avocado is a spoon. A salad called the Arlesienne shares all its secrets right there on the plate: boiled red potatoes, anchovies, salty chickpeas, and fancy canned tuna, all doused with fruity olive oil. Jean-François says that the salad comes from a time of his childhood when his whole extended family would gather at the Bizalion estate in France in the summer. Dinners were formal, but the kids spent the day romping through the woods, and in the morning, the adults would create a smorgasbord that allowed for a self-serve platter that could be eaten by the river.

This salad has several ingredients, and the tuna is a splurge, but they're all useful building blocks for other meals later in the week. If you already have boiled eggs and potatoes in the fridge, this comes together in just a few minutes. Use the recipe below as a guideline, but feel free to improvise in the true spirit of the dish.

1 large egg	¼ cup cooked chickpeas, salted to taste	1 teaspoon capers
2 small thin-skinned potatoes		Extra-virgin olive oil
	2 tablespoons chopped fresh flat-leaf parsley	
2 ounces high-quality tuna in olive oil (like Ortiz or Tonnino)		Finishing salt
	1 teaspoon minced shallot or red onion	
2 or 3 oil-packed anchovies		

1   Bring a small pot of water to a boil. The egg and potatoes cook together, so clean the shell of the egg if necessary. Add the egg and potatoes, cover the pot, and reduce the heat to medium. After 9 minutes, transfer the egg to a bowl of cold water. Let the potatoes continue to cook until fork tender, another 8 to 10 minutes, then drain, run under cold water to cool them, and cut into ½-inch slices.

2   Peel the egg and cut it in half. Arrange the potatoes, tuna, and egg tightly on a plate. Drape the anchovies over the potatoes. Scoop the chickpeas onto the plate and top the whole thing with the parsley, shallot, and capers. Drizzle olive oil and sprinkle salt over the whole plate.

THE HOMEMADE KITCHEN

64

BLUE CHEESE WEDGE

One of my favorite restaurants is a converted old brothel deep in the woods of Becket, Massachusetts. If you're lucky enough to find it, there will be cocktails on the porch, pictures of naked women in the bathroom, and a labyrinth out back. When it's summer and we want a treat, it's the Dream Away Lodge.

Joey always sticks with the burger, but I'm a terrible restaurant orderer—I fight with myself and second-guess. I always have to wait to see what everyone orders first, just so I can decide what else I'll get to try. You'd never know all this sitting across the table from me, but this is the process in my head.

For the longest time, one salad that was always on the menu called to me, and every time I'd say no.

"I'm not ordering an iceberg wedge with blue cheese dressing. Iceberg lettuce is barely a vegetable. I could just drink water, and it would be nearly the same thing."

But one day, I gave in.

Now when I go to the Dream Away, I order an iceberg wedge *every single time*. I've inspired other people to give in to temptation too, as it seems I'm not the only one with the prejudice against the iceberg wedge.

I love the basic partnership of the iceberg and dressing, but if you want to pump this up, feel free to add toasted walnuts, a few cherry tomatoes, and chopped cucumber. And if you're making this for more than just yourself, keep in mind that the dressing makes enough to cover three or four wedges.

½ cup plain yogurt (for homemade, see page 34)

2 teaspoons lemon juice

2 teaspoons rice vinegar

Kosher salt

Freshly ground pepper

¼ cup crumbled blue cheese

¼ teaspoon minced garlic

¼ head of iceberg lettuce, cut into a wedge

Whisk together the yogurt, lemon juice, vinegar, and salt and pepper to taste in a small bowl or measuring cup. Stir in the blue cheese and garlic, taste, and adjust for salt and pepper. Lay the iceberg wedge in a wide bowl and smother it with dressing, reserving any leftover for more lunches later in the week. Top with one more grind of pepper.

VARIATION

This is also great with feta (store-bought or homemade, page 113) in place of the blue cheese.

Put Your Hands in the Earth

Every March, I make new garden plans.

This will be the year I finally put up those whimsical hand-hewn stick towers for my peas. This is the year I'll get those peas in the half-frozen ground so that they'll come up before July. I'll fence the garden to keep the deer out, and it will reach deep into the ground to bar entry from the mob boss king of it all, the groundhog. I'll create a diagram and stick to it. I'll build cold frames in the fall so I have spinach all winter. I'll grow artichokes!

Skip to November, when you'll find me on my knees pulling out the rotten tomato vines, prepping a bed for the garlic, and dreaming of all the things I'll do *next year*. Every year, the November garden holds the hopes, memories, and experiences of the previous six months. The autumn cold is replaced by the warm memory of Joey in August, with a wool blanket over his shoulder and our last two beers cradled in his arms. "Stars!" he says, pulling me away from my computer, and the garden grows around us then, too. I clear the square where Sadie diligently planted marigolds in the spring, inspired by a seed packet a friend sent in the mail. My thoughts spin all the way back to years before, when the garden was smaller and the soil not quite as rich. To Rosie, a baby, starting out her list of limited and strange food preferences with a deep adoration of cool, fresh dirt, preferably gathered with her tiny feet.

Back then, there were only a few plants I could get to grow. I'd fill a bed with lettuces and then miss the tiny window before they'd bolt and fill with bitterness, only to pull them out, compost them, and try again. I had yet to discover the wonder and ease of the backyard garden potato. And I was earlier on in the path of knowing what it was I wanted from my own garden, what it could give to me and only me. When I'd visit other gardens, the ordered rows and perfect logic tortured me. Why couldn't I create that?

In my short decade of gardening, I've learned that I love the perennials most. This is a little bit due to laziness, but there's more to it: when I was growing up, my mother and I lived in twenty-five houses in eighteen years. I always felt safe and grounded with her, and she was especially skilled at creating wonderful spaces for me wherever we lived, even if the space was really a walk-in closet or half of someone else's room. But what I always wanted was to know the feeling of having roots in one place. I wanted to see a space grow and change as I did the same. So without even consciously deciding to do so, Joey and I have managed to stay put. And these perennials that I begin from roots and sticks and seeds—they are my commitment to that. I have an elderflower bush on the north side of the house I started from a tiny twig. It grows taller than the house each year, and for the two weeks it explodes into lacy white blooms, our entire house smells of elderflower. There are Jerusalem artichokes that take over and grow into a jungle of sunflower-like stalks that lead down to the tubers I cook in the fall before everyone in my family threatens a revolt over the possibility of one more "sunchoke bisque." There are the perennial herbs, a lavender and sage that struggle through the cold spring before transforming into huge, fragrant clouds of green and buds. There is the rhubarb, the hero of my garden, that makes me feel like a champion every spring when it squeezes out its rosy bath-wrinkled-hand leaves. Again! It worked again! And there is the asparagus, which I planted after hemming and hawing for years over the required three-year period of waiting before you can eat your very first green stalk. When I finally dug the trench and laid those tiny crowns in the ground, I found that, for better or worse, three years go by pretty fast.

> Start where you are.

My advice to those who want to grow food in their yards is just to jump into it. Start where you are and know that no matter how big or small you begin, you will always be overwhelmed by weeds in September, so you might as well start small. There's no shame in container gardening—in fact, it holds many benefits when it comes to weeding and groundhogs. Remember that flowers feed us too, both in our salads and, more metaphorically, on our tables, so make a little space for them. Know that those stunning backyard gardens with tiled paths and vine-covered archways are usually the result of either someone's love and commitment to that space for multiple decades, or a whole lot of money and a small army of landscapers. If life is kind, you too will have those decades ahead. There is always next year, and then you will begin again, with all the knowledge of this year behind you.

COLD STEAMED GREENS *with* SCALLION DRESSING

I always grow too much kale. In April I'll pick up a few six-packs of veggie starts, always in denial of what's to come. Each compartment holds a small leaf and it seems entirely reasonable to plant them all. By July, my garden is a kale forest. I think the deer come to chomp off a few leaves here and there just because they feel sorry for me.

But I've got a few ways to dig myself out of the kale pile. I blanch and chop the leaves, and freeze them for winter soups. I'm always happy for an excuse to make Garden Pie (page 275). And on a hot summer night, there's nothing so delicious as cold steamed greens in a salty scallion dressing. The dressing recipe makes more than you'll need for your greens. I predict you'll want it on everything until the jar is empty.

FOR THE GREENS

2 cups sliced Napa cabbage

1 to 2 bunches watercress, stems and leaves, coarsely chopped (about 3 cups)

1 large bunch curly kale, pulled off the stem and coarsely chopped (about 5 cups)

FOR THE DRESSING

2 cups coarsely chopped scallions (1 to 2 bunches, white and green parts)

¼ cup coarsely chopped fresh flat-leaf parsley leaves

¼ cup coarsely chopped fresh basil leaves

1 cup safflower or sunflower oil

2 tablespoons rice vinegar

1½ teaspoons kosher salt

1   Cook the greens: Fill a large bowl with ice water and put it next to the stovetop. Add a few inches of water to the bottom of a large steamer pot, then pack the greens in the steamer basket in three distinct zones to keep them separate. Cover, bring to a boil, and steam until the greens are just tender, about 3 minutes. Use tongs or a slotted spoon to dunk them (one kind of greens at a time) in the ice water, giving them a gentle squeeze to drain on their way out of the water. Arrange the greens in a large, wide serving bowl, keeping each vegetable separate.

2   Make the dressing: Combine the scallions, parsley, basil, oil, vinegar, and salt in the blender and process until you have a bright green dressing. Taste, and add more vinegar or salt if needed. Pour the dressing generously over the vegetables, reserving any leftovers in the fridge for future meals.

STORAGE NOTES ✦ Scallion dressing keeps well in the refrigerator for up to 5 days.

GARLIC IN ALL ITS MOMENTS

The life cycle of the garlic plant is abundant and extraordinary.

The first year I grew garlic, my friends Jen and Pete, who regularly grow garlic on their farm, gave me a few bags of "seed." Garlic seed is just garlic, and the trick is to pick your best heads from the previous year to get the next crop started. If you're starting from scratch, use something local. Garlic at the grocery store has usually been irradiated, and this, among other things, will stop it from growing in your garden. So buy a bunch of heads at the farmers' market in the early fall, eat some, and save the plumpest heads for seed.

Plant your garlic when the ground gets cold. I tend to plant my garlic right around Thanksgiving, which is a little late, but as long as the ground isn't frozen, the garlic always forgives me.

Turn a bit of compost into the bed. Separate out the cloves from each head, being careful to preserve the thin paper skin around each one. This is a good job for kids, if you have a few who might be complaining of boredom on a chilly Saturday afternoon.

Use your thumb to press each clove into the ground. Your thumb is a good measure of how deep it should be. Better a little too deep than too shallow, because the ground will heave the cloves upward throughout the winter as it freezes and thaws, and it's essential to keep those cloves underground.

You have two options when it comes to spacing your garlic: you can plant the cloves 2 to 3 inches apart, and then thin it out in the spring when it's in the green garlic stage (more on this later). Or you can plant it 4 to 5 inches apart and avoid the thinning. Either way, cover the cloves with a bit more compost, some chopped-up leaves or straw, or just plain old dirt. Whatever it is, it will serve as mulch to protect the cloves and keep the weeds out.

In the spring, the garlic is the first thing I see.

Sometimes I don't remember where I put it, but there it is, shooting tiny lime-green blades out of the half-frozen ground.

Once garlic comes up, it grows quickly. When it's tall and green and tender like a scallion, this is the green garlic phase. The whole green is usable, and it's especially good with eggs. If you've planted your garlic very close together, you can thin out your patch and use the green garlic as a tender green like a scallion, baby leek, or ramp. Otherwise, let all the plants keep growing. Many farmers sell green garlic at the market, too.

The green garlic will get taller over the spring, and then, almost overnight, the flowers, or scapes, arrive. The scape starts out small and tender, and then as it grows, the stem gets tougher and the bud gets larger. Pick the scapes when they're small and just beginning to twirl. Use a sharp knife to cut the flowers off at the base of their stems. Store the scapes in the crisper drawer of your refrigerator. They last for a month or more, and you can chop up both the stem and flower and use them anywhere you'd use garlic. You can also fry or grill scapes whole, pickle them (see page 29), or pound them into pesto (see page 44). They're milder than the bulb, so be generous with your quantities.

Now that the scape is gone, leave the bed alone. Even if weeds have made their way through your mulch, let them be. You don't want to dislodge the bulbs when weeding.

By now, depending on where you live, it might be July. The garlic will start to look tired and crispy. You might think, "All this time? All this work? Only to shrivel and die?" But you're right on schedule. Each leaf is associated with a layer of skin on the bulb, so what you see aboveground tells you a lot about what's happening below ground. The leaves will begin to brown from the bottom up, so keep an eye on your patch when they start to brown. Aim to harvest when there are three green leaves left on the plant.

Pick a dry day. Use a small garden fork and gently loosen each head. Don't pull on the stalk—just create enough space so the head can come out easily. Gently release the head from the ground, tapping off any large clumps of dirt. Separate out a few heads to eat fresh and then cure the rest. You'll need a place with lots of air but no direct sun. Lay the stems flat to air dry for a few days, then hang them from the rafters of a room with good airflow. Leave them to cure for three to four weeks. When the paper is white, the root is dry, and all the layers feel like paper when you peel into a bulb, it's time to cut off the stalks and store the bulbs. Store your garlic in a dry, cool, dark spot, reserving the largest heads for planting in the late fall. Your stored garlic should last into January and February. Turn any dried-out cloves into Garlic Powder (page 75)—that, along with the garlic you'll now start buying from the store (it's okay!) will carry you until spring, when the cycle begins again.

⟫ ROASTED GARLIC ⟪

Roasted garlic is such a treat, and when I have the sweet creamy cloves ready to go, I use them everywhere I can. Preheat the oven to 425°F. Remove the loose outer paper of each head of garlic and, using strong scissors or a knife, chop off just enough from the top of each head to expose the naked cloves. Wrap a small piece of foil around each head like a gift, leaving the top open, and place in the cups of a muffin tin. Pour a tablespoon of olive oil over each head, then seal the foil so it creates a tight package. Roast until the cloves are soft and ooze out of their skins, 45 minutes to an hour. Roasted garlic keeps well in the refrigerator for 4 to 5 days. To freeze it, remove the cloves from their skins and freeze on a baking sheet. Transfer to a freezer bag and store for 6 to 8 months.

⟫ GARLIC POWDER ⟪

This works with garlic cloves at any stage, but it's an especially good use for old, dried-out cloves. Separate out and peel your cloves. Send the cloves through the slicing disk of your food processor, or slice each clove into as close to ⅛ inch slices as you can. Spread the sliced garlic in a single layer on a parchment-lined baking sheet and bake in a 170°F oven until brittle, about 3 hours. Let the garlic cool. Then, working in batches, transfer the garlic to a spice grinder or coffee grinder devoted to spices. Whir until you have a fine powder—then transfer to a jar for storage. If your powder is sticky, transfer it back to the baking sheet and return it to the oven for 20 minutes. If the powder clumps over time in storage, just press it with a spoon or pestle. Make sure you do this on a day you can open your windows, as the dehydrating garlic is particular aromatic. I like to do this with about 2 heads at once, and I usually get about ¾ cup garlic powder. You can also make onion powder this way. Just substitute finely sliced onions for the garlic, and bake for about 2 hours before whirring them into a powder.

QUEEN GARLIC *with* CHÈVRE *and* TOMATOES

John Andrews is one of the few restaurants in the Berkshires that's been here since I was a kid. It occupies a house in South Egremont, Massachusetts, and serves great, locally sourced, go-out-on-your-anniversary food. There's an appetizer that I'm pretty sure has been on the menu since day one, and there would probably be a countywide revolt if they took it off. It's so simple—grilled toasts are topped with Monterey chèvre and sweet roasted tomatoes. A whole head of roasted garlic sits in the middle of the plate like a queen holding court, and, to access the garlic cream inside, dressed-up diners have to tear off an oily clove and squeeze it onto their tomato-cheese toast. It's messy and sticky and the charred garlic paper sticks to your fingers. But after one bite, the whole table starts fighting for the cloves, licking their fingers, and embracing the mess of it. This recipe starts with both roasted tomatoes and roasted garlic, but if you're starting out with fresh, you can roast them together and meet the temperature difference in the middle at 350°F in the interest of simplicity. Just keep your eye on both, and take them out when the garlic is soft and the tomatoes are like sweet candy.

½ baguette or loaf of country bread, sliced thin	4 ounces chèvre (for homemade, see page 99)	1 large head Roasted Garlic (page 75), warm or at room temperature
2 tablespoons extra-virgin olive oil	1 pint cherry tomatoes, roasted (see page 23), warm or at room temperature	
Kosher salt		

1 Preheat the oven to 425°F. Lay the slices of bread on a baking sheet, brush with the olive oil, sprinkle with salt, and bake for 10 minutes. Check the toasts, and if you prefer them toastier, flip them and give them another few minutes in the oven. Let the toasts cool slightly and generously spread them with the chèvre.

2 Arrange the toasts around the perimeter of a plate. Mound the tomatoes in the center of the plate, and nestle the whole head of garlic right into the tomatoes. To eat, start with a chèvre toast. Separate a clove of garlic, squeeze out the flesh, and spread it over the toast. Top with a few roasted tomatoes.

ROASTED RED PEPPERS

Sadie is a huge red pepper fan, so every year I try again, and my wimpy pepper plant sprouts two twisted fruits that we cheer and pray for. Then one starts to rot at the bottom, and we put all our hope into that last pepper, which, like clockwork, disappears into the mouth of some animal the day before we've planned to pick it. I like to think the pepper-loving animal goes through the same process every year, too, hoping and praying for the health of his pepper. The only difference is that he gets the pepper and I do not, so from the groundhog's perspective, he's *great* at growing peppers.

Despite all our pepper challenges, I often end up with a glut of red peppers, either from the market at high pepper time or when the supermarket puts those expensive red peppers on super sale, and I can't help but fill up my cart. Peppers just do not last, and those moments always require some preservation. Peppers can also be roasted on the grill. Turn them with tongs until blackened and blistered, and proceed with the recipe below.

| 8 large red peppers | High-heat oil such as safflower or sunflower | Olive oil |

1 Preheat your broiler with the rack about 6 inches from the broiler element. If your broiler has a temperature setting, set it for medium or 450°F. Line a rimmed baking sheet with parchment paper.

2 Lightly rub each pepper with oil, laying them on the baking sheet as you go. Broil until the tops are blackened. Stay attentive to their progress, as this will take anywhere from 10 to 25 minutes for each side. The peppers are done when they're mostly blistered and collapsed. Use your tongs to transfer the peppers to a big heatproof bowl. Cover tightly with plastic wrap or a plate that fits the bowl exactly. Let the peppers sit for at least 20 minutes, and up to a few hours.

3 If the peppers are fully roasted, they should slide right out of their skins after steaming and cooling in the bowl. Separate the flesh from the seeds and stems as you go. Tear each pepper into strips and collect them in a quart jar. Pour any pepper juice from the bowl over the peppers, and top off the jar with enough olive oil to cover the peppers.

STORAGE NOTES ✦ As long as they're covered with olive oil, roasted red peppers keep in the refrigerator for up to a week. Alternatively, you can freeze the peppers without oil in a freezer bag, saving any juice from the bowl for use in soups or sauces, for up to 6 months.

MUHAMMARA

I ate something like this in Turkey, and then I came back and tried to re-create it. I had no idea that the red peppery spread had such a beautiful name and I didn't realize it was such a staple in so many countries—I just knew that it was something I needed in my life. There are probably as many versions of muhammara as there are people who make it. Some have cheese and some do not, sometimes it's walnuts instead of almonds, and the herbs and spices change from recipe to recipe. Feel free to play around with flavors depending on what you have in your fridge or pantry when you have too many red peppers. This is a great dip for veggies and crackers, delicious on sandwiches, and a perfect stand-in for pesto on pasta. Use it as part of your Ploughman's Snack (page 241) or, most of all, Turkish Breakfast (page 239).

½ pound carrots, halved and cut into 2-inch lengths	1½ cups Roasted Red Peppers (page 78)	1 tablespoon pomegranate molasses
1 tablespoon olive oil	1 tablespoon minced garlic (2 to 3 cloves)	1 teaspoon dried sumac
½ teaspoon kosher salt	⅓ cup chopped fresh dill	¼ teaspoon kosher salt
⅓ cup whole almonds	3 tablespoons fresh lemon juice (1 lemon)	4 ounces feta cheese (for homemade, see page 113), crumbled

1 Preheat the oven to 400°F. Toss the carrots with the olive oil and salt, lay on a baking sheet in a single layer, and roast for 20 minutes. Spread the almonds on a second baking sheet in a single layer and toast in the oven for 6 to 7 minutes while the carrots finish cooking. Allow both the carrots and the almonds to cool slightly.

2 Scrape the carrots and any oil or juice on the pan into the bowl of a food processor fit with the chopping blade. Add the almonds, roasted peppers, garlic, dill, lemon, pomegranate molasses, sumac, and salt to the carrots and process until the mixture is fairly uniform and the consistency of thick pesto. Transfer to a jar or serving bowl. If you want to freeze some of your batch, separate it out now. Stir in the feta, taste, and adjust the salt if necessary.

STORAGE NOTES ✦ This freezes well. Just leave out the feta and freeze in an airtight container for up to 6 months.

▸▸▸▸▸▸▸ ROASTED RED PEPPER CORN CHOWDER ◂◂◂◂◂◂◂

SERVES 6 TO 8

My favorite time in New England is the end of August, when summer sticks around for most of the day until the sun starts to set and the chill comes in. A month earlier I might have tried (and succeeded!) to pass off Popsicles as dinner, but the pre-fall chill brings on the desire to cook again. Lucky thing, as this is the moment when all the best vegetables are ready. This recipe is late summer in a bowl for me, and with frozen roasted red peppers and frozen corn, I can re-create it at any time of year.

2 tablespoons unsalted butter

2 cups minced leeks (1 to 2 leeks, using all the white and most of the green)

1 tablespoon minced shallot

1½ tablespoons coarsely chopped fresh oregano or 1½ teaspoons dried

1 tablespoon fresh thyme leaves or 1 teaspoon dried

4 cups frozen or fresh corn kernels (from 6 to 7 ears)

½ cup uncooked millet

4 cups stock, whey (see page 35), or water

1 cup coarsely chopped Roasted Red Peppers (page 78)

2 cups whole milk

½ cup coarsely chopped fresh flat-leaf parsley

1 tablespoon coarsely chopped fresh mint

3 to 5 chives, finely snipped with scissors

1½ teaspoons kosher salt

Freshly ground pepper

1 Melt the butter in a large pot over medium heat. Add the leeks and shallot and cook, stirring often, until the leeks soften and turn bright green, about 3 minutes. Add the oregano, thyme, and corn and continue to cook, stirring often, until the corn softens and shrinks, about 10 minutes.

2 Meanwhile, put the millet in a small bowl and cover with water. Let it soak for about 5 minutes, then drain and add the millet to the pot along with ½ cup of the stock. Continue to cook, stirring often, for 10 more minutes. Add the rest of the stock and the roasted peppers to the pot. Bring to a boil, reduce the heat to medium low, cover, and cook at a low simmer until the millet is tender, about 20 minutes.

3 Remove the pot from heat and add the milk. Use an immersion blender to blend the soup with a few pulses, just enough to make it a bit creamy while retaining whole kernels. Alternatively, put 2 cups of the soup in an upright blender, blend, and return to the pot. Add the parsley, mint, chives, and salt and pepper. Reheat if necessary, and garnish with additional parsley.

PLATTER SALADS

Sometimes when I'm working at the farmers' market, a customer will walk up to the table with a shopping list.

"I need arugula. Where's the arugula?"

"No arugula this week. It bolted, and we won't have it again until the fall."

He looks at me, lost, frozen, and not sure what to do. I scan the table. Sometimes I have an easy answer, and other times I just make one up. In that moment, the person just needs a confident suggestion, and I know what he might not—that everything on this table tastes good.

"But I have microgreens. How about microgreens?"

"Will they work? What *are* microgreens? Will my wife be mad if I show up with something not on the list?"

Relying on farmers' markets, CSAs, and gardens requires a shift in the way we put together meals. Everyone knows what to do with lettuce. Broccoli, carrots, potatoes—we have the ways our parents cooked them, or our own ways of preparing them that are a reaction to how our parents cooked them. Those are easy. We know what they'll be.

But when we cook a new vegetable, we might have to ask for directions. What part of this do I eat? How do I cook it? Do I have to peel this? Do I eat the stems? For the first time, we come face-to-face with alien vegetables like kohlrabi and celeriac, and the biggest fear is that we'll mess it up, we'll cook it wrong, or worst of all, we'll lose courage and let the vegetable rot in the crisper.

Deborah Madison taught me about platter salads with her book *Local Flavors*. "Platter salads," she says, "are a blessing for those of us who can't make up our minds about what to focus on when faced with abundance." There's room for every single thing on a platter salad, and the rebellious thrill that comes with combining cooked vegetables and raw, eating a tomato alongside a potato, calling it a salad even though it *has no lettuce*—these are just some of the pleasures the platter salad can bring to your dinner.

This is how it works:

Start with the dressing. It could just be olive oil, or you can take it one step further and make a vinaigrette (see page 31). Put the dressing in the bottom of a large bowl. You'll also need a platter. Have that ready, too.

Now the vegetables. Cook, or don't cook, each vegetable "as appropriate," as Deborah Madison says. Steam or roast little potatoes. Halve or quarter raw cherry tomatoes. Steam or roast green beans and asparagus. Roast cauliflower, delicata squash, and red and yellow beets. Roast peppers (see page 78) or leave them raw. Slice raw cucumbers and grill a zucchini. There's room for all of it. Toss each vegetable in the dressing separately in the large bowl before transferring it to the platter. If the vegetable is cooked, make sure you dress it while it's still a bit warm. When you dress all the vegetables before they get to the platter, you avoid the problem of losing all the good stuff at the bottom when you toss the salad.

Now add coarsely chopped herbs and little leaves of whatever you have. This can be basil or mint leaves, parsley, microgreens, arugula, endive, radicchio, or roughly chopped lettuces. Toss those in the dressing, too, or just sprinkle over the vegetables on your platter. You can stop here if you like—just give the whole thing a sprinkle of salt and a few grinds of pepper.

But if you want to keep going, add a protein. This could be cheese: cubed Feta Cheese (page 113), creamy bits of Chèvre (page 99), or peels of Parmesan. It could be sliced hard-boiled eggs or really good canned tuna. Or cold Tofu (page 160), grilled tempeh, or prosciutto.

And finally, you could add whatever salty bits you have in the fridge: olives, capers, or some roughly chopped rind from Preserved Lemons (page 95). Give the whole platter a few grinds of pepper, and set it on the table for everyone to ooh and aah over. And, of course, to eat.

PUMPKIN PUREE

I didn't expect to have a favorite pumpkin, but I should have known that there's nothing so simple as a basic pumpkin. I needed to make pie, and I asked my friends Jen and Pete if they had a spare pumpkin from their harvest. They gave me four pumpkins.

"Do a comparison! You like that sort of thing."

It turns out there is a pumpkin variety called Winter Luxury. It's as round as a nineteenth-century French bosom, and just as luminous. The skin is frosted with white speckles, and the flesh, when baked, is soft and velvety. This is my favorite pumpkin for pie, and when I can find it, it's the one I roast for puree. I'll also settle for the Long Pie or New England Pie varieties, or any common sugar or pie pumpkin I can get my hands on. The only pumpkins I don't eat are the large, tasteless pumpkins grown for jack-o'-lanterns—those, we save for carving.

You can roast small and larger pumpkins alike, and you'll get an average of 1 cup puree from every pound of pumpkin. Roast a few at once, and then fill the freezer with puree.

1 Preheat the oven to 350°F. Use a large, sharp knife to cut the stem end off each pumpkin, creating a flat top. Cut smaller pumpkins in half and larger ones in quarters. Scoop out the strings and seeds, and throw them in a bowl to set aside for roasting separately (see page 120).

2 Place the pumpkins flesh side down on a greased rimmed baking sheet. Bake until the halves are soft when pricked with a fork and on the verge of collapse, 60 to 90 minutes. Remove from the oven and flip over each half, venting the steam away from your face. Let the pumpkins cool.

3 Separate the flesh from the skin, either by peeling the skin with a knife or scooping the flesh out of the skin with a spoon. Transfer the pumpkin flesh to a food processor or high-speed blender and process until smooth, working in batches if necessary. This may require some tamping down, shifting of pumpkin pieces, and patience. If the pumpkin is dry and refuses to transform into a smooth puree, add water, a few tablespoons at a time, until you have a puree.

STORAGE NOTES ✦ Freeze in 2-cup portions. Fill freezer bags, flatten them out, and store in the freezer for up to 1 year.

NOTE ✦ Homemade pumpkin puree has a higher water content. If you're making pie, pumpkin bread, or some other baked good, drain your pumpkin puree through a cheesecloth-lined strainer in the refrigerator for a few hours before using.

SPICY PUMPKIN HOT CHOCOLATE

 **SERVES 4**

One leaf-covered fall afternoon, I got the best kind of call.

"Can you guys come down here? I have something I want you to try."

My friend Brandee had a pumpkin roasting in the oven, and her mother had sent her a recipe for a thick and spicy pumpkin hot chocolate. We were out the door in moments, running our way down the hill between our houses, fueled by the thrill of spontaneity and the promise of a treat.

The result was so good, and entirely different from the run of "pumpkin" flavored drinks that had begun to show up on coffee shop menus. Instead of the indeterminate sweet spiciness of those drinks, this contained and tasted like actual *pumpkin*. That first warm mug was the spark for this recipe, and I've made it again and again. Thick, deeply chocolaty, and somewhere between a drink and a dessert, this is the hot chocolate I make when I want to serve something special and unexpected. The whipped cream is essential here, as it balances out the spice and richness of the hot chocolate in a perfect way.

3 cups whole milk	2 teaspoons ground cinnamon	Optional: ⅛ teaspoon ground cayenne
4 ounces bittersweet chocolate, chopped	¼ teaspoon grated nutmeg	Whipped Cream (page 294), for serving
1 cup Pumpkin Puree (page 86)		

1 Heat the milk in a medium saucepan until hot and steamy. Remove from heat.

2 Put the chopped chocolate in a blender and add enough of the hot milk to cover the chocolate. Wait 5 minutes for the chocolate to soften, then process the chocolate and hot milk in the blender. Add the pumpkin puree, cinnamon, nutmeg, and cayenne, if using, to the blender and blend until smooth. If there's a lot of the chocolate pumpkin mixture stuck in the blender, you can also add a bit of the hot milk to the blender again at this point, blend, and pour it back into the pot. Add the chocolate pumpkin mixture to the remaining hot milk and return the pot to medium heat. Cook, stirring often, until the mixture is hot. Serve topped with whipped cream.

STORAGE NOTES ✦ Refrigerate hot chocolate in a covered jar for up to 3 days. Reheat on the stovetop.

ᚆᚆᚆᚆᚆ GINGER PUMPKIN PIE ᚆᚆᚆᚆᚆ

MAKES ONE 9- OR 10-INCH PIE

This recipe makes enough filling for a 10-inch pie, a bit larger than the standard. If you're working with a smaller pan and have too much filling for your crust, pour the extra into a few buttered ramekins and bake them alongside the pie for the first twenty minutes. Then you get pumpkin custard while you wait for your pie. This makes a super-gingery pie, and the crème fraîche adds a texture and tang to the custard that makes one of my favorite kinds of pie even more delicious. To up the ginger factor (and I always want to), add 2 tablespoons finely chopped crystallized ginger to your crust when you add the butter.

Unsalted butter, for greasing the dish	2 cups (490 g) drained fresh Pumpkin Puree (page 86) or 1 15-ounce can store-bought pumpkin	½ cup (120 ml) maple syrup
All-purpose flour, for rolling the dough		2 teaspoons ground ginger
		1 teaspoon ground cinnamon
1 recipe for a single whole-grain Piecrust (page 41)	2 large eggs	½ teaspoon grated nutmeg
	1 cup (240 g) crème fraîche (for homemade, see page 34)	½ teaspoon kosher salt

1   Grease a pie dish that can easily survive the direct journey from the freezer to the oven (not glass). Lightly flour the counter and roll your crust to between ⅛ and ¼ inch thick. Fold it in half, then in half again; center it over the pan and gently unfold the crust. Trim the crust so it hangs about 1 inch over the side of the pan, fold the extra crust in on itself and crimp to create a decorative edge. Put the crust in the freezer while you make the filling. (The crust can be stored indefinitely in the freezer at this point—just put it in a freezer bag if you plan to freeze it for longer than a day.)

2   Preheat the oven to 375°F. In a large mixing bowl, combine the pumpkin puree, eggs, crème fraîche, maple syrup, ginger, cinnamon, nutmeg, and salt. Stir with a wooden spoon until the mixture is fairly uniform. Remove the crust from the freezer and place the pie pan on a rimmed baking sheet. Pour the filling into the crust. Bake until the pie just barely jiggles in the center, 50 minutes to an hour. Let your pie cool for at least 1 hour at room temperature, then transfer to the refrigerator until you're ready to serve.

STORAGE NOTES ✦ This pie does well tightly wrapped in the refrigerator for up to 3 days.

One summer, my friend Hedley pitched a tent in our backyard and spent a week teaching me about sourdough.

She taught me about dough ratios, the basics of salt, and how to shape a loaf. But mostly I watched. I watched her coax and shape and roll, and she'd often grab my hand and gently immerse my fingers in the dough.

"Feel? Hmmm. So soft, like a pillow. You can't get that kind of rise with *store-bought yeast.*"

Every time we tucked a batch of dough in for rising, she'd lower her face to the bowl or the pans, and whisper as if to a lover.

"I love you. You are so good. What wonderful dough you are."

I was all for the idea of communing with the dough, but when she urged me to profess my love on the second rise, the words got stuck in my throat like a first-year drama student in improv class.

"I love you!" I squeaked.

Hedley, forgiving, kind, and ultimately possessing an excellent sense of humor, just exchanged knowing glances with the dough, giving it a gentle pat for good measure.

"You'll get there, honey. And your bread will show it."

I have yet to make a loaf of bread like Hedley's. But I did learn over the course of that visit that what makes fermentation so special isn't a recipe. It's a *relationship.* And whether you're maintaining a sourdough starter, helping kefir grains to multiply, or just creating the right conditions for your salted lemons to transform into the ideal condiment, the first thing to understand about fermentation is that it has everything to do with your own belief in the tiny bit of starter. You have to believe in it enough to feed it, to remember that it needs care, and even to profess your love to it once in a while.

> What makes fermentation so special isn't a recipe. It's a *relationship.*

In his foreword to Sandor Katz's *The Art of Fermentation*, Michael Pollan says that "to ferment your own food is to lodge an eloquent protest . . . against the homogenization of flavors and food experiences now rolling like a great, undifferentiated lawn across the globe. It is also a declaration of independence from an economy that would much prefer we were all passive consumers of commodities, rather than creators of unique products expressive of ourselves and the places where we live."

I'd go one step further. Fermentation is not only a political act in itself, it's training for engaging as a citizen in a democracy. Just as our sourdough starters require optimism and faith, so does the political process. Our actions might be small, but if we stay engaged, attentive, and optimistic about the process as a whole, every little "starter" in our lives will lead to some greater result, far more wonderful and alive than the raw materials we started with. We need to believe in the power of those few kefir grains or that little jar of aged flour and water, but we also need to feed it and pay attention to it every day. It's activism in the realest sense of the word. If you want the change, you've got to do the work.

MAKES ½ GALLON

My first preserved lemon came to me several years ago in my friend Ron's kitchen. He's one of those cooks who always has some new food on his counter, and on this day, he stuck a fork into a cloudy jar and pulled out a bite of lemon. "Eat this," he commanded.

I remember the moment well because a taste like that will make a memory cling. It was everything about a good fermented pickle, and everything about a lemon, but mostly about a brand-new taste I'd never experienced. I wanted to eat the whole jar. I wrote down the recipe and swore I would start a batch that day. But I'd never fermented anything and, intimidated by the process, I put it off. Time passed, and I forgot the feeling of tangy, salty rind in my mouth. Until, that is, I tasted it again, this time in my friend Janet's kitchen. Again with the fork, and again with the "eat this," and again I thought that this might just be the most wonderful and perfectly balanced taste I had ever experienced. When I finally got it together to create a jar of my own, it was so simple I kicked myself for missing out on all that time I could have had preserved lemons whenever I wanted.

Now I'm never without a big jar in the fridge, and I sneak them into all sorts of dishes. They're pretty wonderful anywhere you might use an olive or capers, really for any dish that could use a little tart saltiness. Preserved lemon rinds also do wonders to a chicken when you slide them under the chicken skin before roasting. Or use your lemon booty to make Preserved Lemon Hummus (page 97) or one of my favorite quick pastas, Fettuccine with Preserved Lemon and Roasted Garlic (page 172). If you have trouble finding lemon juice without additives, check the juice aisle of your local health-food store. I find this a good amount of lemons for six months, but feel free to halve the recipe and use a quart jar. I love Alice Waters's suggestion to add bay leaves and cardamom pods to her recipe in *Chez Panisse Fruit,* and those additions have become standard in my lemons, too.

3 pounds organic or unsprayed lemons (10 to 14 lemons)	1 cup kosher salt 10 cardamom pods 6 bay leaves	2 cups lemon juice, or more as needed (this can be fresh squeezed or bottled, as long as it is 100% lemon juice without chemical additives)

1 Scrub the lemons to remove any residue. For each lemon, cut off the tip. Then cut the lemon lengthwise, leaving the end intact. Cut it again lengthwise at a 90-degree angle to the first cut. The lemons will be quartered, but still attached at one end. Have ready a sterilized ½-gallon jar or two quart jars.

2 Measure the salt into a medium bowl. It might feel like a lot, but it's the salt itself that preserves the lemons, and it needs to fill all the spaces between the lemons in the jar. Put the cut lemons in the bowl, a few at a time, and rub the

flesh of each lemon with salt. Put a few tablespoons of salt in the bottom of the jar. Push the lemons into the jar, making a layer of lemons. They will release juice and smoosh a bit—this is good. Now scoop some more salt from your bowl and add it to the jar, along with a few cardamom pods and a bay leaf. Salt a few more lemons in the bowl and transfer them to the jar, repeating the process until you have filled the jar. You want to use all the salt in the bowl, so be generous in your layers, and dump any leftover salt into the jar at the end. Press the lemons down with a wooden spoon to release more juice. Then pour the additional lemon juice into the jar so that it fills all of the space around the lemons and covers the lemons entirely. Cover the jar with a sterilized lid and shake well.

3 Let the lemons ferment at room temperature, giving the jar a gentle shake or a turnover every day or so. In 3 weeks, the lemons will be ready to eat, and you can transfer the jar to the refrigerator.

TENSE MOMENTS ✦ As you salt and smoosh your lemons, some of them might break apart at their connected end. This is fine! The lemons will salt up just as well in quarters. Also, a few lemons might float up above your brine, and this is okay, too. If this happens, you have two choices: you can simply discard those top lemons after the fermentation process, or you can rig up a system to keep all the lemons down, as one of my blog readers taught me. Break a skewer into pieces the same diameter as the jar so you can fit them into the jar just above the brine in an "X." This makes a little cage to keep all the fruit under the brine.

STORAGE NOTES ✦ Store in the refrigerator in their jar for 6 months to 1 year. Discard if the lemons get moldy or too soft.

NOTE ✦ Sterilize jars either by submerging them in boiling water for 15 minutes or running them through a dishwasher with an extra-hot temperature setting.

PRESERVED LEMON HUMMUS

Joey gets the credit for this recipe. I was making my (admittedly good) regular old hummus when he slipped a preserved lemon into the mix. Now I never make it without the addition, as it turns good hummus into something remarkable.

1 Preserved Lemon (page 95), rinsed under cold water, pulp and rind coarsely chopped

½ cup sesame tahini

1 tablespoon miso paste

1 tablespoon minced garlic (2 to 3 cloves)

¼ teaspoon cayenne pepper

¼ cup olive oil

2 cups cooked chickpeas or 1 15-ounce can, drained and rinsed

4 to 6 tablespoons chickpea cooking liquid (if using canned chickpeas, use fresh water)

Combine the lemon, tahini, miso, garlic, cayenne, olive oil, chickpeas, and ¼ cup of the chickpea liquid in a blender or food processor. Blend until smooth. Add more chickpea liquid if necessary to get to a good, silky consistency. When you taste it to check the consistency, you may have to hold back so you have some left to eat later. It's that kind of hummus.

STORAGE NOTES ✦ Refrigerate hummus in a covered container for up to 4 days. Hummus also freezes well. Freeze in an airtight container for up to 6 months.

CHÈVRE

Susan Sellew at Rawson Brook Farm has been milking goats for more than thirty years. She keeps the self-serve fridge in the milking shed stocked with her three standard goat cheese flavors: garlic and chive (green label), olive oil and thyme (purple label), and plain (brown label). The tubs come in two sizes, but if you make the trek out to the farm, you might as well splurge on the big one.

Rawson Brook chèvre is as much of a Berkshire institution as any local food I can think of, craved by nearly everyone and used by every chef in the county. For this reason, it took me a long time to get around to making my own chèvre—honestly, how could it be as perfect?

I won't go so far as to say that my goat cheese is *as good as* Rawson Brook's, because that feels like a betrayal. But the process is simple and unfussy, and produces a wonderful cheese for half the cost. And now we can make our own "colors" too, as goat cheese is a perfect canvas for herbs, garlic, or even sweet additions like fig jam. Most natural food stores have a good goat milk in the dairy section. You'll need cheese molds for this recipe, which serve to shape the cheese and help it drain. You can buy molds or just rig up a few at home. I use ½-pint plastic containers with several holes poked in the bottom. You'll also need cheesecloth or butter muslin. Boil your cloth for a few minutes before each use to make sure it's totally clean.

½ gallon goat milk (raw or pasteurized) 1 packet direct-set mesophilic starter	1 drop liquid rennet dissolved in ¼ cup cool water 1 teaspoon kosher salt	Optional: 2 teaspoons fresh thyme leaves, ¼ cup nasturtium petals, 2 to 3 tablespoons mashed roasted garlic (see page 75), 1 tablespoon finely minced shallot, a few tablespoons jam or honey

1 Scrub a medium pot you can do without for a day with soap and very hot water. Set over low heat, pour in the milk, and let it warm to 76°F. (If it gets hotter, just let it cool to 76°F again.) Remove the pot from heat, sprinkle the starter over the milk, and let it sit for 5 minutes. Add the diluted rennet and stir gently for 20 seconds. Cover the pot, wrap it in a towel or warm blanket, and put it in a warm place. The goal is to keep the milk at 76°F as it cultures, so however that works in your house—perfect. On a warm day in the summer, you can just keep the covered pot on the counter.

2 Let the milk culture for 20 to 24 hours, depending on your schedule. When the curd is ready, it will be solid and silky, like firm yogurt. There will probably be a bit of whey around the edge of the curd. Gently fold the salt and any herbs or other additions into the curd. Alternatively, you can press herbs or flower petals onto the surface of your finished cheese.

3 Line each cheese mold with doubled-up cheesecloth so that a bit of the edge hangs over on all sides. Set a cooling rack over a mixing bowl or baking dish to catch the whey (see page 35), and set the containers on the rack. Spoon the curds into the molds, gently pressing down as you go. Cover the cheese with a dish towel to protect it while it drains. Let drain at room temperature until firm, 10 to 12 hours. Gently unmold the cheeses, transfer to a storage container, cover, and refrigerate.

STORAGE NOTES ✦ Store in the refrigerator in a covered container for 3 to 4 weeks or freeze, tightly wrapped, for up to 6 months.

CHÈVRE CHEESECAKE *with* MINT *and* BERRIES

Some of my favorite recipes come about from trying to make good food for friends with crazy dietary needs. When my friend Molly was about to have her first child, I promised I'd create a cheesecake for her baby shower that she could actually eat. The requirements were a gluten-free crust, no sweetener of any kind, and only goat's-milk dairy. I broke the cardinal rule of recipe experimentation and served my very first try at the shower itself. Molly tried to warn everyone off the cake, partially so she could have it all to herself, but also with the claim that it might not be so yummy for those who expected a sweet, cream-cheesy slice. To our mutual surprise, the cake not only disappeared, but I also had to hand out the recipe.

This version, with its bit of sugar and dairy, isn't quite Molly-appropriate, but the formula is my new go-to cheesecake. The crust becomes more of a lower cake layer, and it supports the custard in a way that I love. Feel free to add any additional spices and flavorings to the custard that inspire you. I love rose water in the custard, but orange flower water, vanilla, and almond extract are all delicious as well.

FOR THE CRUST	FOR THE FILLING	FOR THE TOPPING
1 cup (150 g) almonds	8 ounces (225 g) chèvre (for homemade, see page 99)	2 cups fresh berries (strawberries can be sliced if you prefer)
1 cup (80 g) unsweetened shredded coconut	1½ cups (338 g) plain whole-milk yogurt (for homemade, see page 34)	2 tablespoons sugar
¼ teaspoon kosher salt		1 teaspoon balsamic vinegar
¼ cup (50 g) sugar	4 large eggs	1 tablespoon coarsely chopped fresh mint
4 tablespoons (½ stick/ 56 g) unsalted butter, melted and slightly cooled	¼ cup (60 ml) honey	
	Optional: 1 teaspoon rose water	

1   Make the crust: Preheat the oven to 350°F. Spread the nuts and coconut on a baking sheet and bake for 5 minutes. Remove from the oven and allow to cool for a few minutes. Line the bottom and sides of a 9-inch springform pan with a large sheet of parchment paper. You don't need to be fussy about it, but try to fold the paper as smooth as possible where it overlaps on the sides.

2   Combine the nuts, coconut, salt, and sugar in the bowl of a food processor. Process until you have a chunky nut butter, about 1 minute. Add the butter and pulse a few times until the ingredients come together into a wet, buttery dough.

(recipe continues)

Gently press the mixture into the prepared pan and put the pan on a rimmed baking sheet. Bake until the crust puffs and begins to brown, about 25 minutes. Remove the crust from the oven and reduce the oven temperature to 325°F. Let the crust cool until it's no longer hot to the touch.

3 While the crust cools, make the filling: Combine the chèvre, yogurt, eggs, honey, and rose water, if using, in the food processor. Blend until the mixture is smooth. Pour the filling into the crust and bake until the pie barely jiggles in the center when you tap it, about 1 hour and 30 minutes. Chill in the refrigerator in the pan for at least 2 hours, and for up to a day. Unmold the cake when you're ready to serve it.

4 Just before serving, make the topping: Combine the berries, sugar, vinegar, and mint in a medium bowl. Stir to combine, mashing a bit with your spoon. Let the mixture sit for 10 minutes, then spoon it over the cake.

VARIATION

In the winter when fresh berries can be hard to come by, combine 1 cup pitted, coarsely chopped dates with ¼ cup water, ¼ teaspoon ground cardamom, and 1 teaspoon rose water in a small saucepan. Cook until thickened, let cool, and spoon over the cake.

STORAGE NOTES ✦ This cake keeps well in the refrigerator, tightly wrapped, for up to 3 days.

My kefir grains were small—so small I was never really sure what I was looking at. Even after weeks of making kefir, I still wondered each time I strained them if this would be the day I would lose them forever. I called the company that had sold them to me and asked why my kefir grains were so tiny. Where were the plump, voluptuous grains I had seen in pictures?

"Are they working?" the woman on the other end of the line asked me.

"Well, yes," I admitted. "But they're just so *small*."

"Some grains are small and mighty. Don't underestimate them."

Not only were they working, but these two tiny grains that nearly disappeared through the mesh of my sieve every day were surprisingly adept at making thick, creamy kefir. And as soon as I accepted the fact that my grains were just where they should be, I confidently added them to the ranks of the many other starters in my kitchen—the brown blob of sourdough starter, the yogurt in my fridge waiting for the next batch, the strange jiggly mother in the vinegar, and if we want to be really thorough, all the wild yeasts in the air that help these things to thrive and grow and turn basic ingredients into something much more extraordinary.

I also had to believe in the potential of the culture. Without belief, I would have given up on the daily maintenance. And if I'm not active, neither is the starter.

The maintenance of starters is some of the simplest and least time-consuming work I do in my kitchen, on par with wiping down the counters or making sure I turn on the dishwasher. I strain the kefir, and I add the grains to a new jar of milk. Like making kimchi or yogurt, kefir is just about giving the starter the support and conditions it needs to do its thing. The very nature of the culture process means they're never actually finished. The culture does its work; then it's ready to go for another round.

Store-bought kefir and homemade kefir are totally different products. Only homemade kefir is made with grains, while store-bought is made with a starter culture. The grains produce a kefir with a tarter flavor and far more beneficial bacteria. And because I always have a batch going and always have kefir in the refrigerator, I've found lots of ways to integrate it into my cooking. It's great in smoothies, but it's also wonderful in baked goods where you might use yogurt or buttermilk, like Kefir Banana Cake (page 107). I use kefir in my quiche (see page 196), where it creates a tangy, silky custard. Make flavored kefir by blending it with jam (see page 24), Chocolate Syrup (page 297), vanilla and maple syrup, or Cold Brew Concentrate (page 233) and maple syrup.

To make kefir, you need kefir grains. Most people who make kefir have extra grains to share, since the grains tend to reproduce. Otherwise, you can find online sources for both dehydrated and ready-to-go hydrated grains. Once your grains are active and begin actually thickening milk, all you need to do is put them in 1 to 2 cups of milk, cover the jar with cheesecloth fastened with a rubber band, and let the jar sit on the counter until you have kefir. This usually takes anywhere from 16 to 36 hours—faster in a warm kitchen and slower in a cold kitchen. That's it. There's no heating, no incubating, and no equipment other than a jar. When the milk is thick and smells like yogurt, strain it through a fine-meshed nylon strainer (metal isn't so good for the grains) and fish out the grains. Put the finished kefir in the fridge, and start a new batch by putting the grains in a new cup of milk. If you don't want to make kefir every day, just store the grains in a bit of milk in the fridge until you're ready to make another batch. They'll be good in there for a week or so, but if you want to store them for more time, just keep changing their milk in the refrigerator.

STORAGE NOTES ✦ Kefir will keep in the refrigerator for 2 to 3 weeks.

MAKES ONE 9 × 9-INCH CAKE

It seems that flours and sweeteners fall into two categories: the delicious, mainstream, and bad-for-you foods (that's white flour and white sugar), and the wholesome and "better" alternatives (everything else) that are less delicious.

It doesn't have to be this way. I think of whole-grain flours and non-white sugar as ingredients, not replacements. They're best when used where they shine, not as stand-ins.

I make this banana cake with spelt flour and maple syrup, so it's a great recipe if you want to experiment with some new flours and sweeteners. It also makes a good birthday cake for kids who might not be up for a supersweet cake, especially topped with Whipped Cream (page 294) or a simple chocolate ganache. If you don't have kefir, feel free to substitute thin yogurt.

⅓ cup (75 ml) sunflower or safflower oil, plus additional for the pan	1 tablespoon vanilla extract	½ teaspoon grated nutmeg
	3 cups (360 g) spelt flour	1 cup (240 ml) plain kefir (for homemade, see page 104)
⅓ cup (75 ml) maple syrup	1 teaspoon baking powder	
2 large eggs	½ teaspoon baking soda	1 cup (170 g) bittersweet or semisweet chocolate chips
3 (about 375 g) large ripe bananas	1 teaspoon kosher salt	Optional: ½ cup (45 g) sliced almonds
	1 teaspoon ground cinnamon	

1 Preheat the oven to 350°F. Grease a 9 × 9-inch pan. Whisk together the oil, maple syrup, and eggs in a small bowl. In a large bowl, mash the bananas with the vanilla. Add the egg mixture to the bananas and stir to combine.

2 Whisk together the flour, baking powder, baking soda, salt, cinnamon, and nutmeg in a large bowl. Add the flour mixture to the banana mixture and stir a few times just to combine. Add the kefir and chocolate chips and stir with a few swift strokes, taking care not to overmix. Scrape the batter into the prepared pan and scatter the almonds, if using, over the top. Bake until a cake tester or toothpick comes out clean when poked in the center of the cake, 35 to 40 minutes.

VARIATION

This is also wonderful with fresh blueberries in place of the chocolate chips.

STORAGE NOTES ✦ This cake stays delicious at room temperature, tightly covered, for up to 3 days. Or you can wrap it tightly and freeze for up to 3 months.

▶▶▶▶▶▶▶ KIMCHI ◀◀◀◀◀◀◀

MAKES 2 QUARTS

When we have kimchi in the house (and I try to make certain that we usually do), we have kimchi on *everything*. Joey will pair it with the strangest foods, and it's always a success. Scoop kimchi over rice and meat dishes, put it on your grilled cheese, or make a peanut butter and kimchi sandwich. But make sure you try Kimchi Breakfast Tata (page 111) too—it's perfect. The spice of this recipe will vary depending on the heat of your peppers, so adjust according to your preference and the peppers. A good kimchi will burn your hands as you mix it, so don't forget the rubber gloves.

1 large head (about 2 pounds) Napa cabbage, quartered, cored, and thinly sliced	3 tablespoons grated fresh ginger	¼ to ½ cup diced hot peppers (depending on their heat and your own heat desire)
½ pound carrots, peeled and sliced thinly on the diagonal	4 scallions, roots removed, cut into ½-inch lengths	Kosher salt
½ pound daikon radishes, red radishes, spring white turnips, or some combination, sliced thinly	6 large garlic cloves, peeled and thinly sliced	Optional: whey (see page 35)
		Optional: 2 teaspoons fish sauce

1 Combine the cabbage, carrots, radishes, ginger, scallions, garlic, hot peppers, and 1½ tablespoons salt in a large bowl. Put on dish gloves to protect your hands from the peppers, and squeeze the mixture until the vegetables release their juice. Work the mixture until it's quite wet.

2 Scrape the mixture and any liquid into a crock or similar vessel. Place a small plate over the vegetables, and top that with a smaller jar to weight down the plate. Lay a dish towel over the crock to protect the mixture, and store in a cool place. Check the contents after 24 hours. If the liquid from the vegetables does not entirely cover them, add a solution of 1 teaspoon kosher salt to 1 cup water. If you have whey (see page 35), you can use that instead of salt water.

3 Monitor your kimchi over the next few days. Some bubbling is a good (but not necessary) sign, and a layer of fine white scum is okay too—just skim it off as it appears. After about 5 days, taste the kimchi. It should still be crunchy, but with no taste of raw cabbage. If it's too salty, crunchy, or not quite funky enough, let it ferment another day and taste again, repeating for up to 2 weeks total. When it's ready, stir in the fish sauce, if using, and transfer to a covered jar in the refrigerator.

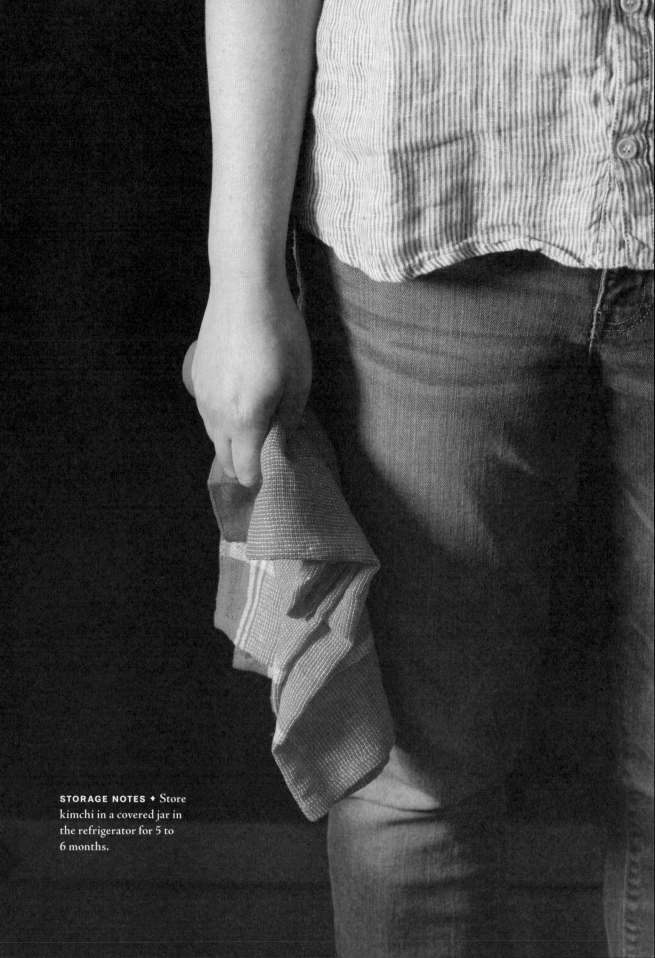

STORAGE NOTES ◆ Store kimchi in a covered jar in the refrigerator for 5 to 6 months.

KIMCHI BREAKFAST TATA

In our early days together when the girls were little and Joey and I had just moved back to Massachusetts from Santa Fe, we found ourselves homesick for New Mexican food. We'd order big cases of green chiles, and those, along with tortillas, made up the basis of most of our meals. Breakfast burritos were for special mornings when we had time to boil potatoes and bake bacon, but for every other day, there was the breakfast quesadilla. Tiny Sadie was especially a fan and she gave the dish the name that stuck, breakfast tata. When I started making kimchi, we tried swapping the green chile for the new and wonderful condiment, and—dare I say it? The tata got even better (just don't tell Santa Fe I said so).

2 tablespoons unsalted butter	7 large eggs	Four 8- or 10-inch flour tortillas
1 cup kimchi (for homemade, see page 108), drained and coarsely chopped	1 tablespoon mayonnaise	¾ cup grated Cheddar cheese
	¼ teaspoon kosher salt	

1 Melt 1 tablespoon of the butter in a skillet larger than one of your tortillas over medium heat, and add the kimchi. Cook, stirring constantly, until the kimchi starts to dry out, about 1 minute. Whisk together the eggs, mayonnaise, and salt in a medium bowl. Pour the mixture into the pan and gently scramble the eggs and kimchi, taking care to let the mixture cook in a few larger pieces. When the eggs are cooked through, transfer them to a plate and wipe out the pan.

2 Melt half the remaining butter in the pan. Add 1 tortilla to the pan and shuffle it around to coat it with butter. Spread a quarter of the scrambled eggs on one half of the tortilla, then fold the other half over. Put the second tortilla in the pan (one side will overlap with the tata already in the pan), shuffle, fill it with eggs, and fold it over so you have 2 folded quesadillas side by side in the pan. Open up each quesadilla and sprinkle a quarter of the grated cheese over the egg, then put the top layer down again. After 2 minutes or so, flip both tatas. Let them cook for a few minutes more before transferring to plates. Repeat the process with the remaining ingredients, for a total of 4 breakfast tatas. Cut each tata in half and serve hot.

THE OPEN DOOR

When I first started making simple cheeses, they seemed similar to any other recipe. There were ingredients (milk, salt, cultures) that I'd stir together and labor over, with the hope that my final result would be something cheese-like. As I made more cheese, I started to see it differently. Any bottle of milk or cream began to hold the potential to be something greater. All it needed from me was a little help and maybe a sprinkle of culture or a bit of heat. In fact, all the fresh cheeses, from cream cheese to mozzarella to cottage cheese, are remarkably similar in their making, but somehow they all create different results. Feta and mozzarella begin with nearly the same curds. Heat and stretch them, and you have mozzarella. Drain and press them, and you have feta. What this means is that as soon as you become comfortable with simple cheeses (and I predict that will happen sooner than you think), a whole world opens up. You can make your cheese softer or harder, tangy or smooth, just by shifting a few simple factors.

Sometimes mistakes lead to even new and better cheeses, so don't get discouraged if the process goes a little differently than you thought it would. It's easy to see why there is an endless variety of cheeses in the world, as every subtle shift in the combination of milk, culture, environment, and method creates its own unique product. It's a process that requires a little more interaction from the cook than the average recipe, as we have to think, taste, and adjust, and even troubleshoot as we go. The result is a cheese that's uniquely your own, and so very worth it.

▶▶▶▶▶▶▶▶ FETA CHEESE ◀◀◀◀◀◀◀◀

MAKES 1 TO 1½ POUNDS, DEPENDING ON THE FAT CONTENT OF THE MILK

You can make this recipe with cow's milk, goat's milk, or, if you can get it, sheep's milk. Although it's not technically feta if made with cow's milk, I actually love that option the most. The yield tends to be a bit higher, and the resulting cheese is more tender and crumbly, just the way I like it. You can find cheese cultures and rennet online, or in most beer-making supply stores. If you don't have unchlorinated water, leave a pitcher of water out on the counter for a few hours, and it will be good to go.

You'll need two or three feta cheese molds for this recipe. They serve to shape the cheese and help it drain. You can buy molds or just rig up a few at home. I use a sharp knife or screwdriver to poke four to six evenly spaced holes around the perimeter of the bottom of ½-pint or pint plastic containers. You'll also need cheesecloth or butter muslin. Boil your cloth for a few minutes before each use to make sure it's totally clean.

1 gallon cow, goat, or sheep milk (pasteurized or raw)	½ teaspoon vegetable-based liquid rennet or a heaping ½ tablespoon animal-based rennet, diluted in ¼ cup unchlorinated water	FOR THE BRINE
1 packet direct-set mesophilic starter		1 quart unchlorinated water
		⅓ cup kosher salt

1 Scrub a large pot with soap and very hot water. I like to use my enameled cast-iron Dutch oven, as it helps to insulate the milk through the whole process. Add the milk to the pot and set it over medium heat until it reaches 86°F. Remove from heat.

2 Sprinkle the starter over the milk and let it sit for 2 minutes. Then gently stir in the starter, cover the pot, and leave it alone for 45 minutes. If it's cold in your kitchen, wrap a blanket around the pot to keep it warm. The goal is to keep the milk temperature as close to 86°F as you can.

3 Add the diluted rennet and give the pot a few gentle stirs with an up-and-down motion. Cover the pot and let it sit for another 45 minutes. Remove the lid and take a look at the curds. They should have solidified into one big mass that looks like tofu. Press your finger about ½ inch into the curd. If it comes out mostly clean, the curd is ready to cut. If the cheese is soft and sticks to your finger, give it another 15 minutes and test it again.

(recipe continues)

4 Now with the curd still in the pot, cut it into 1-inch cubes: Place a long knife 1 inch from the left side of the pot and draw it through the curd in a straight line, taking care to cut all the way to the bottom of the curd. Continue cutting lines parallel to the first set in 1-inch increments. Turn the pot 90 degrees, and repeat so you have a grid. Then make diagonal cuts at a 45-degree angle to the side of the pot. Repeat from the other side. You don't need to be fussy—just do your best to end up with many smaller blocks of curd. Let the curds sit for 5 minutes.

5 Return the pot to low heat and raise the temperature to 90°F, stirring the curds constantly. Remove from heat and let the pot sit for another 5 minutes as the curds sink to the bottom of the pot. Line a sieve with cheesecloth, and set it over a bowl to catch the whey. Use a slotted spoon to transfer the curds from the pot to the sieve. Let the curds drain for about 30 minutes. Save the whey for use in smoothies, soups, and baked goods (see page 35).

6 Line your cheese molds with doubled-up cheesecloth so a bit of the edge hangs over on all sides. Set a cooling rack over a mixing bowl or baking dish to catch the whey as the cheese drains, then set the cheese molds on the rack. Spoon the curds into the molds, gently pressing down as you go. Cover the cheese with a dish towel to protect it while it drains. Let the curds drain for about an hour, then flip the cheeses, which should be solidifying a bit by this point. Let them sit at room temperature for another 6 to 8 hours.

7 Prepare the brine by combining the water and salt in a large pitcher. Shake to dissolve the salt. Unmold the cheeses and either put them into one container together, or give each block of cheese its own container. Pour the brine over the cheese, cover, and refrigerate. The cheese is ready to eat in 24 hours, but will get better by the day.

STORAGE NOTES ✦ Stored in its brine, feta lasts in the refrigerator for 3 to 4 weeks.

TENSE MOMENTS ✦ The strength of rennet can vary a bit, so if your feta is a little softer than you'd like, increase your rennet by just a few drops in your next go-round. If it's too firm and squeaky, reduce the rennet by a few drops. The finished product can require a little tinkering. If it's too salty, soak the cheese in unsalted water for a day, then return it to the brine. And sometimes homemade feta gets a little slippery on the outside as it ages. That's totally fine—it doesn't affect the taste at all.

CULTURED BUTTER

I love the process of fermentation because each recipe breaks down to three essential elements: the good ingredient, the influence of the environment on that ingredient, and the power of my own work to help transform that ingredient.

Take cultured butter, for example.

If you find yourself with a jar of raw cream, eat a spoonful. The cream will reflect the meals of the cow that produced it. It will taste different depending on the time of year and what the cow was eating. That's the *ingredient*, and it's the first step.

Top the jar with cheesecloth fastened with a rubber band, and let it sit on the counter for about 12 hours. The air in which you cook, work, and live carries the culture that will merge with all the grassy flavors of the cream, and if you taste it again, will have more of a tang to it than it did before its rest on the counter. That's the *place* working its way into the food, and it's the second step.

If you want to give the process a boost, or if you're using pasteurized cream, you can add a spoonful of buttermilk, crème fraîche, or yogurt to the jar at the beginning.

Once your cream has ripened, whip it in the bowl of a stand mixer until it turns to whipped cream. Continue beating, and drape a clean dish towel over your mixer. You'll see why in just a moment.

After the cream has whipped, the sound will change to sloshing. The butter will gather around the beater while the buttermilk pools around the bottom of the bowl. (Without that dish towel, the buttermilk will cover you and your kitchen walls.) Stop the mixer, and, holding back the butter with your hand, pour the buttermilk into a jar and transfer it to the refrigerator for tomorrow's pancakes. Gather up the butter in your hands. Transfer it to a clean bowl and knead it against the side of the bowl. Place the bowl in the sink, rinse the butter in cold water, and squeeze it again. Repeat until the water runs clear. Knead salt into the butter if you like. The whipping and the washing is the *work*, the third step.

That's it. Start with a good ingredient, infuse it with the place, and do the work.

GREEK SALAD

This is one of those salads that makes me love summer. All the key ingredients are at their peak at exactly the same time, and for that little window, I eat this every single day. Serve with a pita or other fresh bread, and it's a meal in itself.

2 teaspoons red wine vinegar

1 teaspoon lemon juice

1 garlic clove, crushed into a paste with the side of a knife

1 tablespoon chopped fresh oregano or 1 teaspoon dried

½ teaspoon kosher salt

1 small red onion, diced

6 tablespoons olive oil

2 large cucumbers (or 4 to 5 small), peeled, quartered, and sliced into 1-inch chunks

2 or 3 medium tomatoes, cored and cut into wedges

1 small sweet red pepper, cut into large dice

½ cup pitted kalamata olives, coarsely chopped

6 ounces feta cheese (for homemade, see page 113), cubed or crumbled

½ cup coarsely chopped fresh flat-leaf parsley

Combine the vinegar, lemon, garlic, oregano, salt, and red onion in a large bowl. Let the mixture sit for 10 minutes. Stir in the olive oil, then add the cucumbers, tomatoes, pepper, olives, feta, and parsley to the bowl, gently folding them into the dressing. Let the salad sit for a few minutes, taste, and adjust for salt if necessary.

Oh, the food we waste.

It wasn't always this way. Many of us are descended from immigrants who scraped and saved to get here, miraculously survived the trip, and arrived with nothing. My family (the Jewish side, the side that raised me) stepped off the boat just in time to settle into tiny apartments to sit out the Great Depression. There was no such thing as wasted scraps then. Bones were stunning centerpieces of great meals, cooked, stewed, and celebrated for their marrow. Vegetable peels were pressed together for pancakes, and a soup was an opportunity to make nearly anything edible. My grandmother, the youngest of nine in a tiny apartment in Manhattan's Hell's Kitchen, survived off scraps entirely. Her father made gin in the bathtub (a cliché, but true) and sold it to feed all the open-mouthed birds in his nest.

Of course, for those who stayed hungry, scraps remained a necessity. But as food became cheaper and its production more industrialized, scraps became garbage. Habits shifted. Now even the most well-intentioned and frugal eaters clear out the crisper, pulling out bags of slimy parsley and forgotten carrots that bend at the waist. We throw away bones, discard bread ends, and buy vegetables that have been peeled, cored, or stripped down to their most attractive parts. Animals are bred and raised for the production of one or two popular cuts while the rest of their precious bodies goes to waste. Romaine hearts come bare and naked, as do the inner bits of artichokes.

> Every time we use something we thought was trash, it feels like free food, like a gift.

Food production has become a system of waste and excess, and it's hard to find our way out.

Start here, with a curvy butternut squash. Cut it from top to bottom with your sharpest knife, preparing it for roasting. Then scoop out the sticky seeds at its center and place them in a bowl you've set in the corner of your cutting board. Once you tuck the squash into the oven, fill the bowl with water and agitate the strings and seeds with your hands to make the seeds rise to the top. Fish out the seeds, boil them in salted water for 5 minutes, drain, and dry in a towel. Toss with oil (about 1 teaspoon per cup of seeds) and salt. You can also add chili powder, cumin, rosemary—any herbs or spices you like. Roast in a 350°F oven until they pop and sizzle, 17 to 20 minutes, shuffling the seeds around halfway through the baking time.

You may live in a world of wasted scraps, but today you've used this whole vegetable, and you're sticking it to the man, one bowl of spicy squash seeds at a time. Quiet revolutions add up.

Celery leaves and tough green leek tops go into stock. Bread ends become sweet bread puddings and golden bread crumbs. For the more adventurous, apple cores make vinegar, and tomato skins make a fine powder for flavoring. And every time we use something we thought was trash, it feels like free food, like a gift. It's a boost to our own sense of inner resourcefulness that only grows when encouraged.

For the scraps that just can't be eaten, the last stop is compost. No matter where you live or what you know about composting, try to find a way to incorporate it into your kitchen. The best composters (and I am not one) create a carefully crafted scientifically balanced cocktail of dry and wet and the perfect nutrients, but most of us have a pile of scraps on the side of the yard that go into the garden or dissolve back into the earth right where they are. If you live in the city, there are small composting systems for you, too, or maybe you're lucky enough to live in a city that composts for you. However you compost, you're keeping it from the landfill.

> Quiet revolutions add up.

Of course, this shift in mind-set is not all about using up the scraps. To have scraps in good shape in the first place, we need to be conscious of how we store our food, how often we buy it, and how strategically we use it. Especially when making the shift from store-bought to homemade staples, it can be hard to adjust to creating your own packaging and judging your own expiration dates. The more food you make at home, the more you've got to take food storage and food safety into your own hands.

How to store vegetables in the refrigerator:

+ Place herbs in jars of water, like flowers, in the refrigerator. Put a plastic bag over the foliage. Basil doesn't like the cold, so should be stored similarly, but out on the counter.

+ Keep lettuce and other tender leaves in covered reusable glass or plastic containers in the refrigerator. Wash and dry the leaves, and include a paper towel or a small clean cloth in the container (see page 30). You can also roll up the clean, dry leaves in a clean dish towel. Store in the crisper drawer, right in the towel, for a day or two.

+ Separate all roots from their greens, and store the roots and greens in separate containers. Leaves can be stored like lettuce.

+ Cucumbers and peppers can stay out on the counter for a few days. Tomatoes and avocados should be refrigerated only after being cut. Potatoes, onions, and garlic should not be refrigerated at all. I store those vegetables in baskets in my pantry, but if you have a cool, dark spot somewhere else in the house, that's ideal as well.

Tools that help food last longer:

Tape and a marker: How many times do you throw something away because you just can't remember how many days it's been in the fridge? Keep masking tape and a permanent marker right by the fridge, and label food as it goes in.

The freezer: If you've got leftovers that you're not sure when you'll use, freeze them right away. Got half a jar of pasta sauce left? Freeze it. Half a ginger root? Freeze it. Use the freezer liberally and generously. And label everything.

Mason jars: I try to decant everything in the pantry into a jar to eliminate stale chips and crackers, hard dried fruit, and everything else that happens when my family hastily grabs a bag and puts it back without sealing it properly. Mason jars seal nearly airtight. They're also inexpensive and easy to find at any supermarket or hardware store.

Vacuum sealer: I have a FoodSaver, and it vacuum seals jars as well as bags. Even if you buy a large quantity of something, you can use one portion and vacuum seal the rest.

>>>>>>>>> STUFFED TOMATOES <<<<<<<<

SERVES 4 TO 6

My favorite way to eat an August tomato is whole, like an apple. I sprinkle salt, then I take a bite, sprinkle salt, take a bite. But this method is not particularly dignified, and is best done alone on the back porch. When I want to dress up those bursting tomatoes for dinner, this is what I do. I gather different varieties of tomatoes, mixing red, yellow, orange, and green in the pan. Just make sure they're round, or it's too hard to stuff them. And if you have bread crumbs ready to go, skip that step and go right to the stuffing. These make a great picnic dish or leftover lunch, too.

3 tablespoons olive oil	6 to 8 round medium tomatoes	1 tablespoon finely chopped fresh oregano
2 garlic cloves, smashed	½ cup packed fresh basil leaves, cut into ribbons	½ cup grated Parmesan or pecorino cheese
1 teaspoon kosher salt		
8 ounces sliced stale country or sourdough bread	½ cup packed fresh flat-leaf parsley leaves, coarsely chopped	Freshly ground pepper

1 Preheat the oven to 375°F. Heat 2 tablespoons of the olive oil in a small skillet over medium heat. Add the garlic and ¼ teaspoon of the salt and cook until fragrant, about 2 minutes. Remove the cloves and set aside. Lay the slices of bread on a baking sheet, brush them with the garlicky olive oil, and bake until crispy, about 30 minutes. Remove from the oven and let the toasts cool slightly.

2 Meanwhile, prepare the tomatoes. Carefully core each tomato with a paring knife, cutting wider than the core to create a round opening big enough to stuff, but small enough so the tomato doesn't entirely come apart. Use a spoon to scoop the pulp from each tomato, reserving the flesh in a large bowl. You want to maintain the walls of the tomato, so scoop carefully. Set the tomatoes upright in a roasting pan that holds all the tomatoes snugly, propping them up against each other, and sprinkle the inside of each tomato with the remaining ¾ teaspoon salt.

3 Pick out any big chunks of tomato pulp or seeds from the bowl and discard. The bowl should be mostly juice with some tomato flesh and seeds mixed in. When the toasts are cool enough to handle, run them through the grating disk of a food processor to transform them into crumbs. You can also put them in a sealed plastic bag and roll them with a rolling pin. Reserve a small handful

of fresh herbs for finishing the dish. Add the bread crumbs, remaining herbs, Parmesan, and several grinds of pepper to the bowl of tomato pulp. Finely chop the reserved garlic cloves and add those to the bowl as well, mixing thoroughly to combine. Taste the mixture, and add a bit of salt or pepper if needed. The mixture shouldn't be too salty, as the tomato walls will provide additional salt.

4 Spoon the bread-crumb mixture into the tomatoes, gently packing the mixture down as you reach the top of each tomato. Drizzle the remaining tablespoon of olive oil over the tomatoes and bake until the tops are browned, about 30 minutes. Finish with freshly ground pepper and the reserved fresh herbs before serving.

TENSE MOMENTS ✦ The walls of your tomatoes might crack and break, but that's okay! Pack the tomatoes into the roasting pan together so they can support each other. This dish is meant to be messy and unfussy, so don't get caught up trying to keep the tomatoes perfect.

WHAT TO DO WITH STALE BREAD ✦ The most valuable scrap in my kitchen is stale bread. Bread crumbs, bread pudding, croutons, crostini—stale bread, although often undervalued, is really one of the best ingredients there is. Keep a container or bag in your freezer and throw any stale pieces, ends, or even forgotten toast in the bag. Then you'll have a constant supply of this powerhouse ingredient. Stuffed Tomatoes (opposite page), Panzanella (page 128), and Broccoli Raab and Sausage Bread Pudding (page 129) all use stale bread in different ways. Don't try to use fresh—it doesn't hold up as well. If your grocery store or bakery offers day-old bread at a discount, these recipes are great ways to use it.

PANZANELLA

Panzanella is traditionally made from bread, tomatoes, and basil, but I've come to love it even when it's not high tomato season. With that in mind, I offer three versions: summer, spring, and fall.

6 tablespoons extra-virgin olive oil

8 ounces stale bread, torn into bite-sized pieces

½ teaspoon kosher salt

2 tablespoons red wine vinegar

1 tablespoon balsamic vinegar

1 teaspoon Dijon mustard

1 scant tablespoon finely minced garlic (2 to 3 cloves)

2 to 3 cups any combination of green beans (raw, steamed, or sautéed), chopped cucumbers, and sliced sweet red pepper

3 to 4 medium tomatoes, cut into wedges

½ head of lettuce or tender greens

¼ cup basil leaves, torn or cut into ribbons

Freshly ground pepper

1 Heat 2 tablespoons of the olive oil in a large skillet over medium heat. Add the bread and stir often. When the bread is crisp, 4 to 6 minutes, remove from heat.

2 Meanwhile, make the vinaigrette. Combine the salt, vinegars, mustard, and garlic in a large bowl. Let sit for 5 minutes, then whisk in the remaining ¼ cup olive oil. Add the bread, vegetables, and tomatoes, gently folding them into the dressing.

3 Spread the lettuce on a serving plate, tearing any larger leaves into smaller pieces. Pour the contents of the vegetable bowl over the lettuce. Top with basil and freshly ground pepper.

VARIATIONS

For a spring version, replace the tomatoes and summer vegetables with steamed or roasted asparagus, thinly sliced radishes, and fresh peas. Exchange the basil for tarragon, parsley, chives, or some combination of the three.

For a fall version, use roasted or pan-fried Brussels sprouts and delicata squash. To prepare the squash, halve it lengthwise, remove the seeds, and slice each half into ¼-inch moons. Toss with olive oil and roast on a greased baking sheet at 425°F until crispy, about 25 minutes. Replace the basil with 1 tablespoon chopped fresh sage and thyme. Add shaved Parmesan.

BROCCOLI RAAB *and* SAUSAGE BREAD PUDDING

When I invite friends over for dinner, I always swear to myself I'll have dinner all ready and the kitchen cleaned up when they arrive, but more often than not, we drink our first glass of wine together while I'm still working at the stove and shoving dishes in the sink. Unless, that is, I'm making bread pudding. Then I've got dinner in the oven and I've had time to clean up before they even walk in the door. This also makes delicious leftovers for the next day's lunch.

1 tablespoon unsalted butter, plus additional for the dish	3 large eggs	½ cup (120 ml) water
6 cups (about 1 pound/ 455 g) cubed bread (wheat, sourdough, rye, baguette—as long as it's not seeded)	2 cups halved and sliced leeks (1 to 2 leeks, using all the white and most of the green)	12 ounces (340 g) cooked andouille sausage, cut into 1-inch half-moons
3 cups (720 ml) whole milk	8 cups coarsely chopped broccoli raab (1 large bunch)	2 cups (224 g) grated sharp Cheddar cheese

1 Preheat the oven to 375°F. Grease a 9 × 13-inch or equivalent casserole dish with butter. Scatter the bread over the base of the dish. Whisk together the milk and eggs in a large bowl, and pour the milk mixture over the bread to soak while you cook the vegetables.

2 Melt the butter in a large skillet over medium heat. Add the leeks and cook, stirring often, until soft, about 5 minutes. Add the broccoli raab and the water. Bring to a boil, cover, and lower the heat. Cook, lifting the lid to toss the broccoli raab once or twice, until the greens are tender, about 7 minutes.

3 Fold the sausage and 1 cup of the cheese into the bread. Transfer the greens to the dish as well, leaving any liquid in the skillet. Nestle the greens into the bread mixture. Top with the remaining cheese and bake, uncovered, until the center doesn't weep when pierced with a knife, about 1 hour.

VARIATIONS

• Try this with kale, collards, or turnip greens. Asparagus is also wonderful.

• Feel free to experiment with cheeses, too. Gruyère, Jarlsberg, and Comté are delicious in bread pudding. This is also a good time to use up any stray cheese ends you have sitting in your fridge.

STUFFED WINTER SQUASH

SERVES 4

Every fall, the squash calls begin again. They start just here and there. But in October, the pace quickens, and the calls become more panicked.

"Help. Need squash recipes."

My favorite thing to do with a winter squash is to stuff it. Not only will you use that winter squash taunting you from the counter, you will also use last night's grain, sad apples that came back in the lunch box one too many times, even old corn bread—they all find their home here. The recipe below is a guideline, but most combinations of grain, green, apple, and meat work perfectly.

2 acorn, delicata, dumpling, or carnival squash, cut in half through the stem and seeded	6 ounces chorizo or sweet sausage, crumbled or cut into small pieces	2 cups sliced tender greens (spinach, tatsoi, kale, Swiss chard), cut into ribbons
2 teaspoons olive oil, plus more for rubbing the squash and oiling the dish	1 cup chopped leeks (1 small leek)	4 fresh sage leaves, coarsely chopped
¾ teaspoon kosher salt	1 cup chopped apple (1 to 2 apples)	2 cups cooked millet, rice, or quinoa (see pages 36–38)
	Freshly ground pepper	½ cup grated Cheddar cheese

1 Preheat the oven to 375° F. Rub the flesh of each squash half with olive oil, and oil an ovenproof dish or baking sheet. Sprinkle the whole baking dish with ½ teaspoon of the salt. Lay the squash flesh side down in the dish and bake until it is very tender when pricked with a fork, 30 to 40 minutes. Remove the squash from the oven and raise the oven temperature to 425°F.

2 Meanwhile, heat the remaining olive oil in a large skillet over medium heat. Add the chorizo and fry until browned. Remove from the pan and set aside. Add the leeks to the hot oil and cook until soft, about 3 minutes. Add the apple, remaining ¼ teaspoon salt, and pepper, and cook for another minute. Add the greens, sage, cooked grains, and reserved chorizo. Cook for another minute, stirring to combine, and remove from heat. Taste, and adjust the salt and pepper if needed.

3 Turn the cooked squash over in the baking dish so it is flesh side up. (Be careful, as steam will escape when you turn it.) Scoop the filling into the cavity of each squash half, piling it into a mountain so that it holds as much as possible. Sprinkle with cheese and bake until the cheese melts, about 10 minutes.

🎀 VARIATIONS 🎀

+ Chopped fried bacon is a great substitute for the chorizo.

+ Crumbled corn bread is a delicious substitute for the grain.
  When you make corn bread and have a few pieces left over,
  just crumble them into a container and freeze them for your
  next batch of stuffed winter squash.

+ If you don't have leeks, substitute a medium red onion.

+ If you don't have Cheddar, substitute Parmesan or other
  sharp cheese.

TEN BITS & SCRAPS WORTH SAVING

1 Parmesan rinds

Any time you have a strip of Parmesan rind, throw it in a bag or container in the freezer. Add a chunk to a pot of soup, and it will infuse the soup with a deep, ripe, and wonderful flavor.

2 Carrot tops

This one comes from my friend Jen Salinetti, who grows wonderful carrots and so has lots of beautiful greens. Make a pesto of 2 cups packed cleaned and chopped carrot tops (remove the large stems), 1 tablespoon lemon juice, 1 chopped garlic clove, and ¾ teaspoon kosher salt. Process in a blender or a small food processor, or by hand with a mortar and pestle. Then add ¼ cup extra-virgin olive oil, and process again.

3 Chicken, beef, or pork bones

Save the bones in the freezer until you're ready to make stock. Then pack the bones into a pot along with a leek (or leek tops; see opposite), a carrot, a few garlic cloves, a handful of peppercorns, a tomato if you have one, and any fresh herbs you have on hand. Just barely cover with water. Cook, covered, on low heat for at least 2 hours but up to all day. You can also follow this process in a slow cooker. Pack the cooker at night and you'll have rich stock by the morning.

4 Old bagels, pita, and tortillas

Slice bagels as thin as you can (carefully!) and cut pitas and tortillas into wedges. Brush with olive oil, sprinkle with salt, and bake in a 350°F oven for 12 to 18 minutes, until brown and crispy. Use instead of crackers.

5 Strawberry hulls

Toss those strawberry hulls into a pitcher of water. They infuse it with a mellow refreshing sweetness. You can barely taste them—it just tastes like the best water you've ever had.

6 Peach pits

If you're making peach jam or pie and have a bowl full of peach pits, rub off any excess flesh and give the pits a quick boil to clean them entirely. (Drink the liquid you boiled them in—it's delicious.) Then dry the peach pits in a 200°F oven for about an hour. Let the pits cool, then store in a jar at room temperature. Peach pit tea is good for whatever ails you. To make tea, combine 4 or 5 pits with 5 cups water. Bring to a boil, lower the heat, cover the pot, and simmer for 10 to 15 minutes. Let the pits dry out on the counter—you can use them three times before they won't infuse tea anymore.

7 Root vegetable greens

If you buy beets, turnips, kohlrabi, or radishes with their greens, separate the roots from the greens when you get home, as they store better separately. Cook up the greens as you would kale or Swiss chard, put them all together for Garden Pie (page 275), or pound tender radish greens into pesto.

8 Leek tops and other veggie scraps

Treat leek tops and good veggie scraps as you would bones for stock. Keep a separate bag in the freezer and toss in scraps as you create them. When it's time to make stock, throw them all in the pot.

9 Bacon fat

Whether you fry or bake your bacon, pour the grease into a jar, straining it through cheesecloth or a paper towel to get rid of any bits. Store the jar in the pantry and use it to fry pancakes, collard greens, and other foods that benefit from bacon's smokiness.

10 Orange rinds

Stuff spent rinds into a jar and top off with distilled white vinegar. Let it sit for a few weeks, then combine the orange-infused vinegar with water for a homemade all-purpose cleaner. Or, use the rinds for an easy potpourri. Combine a few orange peels, a cinnamon stick, and a few cloves in a small saucepan. Cover with water and let it simmer away on the stove, scenting the kitchen as it evaporates.

SUMMER SQUASH FRITTATA

Leftover grains in the refrigerator provide an opportunity to get creative the next day. Fried rice is a standard no-brainer, and it always makes a reliable lunch. But the first time I tried folding leftover millet into a frittata, I couldn't get over how delicious it was. Millet and red quinoa are my favorites here, but this method will work with any cooked grain you want to use up. This makes a great breakfast, lunch, light dinner, or even packed lunch.

3 tablespoons olive oil

2 cups chopped leeks (1 to 2 leeks, using all the white and most of the green)

1½ tablespoons finely chopped shallot (about 1 shallot)

1 teaspoon kosher salt

2 cups paper-thin sliced zucchini or summer squash (1 medium zucchini)

6 large eggs

½ cup whole milk

2 cups leftover cooked grains such as millet, rice, or quinoa (see pages 36–38)

⅓ cup packed fresh basil leaves, cut into ribbons

1 cup grated or crumbled cheese [Cheddar, Swiss, Jack, feta cheese (for homemade, see page 113), or chèvre (for homemade, see page 99)]

1 Preheat the oven to 400°F. Heat a 10- or 12-inch ovenproof skillet or frying pan over medium heat. Heat 2 tablespoons of the olive oil for a minute, then add the leeks. Cook, stirring often, until soft and aromatic, about 5 minutes. Add the shallot, salt, and zucchini and continue to cook until the zucchini is soft and translucent, another 5 to 7 minutes. Remove from heat and allow to cool for a few minutes.

2 Meanwhile, whisk together the eggs and milk in a large mixing bowl. Fold in the grains, basil, and cheese, as well as the leek mixture. Wipe out the skillet, then use a clean cloth or paper towel to rub it with the remaining tablespoon of olive oil. Transfer the contents of the mixing bowl back to the skillet and bake for 20 minutes, until the egg is firm and doesn't ooze when you cut into the center. Switch the oven setting to broil and brown the top of the frittata for a few closely watched minutes under the broiler.

VARIATIONS

• If it's earlier in the season, thinly shaved asparagus can stand in for the zucchini.

• Use 1 cup caramelized onions in place of the leeks.

REUSABLES IN THE KITCHEN

One of the best ways to create less waste is to bring reusables into the kitchen where you might have once thrown something away. Fortunately, most disposable kitchen items have a reusable counterpart that is often more beautiful, practical, and easy to use. And although reusable items require a small initial financial investment, they save money in the long run. My favorite kitchen reusable? Cloth napkins.

I think most people come from either a cloth napkin or a paper napkin home, but I hail from a third category where, inspired by environmentalism, lack of money, or both, we refused to buy too many different kinds of paper products. Toilet paper doubled for tissues, and paper towels ripped in half served as napkins. I imagined cloth napkins to be the stuff of homes designed with themes in mind, where ideas like "centerpieces" and "carpet cleaning" were realities. So when Joey and I moved into our first kitchen, paper towels ripped in half (or quarters) were the de facto table setting.

The truth is, you can become a cloth napkin sort of house, even if you don't fit the rest of the profile. I learned this when I finally found myself in a store in our little town that boasted a rainbow of folded cotton napkins imported from India. I could be that much closer to being Martha Stewart for only $3.95 a (endlessly reusable) pop. I splurged on six orange napkins, and then cloth napkins appeared everywhere I looked, often for even less money than my initial stack. (And of course, if you sew, you can whip up a dozen napkins in no time at all.) We now even have enough napkins for big parties. If you'd like to make the switch, here are a few practical tips I've learned along the way:

Buy inexpensive, 100 percent cotton napkins.

Keep a small, dedicated laundry bag or basket in your kitchen.

Designate a napkin for each member of your family.

*Wash napkins with a bit of vinegar and lavender oil to keep them
clean and sweet-smelling.*

POLENTA FRIES *with* SPICY MAYONNAISE

MAKES ABOUT 32 FRIES

If you've had polenta done well, it's hard not to love it. it's wonderful on its own and provides a great base for everything from sautéed vegetables to fried eggs to tomato sauce. When I cook polenta, I often make a double batch so I can slice up leftovers for Broccoli Raab with Cheddar Polenta (page 61) or polenta fries. You can fry these in any high-heat oil, but ghee is my favorite for this recipe. Make the ghee ahead of time, and use it anywhere you might use butter.

FOR THE FRIES

4 cups cooked polenta (see page 38), spread and chilled in a 1-inch layer in a 9 x 6-inch or equivalent baking dish

4 tablespoons ghee (for homemade, recipe follows) or high-heat oil

FOR THE SPICY MAYO

1 large egg yolk

¼ cup olive oil

¼ cup grapeseed oil

Squeeze of lemon

Hefty pinch of salt

Lan chi, sriracha, or any combination of hot sauces in your refrigerator

1 **Make the fries:** Run a spatula along the edge of the chilled polenta to loosen it from the dish. Gently invert the dish on your hand over a large cutting board. The polenta should come out in one rectangular piece. Cut in half lengthwise, then cut each half into ¾-inch slices.

2 Heat 2 tablespoons of the ghee in a large cast-iron skillet over medium-high heat. Put as many polenta pieces in the pan as you can fit without crowding them (they shouldn't touch, and you should have enough room to flip them easily). They tend to sizzle and splatter, so if you have a splatter guard, pull it out now. Cook for 8 to 10 minutes, until crisp and golden. Flip each piece and cook for an additional 8 to 10 minutes. Transfer to a paper-towel-lined plate. Repeat with the remaining ghee and polenta.

3 **Make the spicy mayo:** Whisk the egg yolk with a teaspoon of water in a medium bowl. Combine the olive oil and grapeseed oil in a measuring cup with a spout and, whisking constantly, pour a few drops of the oil into the bowl. Then add a few more drops and whisk again. Continue in this way until you have a thick yellow sauce, then add greater amounts of oil all at once.

4 Add the lemon, salt, and as much hot sauce as you like. Stir to combine, taste, and adjust the seasoning if necessary.

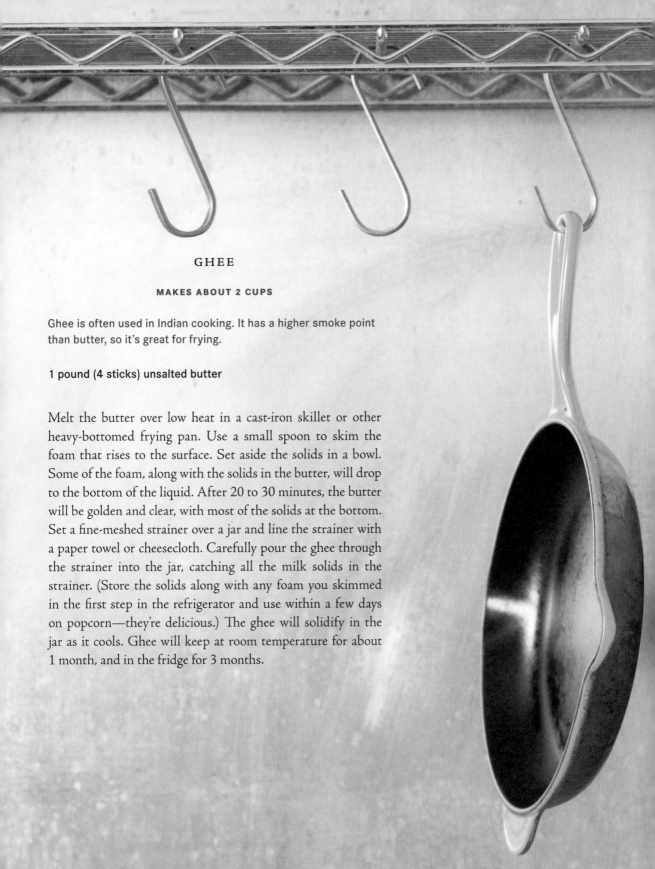

GHEE

MAKES ABOUT 2 CUPS

Ghee is often used in Indian cooking. It has a higher smoke point than butter, so it's great for frying.

1 pound (4 sticks) unsalted butter

Melt the butter over low heat in a cast-iron skillet or other heavy-bottomed frying pan. Use a small spoon to skim the foam that rises to the surface. Set aside the solids in a bowl. Some of the foam, along with the solids in the butter, will drop to the bottom of the liquid. After 20 to 30 minutes, the butter will be golden and clear, with most of the solids at the bottom. Set a fine-meshed strainer over a jar and line the strainer with a paper towel or cheesecloth. Carefully pour the ghee through the strainer into the jar, catching all the milk solids in the strainer. (Store the solids along with any foam you skimmed in the first step in the refrigerator and use within a few days on popcorn—they're delicious.) The ghee will solidify in the jar as it cools. Ghee will keep at room temperature for about 1 month, and in the fridge for 3 months.

 Minestrone is a soup of scraps, and because the recipe is infinitely changeable depending on what you have, it's a soup of the moment.

Start with the aromatics. Dice a large onion and, if you have them, a few carrots and ribs of celery. Cook in a mix of butter and olive oil, stirring often, for 15 minutes. Add a few finely chopped garlic cloves along with a handful of fresh herbs. If you don't have fresh, use dried, but just a teaspoon or so of each. Thyme, rosemary, sage, and marjoram are great here. If you have basil, save it for the finished bowl. Throw in a teaspoon of salt and a bay leaf and continue to cook for a few minutes.

From here, you have a great base. Add any combination of diced leeks, hearty greens sliced into ribbons, peeled and cubed winter squash, diced zucchini, and green or yellow beans cut into 1-inch lengths.

Add the tomatoes. This can be 2 cups of roasted tomatoes (see page 23), 2 cups chopped canned tomatoes, or 2 medium fresh tomatoes, cored and diced. Include any liquid from the can, jar, or bag.

Finally, add the extras. Add any or some combination of cooked beans (cannellini and chickpeas are my favorites here), cooked pasta, or cooked grain.

Scoop into big bowls and finish with your toppings. A drizzle of olive oil, grated parmesan, Pesto (page 44), or coarsely chopped basil are all wonderful here.

STORAGE NOTES: This freezes well, as long as it doesn't have pasta. Freeze in airtight containers for up to 6 months.

DO YOUR BEST,
AND THEN
LET GO

Most Saturdays from May to October, I work at our local farmers' market for Indian Line Farm.

The farm, run by my friends Elizabeth Keen and Al Thorpe, feeds 120 families through its CSA and fills tables with produce at the Saturday market. In fact, Indian Line Farm has the distinction of being one of the first CSAs in the country. The soil there grows miraculous vegetables, heads of lettuce as big as the moon with names like Deer Tongue and Firecracker, radishes that I eat on buttered bread in the spring and fall, and tomatoes that make me count the days till July.

I love the farm, and I'm committed to supporting it. And for all the things it is, there is one thing it is not: organic.

Every week I work at the market, I answer the same question, over and over.

"No. We're not organic. We're Certified Naturally Grown." I change my words depending on the length of the line at the market table, but my most common summary of the certification goes like this: it's just as good as organic, but we're certified by farmers instead of the government.

The Certified Naturally Grown label is based on the standards of the National Organic Program. In some cases, the criteria for CNG certification are even more rigorous than for organic. But organic certification comes with a mountain of paperwork and a high price tag that just isn't feasible or even desirable for many small growers who sell mainly to farmers' markets and CSAs. If a small farm is growing primarily for the local community, customers most likely know the integrity of the farm's growing practices. People can visit the farms, ask the farmer any questions they may have, and even sometimes volunteer to work themselves. Those small farmers don't necessarily need the organic label to help sell their produce or meat. The CNG certification process is far more affordable and accessible for small farmers, and because CNG farms are inspected by other farmers in the program, the process can even help to build community among small farmers. It's a good label, and I feel great buying CNG products. The only issue is that customers don't recognize the CNG label. But hopefully, one conversation at a time, it will gain recognition.

I understand why people seek out the organic label, and why they ask for it when they choose their veggies. But it's helpful for me to dig a little deeper to try to understand their priority behind the question before I shape my answer. Is it pesticide use? GMO seeds? Locally produced food? Or is there just an ease that comes with knowing the food is organic? As more troublesome information comes to light about the sources of our food, the natural response is to draw lines between this label and that. To state clearly and definitively that it is how we eat. Or that I won't eat anything that's not [fill-in-the-blank]. But like most aspects of our food system, each of these labels is complex, and carries both positive and negative consequences. As consumers, it's essential to prioritize what we want from our food, and to understand that a label is not an end in itself; it is simply a tool to help us find the food we want to buy. The more we know about the various labels and how much they reflect our own priorities, the more informed our choices can be. I could fill pages about these labels, but there are a few that lead the way: Local. Seasonal. And, of course, organic.

> How do I eat? Organicish. Locenough. Homemade when I can. Fresh. Good. Mine.

The prevalence of the organic label has changed the way we shop at the grocery store. When we buy "organic," we know that the food was grown or raised without the traditional chemicals of conventional counterparts, but we also can assume that a certain amount of thought went into the production of that item. The organic label serves to provide peace of mind and, on the whole, signals a better product than a conventional option.

But there's a flipside as well. Organic food tends to cost more, and with that, the promise of healthy and conscious eating becomes available only to a certain part of the population. The expense is sometimes real and sometimes perceived, but the higher cost of organic and local food not only excludes those who might not be able to afford it, it also limits the capability of organic and local food to reach a greater audience. It's getting better, but slowly. A decade ago, I was lucky enough to find WIC, a government-subsidized program that helps pregnant women and families with young children pay for groceries. There was a restriction against using WIC checks for organic food, even if it cost less. But today, many WIC, SNAP, and senior assistance programs supply beneficiaries with farmers' market checks. It's good for everyone involved. People who might not otherwise have such clear access to local food now do, and farmers have an enthusiastic and committed addition to their customer base. The more we can erase the line between who gets to eat well and who doesn't, the better it is for all of us.

When I shop, my first hope is that my money supports producers and farmers—even better if they're in my own community. Large-scale industrial organic production usually doesn't meet these criteria, and often the food has traveled thousands of miles to get to my cart, another check against it when I'm deciding how I want to spend my grocery money. My priorities are clear, and I often go to great lengths to find food that reflects them.

And yet.

There are weeks when money is especially tight and I can look only at what's on sale at the grocery store. There are weeks that are way too busy for me to drive to four different farms and two different stores to buy my ideal version of every ingredient on my grocery list. There are nights when I know that a happy and relaxed mother bringing home a pizza for dinner is better than a stressed and tired mother making her own dough, cheese, and sauce from scratch. In the end, my priorities are as complicated and in flux as the food system that feeds me. I do the best I can, and then I let go.

So yes. These labels are important, especially when they're connected to a concrete set of standards. Choose the labels that you're committed to, and seek out food that makes you feel good about what you're creating in your kitchen. Even more, delve a little deeper into those labels and figure out what they mean and how they relate to what's important to you. But I encourage you to be wary of rules and standards that make you feel guilty or ashamed about how you choose to feed your family. Try not to judge other people's shopping carts, either. Remember that every family has a different way of making it work, and you, too, can find your own way, even if means you have to make up a few words.

How do I eat? Organicish. Locenough. Homemade when I can. Fresh. Good. Mine.

SKIRT STEAK SALAD OR HOW TO BUY A COW

I often buy portions of animals from farmers, which gives me the opportunity to figure out how to make the best use of all sorts of great cuts I would never find at the store. It's good for the farmer, too, as selling animals in large portions directly to customers helps the farmer sell parts of the animal that are more difficult to unload in a commercial market. Some of these, like crosscut beef shanks and lamb shoulder, have become my favorite cuts. Others, like pig's heads and lamb necks, have given me an education in the kitchen I never could have gotten without having them right there in front of me needing to be prepared. (You don't need to take the head if you buy a pig. But you can ask, if you want it. And there's nothing so delicious as a pig's cheek.)

If you want to buy a whole or large portion of an animal, the farmers' market is a good place to start. Get to know the meat farmers at your market and ask if they sell larger quantities. Usually, farmers ask people to preorder their meat, and your deposit will help to raise the animal. It's an investment, but a big money saver over the long term. Of course, you need somewhere to *put* all that meat. But if you have a chest freezer, this is a great way to use it.

Skirt steak is a lesser-used cut that came to me the first time I bought a quarter of a cow. It cooks quickly like flank steak, but I find the texture of the meat holds flavor even better. It's delicious grilled, too, but I prefer my trusty skillet for quick weeknight cooking.

SKIRT STEAK SALAD *with* CUCUMBERS *and* MINT

The spark for this recipe comes from my friend Isabella. "Have I ever told you," she asked, "about how my mother wrote a Vietnamese cookbook that included the *best* pork recipe ever?" Although the book was never published, I begged Isabella for the recipe, and *thit heo ram man,* or salty pork, has become a standard in our dinner rotation.

This dish, with all its sweet, salty, and fresh flavors, is another take on that brilliant weeknight meal. You can eat this with utensils or use the lettuce to scoop up the meat and cucumbers, which I prefer. You can also use flank steak here; just add about a minute of cooking to each side.

1¼ pounds skirt steak

2 tablespoons tamari

2 tablespoons fish sauce

2 tablespoons fresh lime juice (1 lime)

1 tablespoon grated fresh ginger

2 tablespoons toasted sesame oil

2 garlic cloves, smashed

4 to 6 small cucumbers, sliced into ½-inch rounds

2 tablespoons seasoned rice vinegar

¼ teaspoon kosher salt

Pinch of dried red pepper flakes

5 to 7 mint leaves, cut into ribbons

1 small head of butter or red leaf lettuce

1 tablespoon any high-heat oil

For serving: ½ cup peanuts, toasted and roughly chopped; torn basil, mint, or chopped cilantro leaves; lime wedges

1 Lay the steak in a large rimmed baking sheet. If there is a tough membrane on the steak, remove it. Skirt steak is long, so you can cut it in half in order to fit it in a single layer in the pan.

2 Whisk together the tamari, fish sauce, lime juice, ginger, and sesame oil in a small bowl. Add the garlic cloves to the bowl, and pour the mixture over the steak. Marinate for 30 minutes at room temperature, turning it over once or twice.

3 Meanwhile, combine the cucumbers, rice vinegar, salt, red pepper flakes, and mint in a bowl. Toss to combine, and set aside. Lay the lettuce leaves on a large platter.

4 Heat a large cast-iron skillet over medium-high heat. Add the high-heat oil and, after a moment, add a drop of water. When the water sizzles in the oil, add

the steak, working in 2 batches if necessary. Remove the garlic cloves from the marinade, and spoon additional marinade over the meat for the first minute of cooking. Cook the steak for about 3 minutes on each side. This should get you to medium/medium rare. Transfer the steak to a cutting board, and let it rest for 10 minutes.

5 While the steak rests, pour the cucumbers and their dressing over the lettuce, creating a bed for the steak. Then, use a sharp knife to slice the steak against the grain as thinly as you can. Pile the steak over the cucumbers and top with the peanuts, herbs, and lime wedges.

HOW TO FIND A CHICKEN

Let's talk chicken labels. There are more labels on your average chicken than a teenager trying to wear the right designers. And like most designer labels, most chicken labels don't really mean anything.

FIRST, THE MEANINGLESS LABELS:

Hormone Free: All chicken grown in the United States is hormone free. Whether there is a label or not, you can be sure that's the case. Hormones and antibiotics are two separate things, however, and although all U.S. chicken is hormone free, most is not antibiotic free.

Free Range: This means that chickens have access to the outdoors, although it doesn't mean they ever actually went outside.

Cage Free: Chickens are raised inside, uncaged with no requirement to ever let them outside. So this is no real improvement on conventional methods.

Natural: This means absolutely nothing.

NOW, FOR THE LABELS THAT GIVE US A LITTLE MORE INFORMATION:

Pastured: The chicken went outside regularly and ate plants and bugs. When you go to a farm to buy a chicken and have to dodge the chickens pulling up worms along the side of the parking lot, that's a good sign.

Organic: The chickens received no antibiotics after the first day, and all feed was certified organic. Organic certification doesn't specify much about living conditions, but the fact that the chickens don't receive antibiotics gives us a big clue. Chickens in tight conditions get sicker and need antibiotics. So for the most part, you know an organic chicken was raised well.

Certified Humane: The chicken had more space (inside) and consideration was given to the ammonia levels in the air.

Non GMO Product Verified: The chicken was given feed free of genetically modified organisms.

Certified Naturally Grown: The chicken was raised according to organic standards, but with greater strictness and clarity when it comes to how much time the animals must pasture outside. All feed must be grown according to CNG standards. Unlike organic certification, CNG is not regulated by the USDA.

CHICKEN POTPIE

Once you've put all that work into choosing your chicken, honor it with something truly delicious. Humble as it may be, chicken potpie is, hands down, the most requested birthday, friends-over, and regular old Thursday when-we-all-need-something-special dinner. It uses a few pots and involves a bit of time in the kitchen, but it's very worth it. For an extra boost to the broth, throw all the vegetable scraps into the chicken pot as you prep the vegetables.

FOR THE FILLING

One 3½- to 4-pound chicken

Kosher salt

1 bay leaf

2 tablespoons olive oil

1 cup diced onion (about 1 small onion)

3 cups halved and thinly sliced leeks (2 to 3 leeks, using all the white and half the green)

2 cups peeled and small diced carrots (4 to 5 carrots)

½ cup chopped celery (2 ribs)

1 cup coarsely chopped fresh flat-leaf parsley leaves

1 tablespoon fresh thyme leaves or 1 teaspoon dried

2 cups frozen or fresh green peas

2 tablespoons unsalted butter

½ cup (60 g) all-purpose flour

2 tablespoons whole-grain or Dijon mustard

Freshly ground pepper

FOR THE BISCUITS

2 cups (240 g) all-purpose flour

1 tablespoon baking powder

½ teaspoon kosher salt

8 tablespoons (1 stick/ 115 g) unsalted butter, cut into ½-inch cubes

1 cup (240 ml) buttermilk

1 large egg

1   Make the filling: Put the chicken, 1 teaspoon salt, the bay leaf, and any scraps and stems from your vegetables into a large pot. Just barely cover the chicken with water, set over high heat, cover, and bring to a boil.

2   When the water boils, skim off any foam on the surface, reduce the heat to medium low, and replace the cover. Cook until the chicken falls off the bone, about 1 hour. Carefully transfer the chicken to a large plate to cool. Remove the stock from heat.

3   Meanwhile, cook the vegetables. Heat the olive oil in a large ovenproof roasting pan or cast-iron skillet over medium heat. Add the onion and cook, stirring occasionally, until soft, about 3 minutes. Add the leeks, carrots, and celery and

cook, stirring occasionally, until the carrots are soft and the mixture starts to smell wonderful, about 10 minutes. If the mixture seems dry, add about ¼ cup of skimmed stock from the chicken pot. Add the parsley and thyme and cook, stirring occasionally, for another 10 minutes. Add the peas, cook for another minute, and remove from heat. Preheat the oven to 450°F.

4 In a separate medium saucepan, melt the butter over medium heat. Skim off about ½ cup of the fattier stock from the surface of the stock and add it to the butter. Add the flour, whisking the mixture constantly until it browns slightly, 3 to 4 minutes. Dip a 1-cup measure into the stock, and, straining to remove any scraps, pour the stock into the flour mixture. Whisk until smooth and repeat twice, using a total of 3 cups stock. The rest of the stock can be strained and frozen for other recipes. Whisk the mustard into the sauce, add several grinds of pepper, and continue to whisk over medium heat until thick, about 5 minutes. Pour the sauce over the vegetables.

5 Remove the meat from the chicken, tearing it into bite-sized bits. Add the chicken to the sauce and vegetables. Taste, and adjust for salt and pepper if necessary.

6 Make the biscuits: Whisk together the flour, baking powder, and salt in a medium mixing bowl. Add the butter and gently rub it into the flour with your fingers until it's well integrated but some chunks of butter remain. Combine the buttermilk and egg in a measuring cup and stir it into the flour mixture with a few swift strokes to create a sticky batter. Use wet hands to scoop 8 evenly spaced biscuit-sized rounds of batter on top of the filling. Bake until the biscuits are golden and a knife inserted into the center biscuit comes out clean, 20 to 22 minutes.

VARIATIONS

Add whatever needs cooking in your refrigerator. A cup of chopped mushrooms can be cooked along with the onions. Or include a cup of asparagus, cut to 1-inch lengths, when you add the peas. For a fall vegetable pie, substitute cubes of celeriac for the celery, omit the peas, and use 2 cups cubed winter squash in the mix.

TENSE MOMENTS ✦ Once in a while, my sauce doesn't quite thicken, no matter how patiently I stir. If this happens to you, you have two options. The first is to use it as is, and have a slightly looser sauce and stew-like pie. The second is to pull out another saucepan and make a new base for your sauce. Melt a few tablespoons of butter in the pot, add a few tablespoons of flour, and stir until you have a golden paste, about 2 minutes. Then slowly pour your too-thin sauce into the butter mixture, whisking as you go. The additional butter and flour should do the trick.

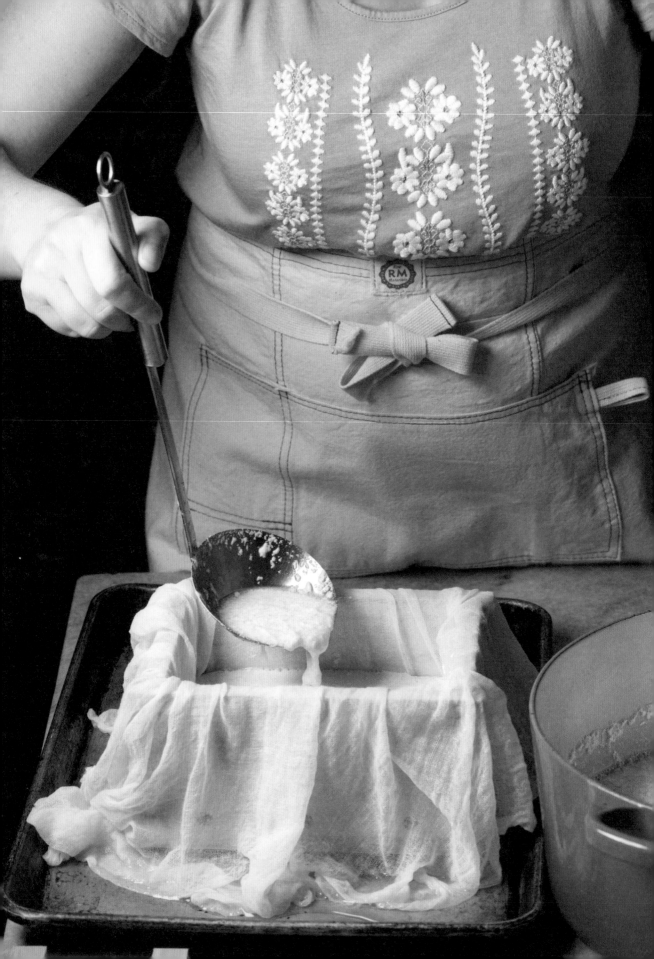

TOFU, OR THE ALTERNATIVE

Few food issues are as divisive as meat. Those on one side of the divide or the other will often defend their stance with a ferocity usually reserved for religion or politics. But most of us can agree on a few key elements: (1) Our process around raising and harvesting meat needs vast improvement, and (2) most of us who do eat meat could stand to eat a little less. Over the last decade, movements like Meatless Mondays have gained popularity, and little by little, we might just be easing our way to a more plant-based diet.

The shift away from meat can be hard for a home cook. We all get used to our standbys, and there are few dinners easier than a simply cooked steak or chicken breast. Meat "alternatives" like tofu, tempeh, and seitan are shaped into links, bacon-like slices, and even turkeys (!) as if what we need is just to close our eyes and imagine we're eating the real thing. But these foods are truly delicious in their own right, especially when they're taken for what they are, not as imitations of another thing.

Sometimes I try to make a store-bought food from scratch and find it's just not worth it. The end result might be totally lacking, or the process too tedious to merit spending the time. I thought tofu might fall into that category. But, in the interest of adventure, I lined up my supplies and got to work.

Several batches of perfect tofu later, I had to admit I was making so much tofu not because I was recipe testing, but because I love making tofu. Sure, the end result is wonderful. It's silky and fresh, and lacks the bitterness I didn't even know was there in store-bought until I tasted my own tofu. But I might love the doing more than the eating. Of course, the eating is wonderful, too.

TOFU

MAKES 2 POUNDS

If you've made fresh cheese, this follows the same simple process of separating curds from whey. This recipe is inspired by the basic tofu recipe from Andrea Nguyen's *Asian Tofu*, a beautiful book that's a definite must-have for anyone ready to be seduced by the wiles of homemade tofu. Nigari, the coagulant that transforms your homemade soymilk into tofu, is available online. You can also purchase a tofu mold, or you can rig one up with a colander lined with cheesecloth.

2 cups (335 g) dried soybeans	17 cups water	1 tablespoon nigari

1 Rinse the soybeans, transfer them to a large bowl, and cover generously with water. Lay a dish towel over the bowl and let it sit for 12 to 14 hours. Squeeze a bean, and if it splits down the middle, the beans are ready.

2 Measure 10 cups of water into a large, heavy-bottomed pot. Set the pot over high heat and bring to a boil. While the water heats, drain the beans and transfer them to a blender with 4 cups water, working in batches if necessary. Blend on high until you have a smooth puree, about 2 minutes in a regular blender or 1 minute in a high-speed blender (such as Vitamix or Blendtec). Add the mixture to the large pot of boiling water, stirring well. Measure 1 more cup of water into the blender and blend for a few seconds to rinse the blender. Add that water to the pot as well, and reduce the heat to medium. Cook, stirring constantly, until the entire mixture is steaming and foamy, about 5 minutes.

3 Set up a large strainer over a large bowl and line the strainer with a large piece of damp cheesecloth. Ladle the hot soy mixture into the strainer, stirring the solids as you go to help the liquid drain through. Let the solids cool enough for you to handle them.

4 Gather the edges of the cheesecloth together to make a sealed bag, and squeeze to release more milk. Take care, as the bag will still be warm. Transfer the bag to a smaller bowl, open it within the bowl, and gently stir 1 cup of water into the solids. Reseal the bag, hold it over the strainer over the bowl, and massage again until no more milk escapes from the cloth. Rinse the big pot, and pour the hot soymilk from the large bowl back into the pot. (Transfer the solids from the cheesecloth to a container. That's the *okara*.) Rinse your cheesecloth and keep it ready for the next step.

5 Set the pot of soymilk over medium-high heat and cook, stirring often to prevent scorching, until it reaches a high simmer, 10 to 15 minutes. If a skin forms on the surface of the milk, skim it off (that's the yuba). Remove from heat. Combine the nigari with 1 cup cool water and stir to dissolve. Line a tofu mold or colander with the cheesecloth and set it in a roasting pan to catch the whey. Keep both the nigari and the tofu mold at the ready. Stir the milk vigorously to get the liquid moving. Pour the nigari mixture into the pot and give the soymilk a few swift strokes to incorporate it. Cover the pot and let it sit undisturbed for 6 minutes.

6 The soymilk should now be transformed into curds and whey, similar to ricotta. Use a ladle to scoop the curds out of the pot, transferring them to the tofu mold. As the whey gathers in the roasting pan, pour it into a jar to use for soups and smoothies later (see page 35). Fold the cheesecloth over the top of the curds, and top the mold with its lid (if you're using a colander, find a plate that fits just inside the circumference). Fill a jar with water so that it weighs about 5 pounds, and use that as a weight on top of the lid. Let the curds sit for 20 to 25 minutes, until they are reduced by about half. Very gently place the tofu, still wrapped in its cloth, in a large bowl of cold water. Unwrap the cheesecloth and let the tofu sit in the water for about 30 minutes, changing the water occasionally to keep it cold.

STORAGE NOTES ✦ Store tofu, submerged in water, in a covered container for up to 5 days. Change the water every 2 days. You can also freeze tofu, although it dramatically changes the texture of both store-bought and homemade tofu. It makes it spongy and heartier, and perfect for stew. Freeze in water in an airtight container for up to 3 months. Then thaw in the fridge and drain off the water.

ALL THE DELICIOUS BY-PRODUCTS OF THE TOFU PROCESS
OKARA ✦ When you strain your soymilk, the cheesecloth will catch the solids. Store them in the fridge and stir-fry with vegetables for tomorrow's lunch.
YUBA ✦ This is the skin that collects on the surface of the soymilk as it heats, and it's a treat. Skim it off with chopsticks, dip in soy sauce, and eat it right there at the stove.
WHEY ✦ Like the whey from milk, soy whey is packed with nutrition, and has a delicate flavor. Use it in soups, smoothies, and breads.

▶▶▶▶▶▶▶ HIYAYAKKO ◀◀◀◀◀◀◀

SERVES 4

Fresh tofu is so subtle and creamy and delicate, I love to eat it raw. This traditional Japanese summer dish is cold, quick, and a great way to show off your tofu-making skills.

1 pound chilled tofu (for homemade, see page 158) Optional: ¼ cup dried bonito flakes	¼ cup chopped scallions (white and tender green parts) 2 teaspoons grated fresh ginger	3 tablespoons tamari or soy sauce 2 tablespoons sesame seeds, toasted (see page 54)

Cut the tofu into 4 equal rectangles. Lay each piece on a small plate. Divide the bonito flakes, if using, among the pieces of tofu, topping each with a small puff of flakes. Sprinkle the scallions over the bonito, then the ginger, tamari, and the sesame seeds. Finish with a final puff of bonito flakes.

HOW TO BUY A FISH

Once we sort through the mess of what meat to eat and not to eat, we still face the hardest proteins of all to navigate: fish.

The food that was once lauded as the right choice is now as bad as the rest of them. Whether they're bad for our bodies because they're filling us with mercury, bad for the fish themselves, or just plain ruining the planet, most fish have a reason to be off limits. Not only do we have to remember what fish we should and shouldn't be eating, but also we have to keep track of whether we should be eating fish from the Pacific or the Atlantic. Should it be wild or farmed? Are the fishermen being paid a fair wage? What kind of oil/chemical/radiation has leaked into the water lately? And shrimp! IS IT OKAY TO EAT SHRIMP? It's enough to make anyone quit seafood all together.

There are a few guiding principles when it comes to fish, and at least at the time I'm writing this, they usually lead me in the right direction:

Small, oily fish like anchovies, sardines (fresh or canned), and smelts are a good bet, and easy on the wallet, too. Because they're low on the food chain, they're also low in mercury, and they're packed with nutrition.

A few fish are always on the "no" list, whether because of mercury, PCBs, or the fishing process. These include imported shrimp, all shark, Chilean sea bass, and swordfish. Don't eat too much tuna, whether fresh or in the can. Chunk light tuna is lower in mercury than other choices.

For the most part, wild salmon is reliably okay. You can buy it frozen and it's still delicious, and it makes a great easy weeknight meal. I'm thankful for salmon.

If you love fish, keep an eye on Monterey Bay Aquarium's Seafood Watch (www.seafoodwatch.org). This organization makes a little pocket guide you can take to the store with you, and their app is great for keeping you up to date on safe fish news.

ROASTED SALMON *with* YUMMY SAUCE

Simple roasted salmon is a weeknight dinner staple in my house, and it's as good unadorned as it is with any sauce I might pull together in the moment. My favorite dressing for salmon, however, is an unexpected combination I found in an old pamphlet vegetarian cookbook from a conference center my mother cooked at in the early eighties. The cookbook itself is precious to me. It's illustrated by my mother, filled with photos of women in overalls and bandanas sharing health food revelations like "tofu meatballs" and "apple-cheese sandwiches." The recipes I've tried all taste like my childhood, but none so much as "yummy sauce," a rich and salty mix of butter, garlic, tamari, and nutritional yeast. It's perfect on salmon, and just as good on grains and vegetables.

FOR THE FISH

1½ pounds boneless wild salmon fillet

1 tablespoon fresh lemon juice (½ lemon)

1 teaspoon tamari or soy sauce

1 tablespoon olive oil

FOR THE SAUCE

4 tablespoons (½ stick) unsalted butter

1 tablespoon finely minced garlic (2 to 3 cloves)

2 tablespoons nutritional yeast

1 tablespoon tamari or soy sauce

1 **Roast the fish:** Preheat the oven to 400°F. Line a baking sheet with parchment paper. Lay the fish skin side down on the parchment and top with the lemon juice, tamari, and olive oil. Roast until the fish flakes when you pull it with a fork, about 15 minutes.

2 **While the fish roasts, make the sauce:** Melt the butter over low heat. Add the garlic, yeast, and tamari. Cook, stirring occasionally, until the sauce thickens, 5 to 7 minutes. Spoon the sauce over the fish, reserving some for anything else on your plate. The sauce is wonderful on grains and vegetables, too.

FOUR QUICK AND SPECIAL PASTAS OR THE STORY

For years, I told the same story. It began like this: I have one picky kid and one good eater.

But then, as my two eaters grew and changed, the story got more complicated. *I have one picky kid who eats kale now and then, and one good eater.* The next week, the story would shift again. *I have one picky eater and one good eater going through a picky phase.* We've been through times when the picky one would go weeks without touching a vegetable. Even now there are times when a food, once loved by one or both the girls, becomes mysteriously exiled. Sometimes I'm totally fine with it; other days I just want to bang my head on the dinner table. And through it all, I read every article about picky kids, and I even write a few. The experts will tell you that all picky kids can be converted. Get them into the kitchen and have them make dinner. Pull them into the garden and let them discover the wonder of fresh peas. Don't talk about food. Do talk about food. Most of all, enjoy your food! Show them how much you love food. Do all these magical things for thirty days, and then they'll come around.

Some of these gems of advice work . . . sometimes.

But I'd like to throw my hat into the ring of picky kid advice, and here it is:

Don't get wrapped up in the story of what kind of eater your kid is. Feed your family well, but also know that many children have thrived on bread and yogurt, going on to a full and happy adulthood filled with all those foods they'd never eat as a kid.

This is how I got there. My picky child is just as healthy, if not healthier, than my good eater. Rosie's energy is good, her hair is long and glossy, and she hardly ever gets sick—all on a diet of mostly bread, bananas, noodles, and cold cuts. Sadie, on the other hand, will try anything. But the differences don't end there. Rosie never gets ravenous. She's happy to eat (as long as one of her favorite foods is on the menu), but even then, the bites are more of an experience than anything. She closes her eyes and takes the tiniest bit of food. She thinks about its texture and overarching qualities. But Sadie gets so hungry, she needs something, anything, to fill her belly. Luckily, she knows this, and as soon as she starts to feel the need, she eats. But when I framed the story this way for myself, taking into account that my two kids experience taste and texture differently, my thinking on picky eating shifted. My two children are *different*, and the way they each relate to food is different, too.

Try not to label your children as good eaters or bad eaters—not just to the world, but to yourself. Children are, after all, just small humans, and they have all sorts of loves and preferences that will continue to change as they make their way through life. Know that they'll be okay, that someday they'll eat something else, and that until then, their bodies will tell you when you have to step in. If they're healthy and energetic, trust that they're getting what they need.

Also, know that you have lots of company. There's a noodles-with-butter eater in nearly every family. We speak in hushed tones. We thought our kids would want real food, but we fall back again and again on the tried-and-true bowl. "Noodles. So many noodles! Can a person live on noodles and butter?"

Yes, they can. But a few other ingredients in the mix help keep it interesting, and they might even slowly, over the years, gain acceptance from the pickiest at the table. Do your best, then let go. And when we're busy, and a little overwhelmed at six o'clock, in need of a true thirty-minute dinner that will make everybody happy, pasta is just the thing.

BUTTERNUT SQUASH PASTA *with* BACON *and* SAGE BROWN BUTTER

SERVES 4, WITH LEFTOVERS

The browned butter and roasted vegetables make this special, but roasting everything in the oven at once makes it easy to prepare.

1 small butternut squash, (1 to 1½ pounds) seeded, peeled, and cut into 1-inch cubes

1 medium onion, cut into ½-inch wedges

1½ tablespoons olive oil

½ teaspoon kosher salt, plus more for the pasta water

4 ounces sliced bacon

1 pound store-bought bowtie pasta or 1¼ pounds homemade (page 46)

4 tablespoons (½ stick) unsalted butter, cut into chunks

10 fresh sage leaves

½ cup finely grated Parmesan cheese

Freshly ground pepper

1 Preheat the oven to 425°F. In a large bowl, toss the squash and onion with the olive oil and salt. Spread on a parchment-lined baking sheet and roast in the upper half of the oven until the squash is tender and the onions are golden, 30 to 35 minutes.

2 Meanwhile, lay the bacon on another baking sheet. Bake until crispy, about 18 minutes. Transfer to a paper-towel-lined plate.

3 While the bacon and vegetables cook, bring a large pot of salted water to a boil and cook the pasta until tender, 7 to 10 minutes for dried, or 2 minutes for fresh. Reserve 1 cup of the pasta water, drain and rinse the pasta, and transfer it to a large serving bowl.

4 Melt the butter in a small saucepan over medium heat. Stir constantly, keeping a close eye on the color of the butter. When the foam subsides and the butter turns slightly brown, add the sage leaves. Remove from heat and as soon as the sage leaves start to curl, transfer them to the plate with the bacon.

5 Add the squash and onions to the pasta, then pour the butter over the bowl, tossing to coat the pasta and vegetables. Crumble the bacon over the pasta and top with the crispy sage leaves and the cheese. Pour enough pasta water over the cheese to create a light sauce. Finish with a bit more salt and lots of freshly ground pepper.

❊ VARIATIONS ❊

Fry up a few chopped leeks before cooking the bacon and trade the tarragon for basil. Or use chard, kale, or collards instead of asparagus. Remember that carbonara is the queen of all resourceful dishes. Make it without any vegetables at all—just give it a few extra grinds of pepper.

ASPARAGUS CARBONARA

Making carbonara is a little bit like conducting an orchestra. One pot cooks, another fries the bacon, veggies here, herbs there, egg poached—then BAM! Dinner is ready.

Kosher salt

4 ounces slab or sliced bacon, cut into ¼-inch pieces

1 pound store-bought spaghetti or 1¼ pounds homemade (page 46)

1 bunch asparagus, ends snapped off, sliced into 1-inch lengths

2 tablespoons unsalted butter

½ cup grated Parmesan cheese, plus additional for sprinkling

4 large eggs

¼ cup coarsely chopped fresh tarragon or parsley

Freshly ground pepper

1 Set a large pot of salted water over high heat. Simultaneously heat your largest skillet or frying pan over medium-high heat. Add the bacon to the skillet and fry, stirring often, until it's crispy, 3 to 5 minutes. Remove from the heat and use a slotted spoon to transfer the bacon to a small bowl. Leave the bacon fat in the pan and set aside.

2 When the water boils, add the pasta and cook until tender, 7 to 10 minutes for dried or 2 minutes for fresh. If using dried pasta, add the asparagus when the pasta is about halfway done. If using fresh pasta, you can start the pasta and asparagus together. Pour a few cups of the pasta water into a smaller pot set over medium-low heat (you'll use this to poach the eggs), then drain the pasta and asparagus in a colander and rinse in cold water.

3 Return the reserved skillet to medium-high heat. Whisk the butter into the bacon fat, then whisk in about ½ cup of the reserved pasta cooking water.

4 Add the pasta, asparagus, Parmesan, and reserved bacon to the skillet, gently tossing until the pasta and asparagus are fully coated in the sauce. Divide the pasta evenly among 4 plates.

5 Crack an egg into a ramekin or teacup. Pour off the most watery part of the white, and give the small pot a little swirl to get the water moving. Gently slide the egg into the water and cook until the white is firm, for 2½ minutes. Use a slotted spoon to lay the egg over one of the bowls of pasta, then repeat with the other 3 eggs. Top with the herbs, lots of pepper, and a bit of extra Parmesan.

TAGLIATELLE *with* FRESH TOMATOES *and* BALSAMIC VINEGAR

In the summer, the whole family-dinner thing tends to fall apart. The days are long, the kitchen is hot, and more often than not, I end up looking in the fridge or the garden at seven o'clock for something, anything, to turn into dinner. I'm not ashamed to admit that we've eaten popcorn for dinner in the summer. But in late August, when there are piles of ripe tomatoes on the counter and there is plenty of basil in the garden, I make this dish, inspired by one of the books that taught me how to cook, *The Splendid Table: Recipes from Emilia-Romagna*, by Lynne Rossetto Kasper. If you can swing it, this is especially good with homemade pasta.

3 tablespoons balsamic vinegar	3 large ripe tomatoes, cored and cut into bite-sized pieces	1 pound store-bought tagliatelle or 1¼ pounds homemade (page 46)
1½ teaspoons minced garlic (1 clove)	½ cup tightly packed fresh basil leaves, cut into ribbons	¼ cup extra-virgin olive oil
2 tablespoons minced shallot (1 shallot)	Freshly ground black pepper	1½ ounces Parmesan cheese, shaved with a vegetable peeler
Kosher salt		

1 Combine the vinegar, garlic, and shallot in a large serving bowl and let sit for a few minutes. Bring a large pot of salted water to boil.

2 Fold the tomatoes, basil, and black pepper into the vinegar mixture and let marinate while you cook the pasta. Add the pasta to the water and cook until just barely done, 6 to 8 minutes for dried or 2 minutes for fresh. Drain the pasta and add to the bowl with the tomato mixture. Pour the olive oil over the top and gently fold in the pasta, taking care not to crush the tomatoes. Top with the shaved cheese and more pepper.

FETTUCCINE *with* PRESERVED LEMON *and* ROASTED GARLIC

I would never have thought to combine the caramelized cream of roasted garlic with preserved lemons, but when my friend India suggested this recipe, I was floored by how good it was. The garlic and lemon melt together in a sauce that tastes entirely different (and better!) than its separate components. India had gotten this recipe from a friend who had gotten it from a friend who had gotten it from a friend's aunt, and, well . . . you get the idea. I went on a search to try to find where the recipe originated, and tracked it back to Molly O'Neill, who introduced the world to the recipe in the *New York Times* in 1999. My version uses olive oil instead of butter, and I add rosemary to the mix. Adding pasta water to the sauce also makes it a little lighter and saucier than the original, which suits my family's tastes. I love both recipes, though, and the preserved lemon/roasted garlic combination has become one of my favorites.

Kosher salt

1 pound store-bought fettuccine or 1¼ pounds homemade (page 46)

¼ cup extra-virgin olive oil

Heaping ⅓ cup coarsely chopped Preserved Lemon (page 95; about 1 lemon, rinsed before chopping)

¼ cup mashed Roasted Garlic (page 75; about 2 heads)

1 tablespoon finely chopped fresh rosemary

1 cup grated Parmesan cheese

2 tablespoons coarsely chopped fresh flat-leaf parsley

Freshly ground pepper

1 Bring a large pot of salted water to boil. Cook the fettuccine until tender, 7 to 10 minutes for dried, or 2 minutes for fresh. Reserve 1 cup of the pasta water, then drain and rinse the pasta. Transfer to a large serving bowl.

2 Meanwhile, heat the oil in a medium saucepan or skillet over medium heat. Add the preserved lemon, roasted garlic, and rosemary, smashing and stirring them all together in a thick relish. Cook, stirring often, until the sauce melts together, 3 to 5 minutes. Remove from heat and scoop the garlic mixture over the pasta. Sprinkle the cheese over the bowl, then pour about ½ cup of the pasta water over the top. Stir gently to melt the cheese and coat the pasta in the sauce. Add more water if the sauce seems too thick. Top with the parsley and lots of fresh pepper.

HOW TO MAKE IT BETTER

At my girls' school, a group of middle school students run a snack program for the younger grades. A few years ago, the older students wanted to try creating some homemade options as part of their program, and the head of the middle school asked me to help the kids brainstorm the possibilities. We started by talking about the store-bought snacks they already offered, and which of those could easily be made from scratch.

"What's the most popular snack you serve?" I asked.

"Goldfish. Always Goldfish."

That, I could do! I asked if they were interested in learning how to make their own cheese crackers. I'd even bring in my goldfish cookie cutter. And that's when the real conversation began.

As the middle schoolers considered whether to make foods from scratch, they wondered if the younger kids would actually order them. As it stood, there were healthy snack days (cucumber slices, oranges) and "other" days with snacks like Goldfish or animal crackers. If the kids replaced the beloved snacks with "healthier" homemade options, would the younger kids still want them?

"Whoa, hold on a minute there!" I couldn't help but jump in: "Who said anything about making healthy food?"

I was raised on health food. I have always been able to list the seven ancient grains, and I know the difference between white and red miso. But I don't think the "healthy" label is helping anyone.

How about if the goal is to make *good* food? That's how we make it better when we make it at home.

Especially for families with small children, store-bought classics like Goldfish and animal crackers tend to be fixtures in the pantry. Sometimes what we just need is a ready snack that everyone's excited to eat. And for those who want to go homemade, both crackers are easy to make at home. Are they healthier? I couldn't say. Better? Absolutely.

⇢⇢⇢⇢⇢⇢ CHEESY FISH CRACKERS ⇠⇠⇠⇠⇠⇠

MAKES ABOUT 160 TINY CRACKERS

Few snacks are so beloved as cheddar goldfish. Fortunately, they're easy to re-create. If your crackers must be fish shaped, you need to track down a mini fish-shaped cookie cutter. I found mine online as part of a set of animal cookie cutters (also useful for Animal Crackers, page 180). You can also MacGyver up one of your own by chopping up an aluminum can and shaping it with tape. And of course the better the Cheddar, the tastier the cracker.

1 teaspoon rice vinegar or distilled white vinegar

1 teaspoon kosher salt

7 tablespoons (105 ml) water

1 cup (120 g) all-purpose flour

1 cup (120 g) whole-wheat flour

2 tablespoons (28 g) cold unsalted butter, cut into ¼-inch cubes

8 ounces (225 g) grated sharp Cheddar cheese

1 Preheat the oven to 375°F. Combine the vinegar, salt, and 6 tablespoons of the water in a measuring cup, stir to dissolve the salt, and put the cup in the refrigerator. Combine the flours and butter in the bowl of a stand mixer fit with the paddle attachment and run the mixer on medium low for about 30 seconds. Add the cheese, start the mixer again, and slowly add the vinegar mixture. Run the mixer on medium speed until the dough comes together into a ball around the paddle, 2 to 3 minutes. If it's still crumbly, add the remaining tablespoon of water and process until the dough comes together, about a minute. Gather the dough into a ball, wrap in plastic or wax paper, and let it rest in the refrigerator for 20 minutes.

2 Roll the dough about ⅛ inch thick on a lightly floured counter or board. Use a fish cookie cutter to cut your crackers, transferring them to 2 ungreased baking sheets as you go. When you've cut as many crackers as you can, gather the dough together, reroll it, and start cutting again. The more beat-up this dough gets, the happier it is, so gather the scraps and reroll until every bit of dough is gone. Use a toothpick to poke an eye in each fish—this will stop the crackers from puffing up too much. Bake until the crackers are light golden on the bottom, 12 to 15 minutes, rotating pans between upper and lower racks halfway through baking.

STORAGE NOTES ✦ Store at room temperature in a tightly covered container for up to 10 days. Or freeze unbaked dough, tightly wrapped, for 3 to 4 months. Thaw in the refrigerator and let soften on the counter before rolling.

ANIMAL CRACKERS

I've become partial to the sweet and oat-y variety of animal cracker the girls always ask for at our local co-op, so that cookie is my inspiration here. It's sweet enough for a tea snack, but with enough whole grain to be a healthy lunch box treat. You'll get authenticity points if you have animal cookie cutters, but any other small shape works just as well.

8 tablespoons (1 stick/ 115 g) unsalted butter, at room temperature

¼ cup (55 g) packed light brown sugar

½ teaspoon kosher salt

1 teaspoon ground cinnamon

½ teaspoon grated nutmeg

½ teaspoon ground ginger

¼ cup (60 ml) honey

1 large egg

1 tablespoon vanilla extract

1 cup (100 g) rolled oats, blitzed in a food processor or finely chopped with a sharp knife

1 cup (120 g) all-purpose flour, plus additional for the counter

½ cup (60 g) whole-wheat flour

1 Combine the butter and brown sugar in the bowl of a stand mixer fit with the paddle attachment. Beat at medium speed until the mixture is smooth, about 1 minute. Add the salt, cinnamon, nutmeg, and ginger, and beat for 10 seconds. Add the honey, egg, and vanilla, beat for a moment, scrape down the sides of the bowl with a silicone spatula, and beat for another 10 seconds.

2 In a separate bowl, whisk together the oats, all-purpose flour, and whole-wheat flour. Add the flour mixture to the butter mixture and beat again until you have a cohesive dough, about 15 seconds. Gather the dough into a ball, wrap in plastic or wax paper, and refrigerate for at least 2 hours and up to 12 hours.

3 Preheat the oven to 350°F. Remove the dough from the refrigerator about 15 minutes before you're ready to roll it. Lightly grease 2 baking sheets or line them with parchment paper. Generously flour the counter or a board and roll out half the dough to between ⅛ and ¼ inch, continuing to add flour to the counter when the dough gets sticky. Use a cookie cutter to cut shapes in the dough. Transfer the cookies to the prepared pan, leaving about ½ inch between cookies. Any scraps can be gathered and rerolled. Bake for 8 to 10 minutes, switching the trays midway through baking, until the edges of the cookies are golden.

⊱⊰ ▷ VARIATION ◁ ⊱⊰

To fancy these up, dip them in chocolate: Melt a 4-ounce dark chocolate bar in a double boiler. Remove from heat and dip each cookie halfway into the chocolate, transferring to a parchment-lined baking sheet as you go. Refrigerate for 15 minutes.

STORAGE NOTES ✦ Store at room temperature in a covered container for up to 3 weeks. Or freeze unbaked dough, tightly wrapped, for 3 to 4 months. Thaw in the refrigerator.

POPOVERS

I have one back-pocket recipe that can save any breakfast, lunch, or dinner. Special birthday breakfast on a school morning when we have to get out at 7:00 a.m.? Popovers. A soup pulled from the freezer that's not quite as delicious as I remember it? Serve with popovers. Friends coming over with picky kids? Anything + popovers. Of course, I wish all my meals were flawless and delicious, and all my experiments came out cookbook-worthy. But for the meals that don't quite make it, popovers save the day.

This is also a great recipe for kids, because once it's in your blood, you can rely on it for life. The blender, along with the hot oven, creates a lofty popover with a hollow center. Although you can buy a special fancy popover pan, this recipe works just fine in a regular muffin tin. If you prefer a more custardy popover, mix the ingredients by hand and bake in a 375°F oven for 30 to 35 minutes.

3 large eggs	½ teaspoon kosher salt	Safflower oil or melted butter, for greasing the pan
1½ cups (360 ml) whole milk or buttermilk (for homemade, see page 34)	4 tablespoons (½ stick / 56 g) unsalted butter, melted and slightly cooled	Optional: ¼ cup fresh herbs; 4 ounces (115 g) chèvre (for homemade, see page 99)
1½ cups (180 g) all-purpose flour		

1   Preheat the oven to 425°F. Combine the eggs, milk, flour, salt, and butter in a blender. Blend until you have a smooth batter, 15 to 20 seconds. Let the batter rest for about 10 minutes.

2   Generously grease a 12-cup muffin or popover tin with oil. Divide the batter evenly among the cups, filling them most of the way. Add a pinch of fresh herbs and a dollop of chèvre, if using, to the center of each muffin cup. Bake until puffed and golden, WITHOUT OPENING THE OVEN, 25 to 28 minutes. Serve immediately.

The day after I had Sadie, the first dinner appeared.

My mother's friend Emily, a wonderful cook who had spent a year feeding scientists in Antarctica, came in with a little pot of soup. She had given birth to her first child months earlier, and Joey had been practicing on her son Oscar—changing diapers, holding him, smelling his head. Emily brought a creamy lentil dal with baby spinach stirred in, a little pot of rice, and a stack of chocolate chip cookies for dessert.

It went on from there. Lasagna, chicken potpie—we didn't cook for weeks. And since then, when there's a birth, a death, or anything big in between, I bring dinner.

It can be easy to talk yourself out of bringing dinner. Particularly when there's a birth, death, or illness, walking into someone else's experience can feel awkward. We want to give space. The thought of walking in on someone who's not a close friend when she's postpartum and in pajamas, trying to work out the whole breastfeeding thing, can feel just plain wrong. But on the whole, we usually think people want more space than they actually do. You don't have to visit, or to fill the house with conversation. You only have to bring dinner. The presence of that little box, the pot, the food into which you put care—it will remind them they should eat, and it will make them feel taken care of when they need it most.

When we bring dinner, we say: I'm your community. I'm here for you. Eat.

People need to be fed when they are soft and open, freaked out or grieving. When the only way they'll eat is if someone puts something in front of them. And at the same time, we have to feel brave enough to tread around their vulnerability, to tiptoe up their front porch steps and tap gently on the window, use our intuition to gauge whether we should open the door and wrap them in our arms before we go, or just leave dinner with a wave through the window. We have to be vulnerable ourselves, willing to take a risk, to do the wrong thing, to make a meal they don't love, to show up at the wrong time. We can even help them if they ask for it. It requires a softening on both sides, and it takes practice. When we bring dinner, we say: I'm your community. I'm here for you. Eat.

DAL *with* RADISH RAITA

SERVES 6 TO 8

This recipe is similar to the dal my friend brought after Sadie was born. Feel free to kick up the heat by increasing the cayenne and ginger. If radishes aren't available, substitute 1 small seeded, grated cucumber.

FOR THE DAL

1 tablespoon olive oil

2 tablespoons unsalted butter or ghee

2½ cups chopped onions (about 2 onions)

1½ cups diced carrots (3 to 4 carrots)

1 teaspoon kosher salt

1 tablespoon grated fresh ginger

½ teaspoon ground cayenne

½ teaspoon ground cumin

1 teaspoon turmeric

2 cups red lentils, rinsed

6 cups water or whey

2 cups roasted tomatoes, with all oils and juices (see page 23) or 2 cups canned tomatoes

1½ cups packed chopped spinach or other green

2 tablespoons fresh lemon juice (1 lemon)

FOR THE RADISH RAITA

1 cup plain whole-milk yogurt (for homemade, see page 34)

1 tablespoon fresh lemon juice (½ lemon)

1 tablespoon extra-virgin olive oil

1 teaspoon kosher salt

3 radishes, finely grated

1 tablespoon finely chopped fresh mint

1 **For the dal:** Melt the olive oil and butter in a large, heavy-bottomed pot over medium heat. Add the onions and cook, stirring often, until soft and translucent, 4 to 5 minutes. Add the carrots, salt, ginger, cayenne, cumin, turmeric, lentils, and ½ cup of the water and cook, stirring often, for another 5 to 7 minutes. Add the rest of the water and bring to a low boil. Reduce the heat to medium low, cover, and cook for 10 minutes. Add the tomatoes and their juices to the pot, squeezing them with your hands to crush them. Continue to cook, covered, stirring occasionally, until the lentils are cooked and the soup is thick, 30 to 45 minutes. Stir in the spinach and lemon, remove from heat, and add salt to taste.

2 **While the soup cooks, make the raita:** Stir together the yogurt, lemon, olive oil, salt, radishes, and mint in a small bowl. Serve the soup with a dollop of raita in each bowl.

STORAGE NOTES ✦ Dal freezes well in airtight containers for up to 6 months.

CALZONES *with* BUTTERY TOMATO SAUCE

When I'm bringing dinner, I try to choose a meal with options. If I'm just one of many people trying to help out, the recipients might be overwhelmed with leftovers, so it's ideal to bring a dish that can just as easily be eaten in a few days or frozen for a time when the dinner donations thin out. Sometimes I'll bring a bag of frozen calzones that can be pulled out when the need arises. And of course this recipe is also useful for stocking up your own freezer.

2 tablespoons olive oil, plus additional for brushing the dough and baking sheets

¾ cup thinly sliced onion (about 1 small onion)

1 pound sweet or spicy Italian sausage, casings removed

1½ cups coarsely chopped fresh spinach

Kosher salt and freshly ground pepper

1 recipe Basic Pizza Dough (recipe follows), cut into 6 pieces

Flour for rolling the dough

¾ cup (188 g) ricotta (for homemade, see page 35) or farmer's cheese

¾ cup (90 g) grated mozzarella

Buttery Tomato Sauce, for serving (recipe follows)

1 Heat the olive oil in a large skillet over medium heat. Add the onion and cook, stirring often, until soft, fragrant, and slightly browned, about 15 minutes. Transfer the onion to a bowl and add the sausage to the skillet, stirring to break it up as it browns, about 10 minutes. Add the spinach, cover the skillet, and let the spinach wilt over the sausage, about 2 minutes. Remove from heat, add the onion back to the pan, and stir to combine. Add salt and pepper to taste. (Depending on your sausage, this can really vary, so taste as you go.) Drain off any liquid from the pan so the mixture is dry. Make sure your cheeses are at the ready. Taste the soft cheese, and add a touch of salt if it needs it.

2 Preheat the oven to 425°F, grease 2 baking sheets with olive oil, and lightly flour the counter. Use a rolling pin to roll each section of dough on the counter into something close to a circle 8 to 9 inches in diameter, and stack with plastic or parchment between them. Lay one round on the counter and scoop a heaping ¼ cup of sausage mixture nearly in the center of the dough, but skewed off to one side. Top with a generous tablespoon of ricotta and a hefty pinch (about 1½ tablespoons) of mozzarella. Fold the dough over on itself to make a semicircle, gently pulling the bottom layer of dough over the top and crimping to seal. Try not to tear the dough—better to leave it slack if you can. Transfer

the calzone to the baking sheet and repeat with the remaining dough, spreading out to the second pan when you need to. (You should be able to fit 4 or 5 calzones on one baking sheet.) Brush olive oil over the top of each calzone and bake for 35 minutes if you're going to eat them right away, or 20 minutes if you're planning to freeze them.

3 Serve with the tomato sauce on the side for dipping. Or to freeze, allow to cool, then transfer to freezer bags with parchment between them. Frozen calzones can be thawed overnight in the fridge or more quickly in the microwave, then baked in a 400°F oven for 15 to 20 minutes.

BUTTERY TOMATO SAUCE

MAKES 3½ CUPS

This recipe is inspired by Marcella Hazan's tomato sauce with butter and onion. Get it started before you fill your calzones, and it will be ready to go as soon as they're done.

1 28-ounce can whole tomatoes, 1 quart home-canned tomatoes, or 2 pounds roasted tomatoes (see page 23)	1 medium onion, halved 3 garlic cloves, peeled 6 tablespoons unsalted butter or olive oil	1 teaspoon kosher salt, or to taste 1 tablespoon chopped fresh oregano or 1 teaspoon dried

Combine the tomatoes, onion, garlic, and butter in a medium saucepan. Bring to a boil over medium-high heat, then cover, reduce the heat to low, and simmer, stirring occasionally to break down the tomatoes until the sauce thickens, 40 to 45 minutes. For a rough sauce, mash up the onions and the garlic in the sauce. Or for a smoother sauce, blend with an immersion blender or in an upright blender. Add the salt and oregano, adjusting the salt to taste.

BASIC PIZZA DOUGH

MAKES JUST OVER 1 ½ POUNDS DOUGH, ENOUGH FOR 4 MEDIUM PIZZAS OR 6 CALZONES

1 ¼ cups (300 ml) warm water

1 teaspoon sugar

2 teaspoons active dry yeast

3 cups (360 g) all-purpose flour, plus more for shaping the dough

⅓ cup (33 g) rye flour or whole-wheat flour

1 teaspoon kosher salt

1 tablespoon olive oil

1 Combine the warm water and sugar in a liquid measuring cup, stirring to dissolve the sugar. Sprinkle the yeast over the surface of the water and let stand for 10 minutes.

2 Combine the flours, salt, and 2 teaspoons of the oil in the bowl of a food processor. Pulse to combine and then, with the machine running, add the yeast mixture as fast as the flours will absorb it. Process until the dough forms a ball and clings to the blade, then process for another 30 seconds. Use the remaining teaspoon of oil to grease a medium bowl. Place the dough in the bowl, cover it with plastic wrap or a reusable equivalent, and leave in a warm place to rise. You can use the dough in 2 to 3 hours, but the longer you leave it, the more tangy and developed the flavor will be. I like to make the dough in the morning for that night's dinner, but you can make the dough up to 24 hours in advance. Just keep an eye on it, and if the dough looks like it will spill over the bowl, give it some time in the refrigerator to slow the fermentation.

3 When you're ready to use the dough, turn it out onto a lightly floured counter. Use a bench knife to divide the dough into your desired number of pizzas or calzones. Gently shape each piece of dough into a ball, lay the plastic wrap over the balls, and let them rest for about 20 minutes before shaping.

BURRITOS

MAKES 10 TO 12 BURRITOS

Here's another great recipe for filling the freezer. Leave any fresh vegetables like lettuce, tomato, and avocado out of the mix—they won't freeze or reheat well. Add them to finished burritos just before serving.

10 to 12 large flour tortillas, at room temperature	6 cups filling (grains, meat, and vegetables—see my favorite combinations below)	1 cup salsa (recipe follows) 2 cups (224 g) grated Cheddar or Monterey Jack cheese

1 Lay a tortilla on your work surface and scoop about ½ cup filling just below the center line of the circle. Top with a few spoonfuls of salsa and a sprinkle of cheese. Roll your burrito by first folding in the sides over the filling, then rolling tightly away from you. Repeat with the remaining ingredients.

2 To eat burritos right away, cook in a lightly greased skillet over medium heat for about 5 minutes, turning the burrito to crisp up all sides and melt the cheese. To freeze, transfer rolled (uncooked) burritos to a freezer bag. You can thaw the burritos overnight in the refrigerator before cooking, or cook them straight from the freezer.

NOTE ✦ Cook thawed burritos in a lightly greased skillet for 5 to 10 minutes. Frozen burritos can be reheated either in the microwave for 4 to 5 minutes or directly on the oven rack in a 375°F oven for 25 to 30 minutes.

TOMATO SALSA

MAKES 2 CUPS

2 medium tomatoes, cored and quartered	½ cup coarsely chopped sweet red pepper	1 teaspoon chopped fresh oregano
½ small red onion, coarsely chopped	1 to 2 small hot chile peppers, stemmed and seeded	2 tablespoons fresh lime juice (1 lime)
1 tablespoon coarsely chopped garlic (2 to 3 cloves)	¼ cup loosely packed fresh flat-leaf parsley or cilantro, coarsely chopped	1 teaspoon kosher salt

1 Set the tomatoes in a fine-meshed sieve and drain for at least 5 minutes.

2 Combine the tomatoes, onion, garlic, red pepper, and hot peppers in the food processor. Pulse until the ingredients come together in a fairly uniform mix. Add the parsley, oregano, lime juice, and salt and pulse one more time. Taste, and adjust the salt if needed.

VARIATION

For tomatillo salsa, substitute 1 pound husked, halved tomatillos for the tomatoes. Use white onion instead of red, omit the red pepper, and use green hot peppers (such as jalapeños). Roast the tomatillos, onion, and hot peppers in a 400°F oven for 45 minutes. Let cool, then combine in the food processor with the parsley, oregano, lime juice, and salt.

here are a few of my favorite fillings

2 cups mixed roasted vegetables; 2 cups cooked black beans;
2 cups millet or quinoa; Cheddar; tomatillo salsa

———

3 cups shredded broiled chicken thighs; 3 cups thinly sliced green cabbage
that's been sautéed with chili powder and lime; tomatillo salsa

———

2 cups refried beans (cooked pinto beans mashed in a skillet with butter
or lard, salt, and green chiles); 2 cups white rice; 2 cups browned ground
beef; tomato salsa

———

3 cups chopped roasted sweet potatoes; 2 cups browned sausage;
1 cup cooked brown rice; either salsa

———

3 cups scrambled eggs with chopped green chiles; 3 cups roasted potatoes;
a few slices of crispy bacon per burrito; Jack cheese

MISO SOUP

When someone is grieving, I always bring food and I always feel like I'm fumbling, trying to do the right thing. This is despite the fact that in the mercifully few times I've been the one who has lost someone I love, I've just been thankful for any gesture from anyone. But it's so hard to know what to do when someone is grieving, because we can't do the thing we wish we could, that is, bring back the one they love.

Miso soup is what I can give. The fermented saltiness of miso provides a deep briny comfort that I can only describe as both the taking in and replenishing of tears. Even a few sips of good miso help to focus and soothe, and the simple vegetables go a long way when it comes to providing fuel for whatever is ahead. And at least in that most basic way, we can bring a warm pot of just a little bit of what they've lost.

One 6-inch length of kombu or wakame seaweed

6 cups water

1 tablespoon olive oil

1 cup thinly sliced onion (about 1 small onion)

1 cup diced carrots (2 to 3 carrots)

1 teaspoon grated fresh ginger

1 cup thinly sliced purple cabbage

4 curly kale leaves, de-stemmed and torn into bite-sized pieces

1 pound tofu (for homemade, see page 158), cut into ½-inch cubes

¼ cup miso paste (brown, red, white, or a combination)

1 tablespoon tamari or soy sauce, or more to taste

¼ cup finely chopped scallions (white and green parts), for serving

1 Soak the kombu or wakame in 2 cups of the water. Heat the olive oil in a large, heavy-bottomed pot over medium heat. Add the onion and cook, stirring often, until soft, about 3 minutes. Add the carrots, ginger, and cabbage and continue to cook, stirring often, until the vegetables are tender, another 5 to 6 minutes.

2 Remove the kombu from the water, set aside, and add the water to the pot along with the remaining 4 cups water. Bring to a boil, reduce the heat to medium low, add the kale and tofu, and cover the pot. Cook until the kale is tender and bright green, about 5 minutes. Scoop out about a cup of the broth into a small bowl. Add the miso to the small bowl and stir until you have a thick sauce. Pour the miso mixture back in the pot. Roughly chop the reserved kombu and add that to the pot as well. Add the tamari, taste, and adjust as necessary. Top with scallions just before serving.

This can be made into a hearty meal with the addition of ½ pound cooked
udon or soba noodles or 1½ cups cooked rice.

QUICHE

MAKES ONE 9- OR 10-INCH QUICHE

"If you can make a pie crust, you can make a quiche," claims Mollie Katzen in *The Enchanted Broccoli Forest*. I'm thankful that I believed her, as her "quiche formula" inspired my very first quiches, and I never stopped. It really is just a simple vegetable pie, essentially—an omelet in a crust. Quiche is good party food, good picnic food, and perfect regular dinner food. It's nice at every temperature. And I've never met a person who didn't love a good slice of quiche, so if you're feeding friends, it's an excellent choice. I offer a formula rather than a recipe, as quiche has the benefit of endless filling possibilities.

Prepare the crust. Make a single piecrust (page 41) and roll out the dough so it's about ⅛ inch thick and 12 to 14 inches in diameter. Transfer to a lightly greased and floured pie or straight-sided quiche pan, and crimp the edges of the dough into a crust. Put the pan in the freezer and preheat the oven to 375°F.

Make the filling. You can really use anything you have on hand. The only rule is that, with the exception of fresh herbs, marinated artichoke hearts, and olives, the vegetables in the filling should first be steamed, sautéed, or roasted. Otherwise they release water into the filling, making it runny and the crust soggy. You want to have enough to fill the crust at least halfway, so you'll need about 1½ cups filling for your quiche. Keep vegetables to the size of small bites. You can also add ¼ cup coarsely chopped ham or cooked bacon. Season the filling with salt until it tastes good to you and let it cool slightly.

Meanwhile, make the custard. Whisk together 4 large eggs and 1½ cups (360 ml) of any combination of whole milk, half-and-half, heavy cream, crème fraîche, buttermilk, or kefir. Add a pinch of salt and a few grinds of pepper.

Assemble the quiche. Remove the crust from the freezer. Sprinkle 1 cup (112 g) grated Cheddar over the bottom of the crust. Add the filling (leaving any cooking liquid behind in the pan), then spread the filling on the crust over the cheese. Put the quiche on a baking sheet and pour the custard over the filling. If you like, you can paint the crust with a bit of olive oil or egg wash and sprinkle finishing salt on the crust. Bake until the crust is golden and the center of the quiche is firm, 50 minutes to 1 hour. Let cool for at least 30 minutes before serving.

Some of MY FAVORITE QUICHE FILLING combinations

1 small bunch **asparagus**, chopped and roasted or steamed,
with 2 tablespoons chopped fresh **tarragon** and ¼ cup cooked,
coarsely chopped **bacon**

———

1½ cups roasted **cherry tomatoes** with ribboned **basil**
and chopped **oregano** and **thyme**

———

1½ cups sautéed sliced **zucchini** with basil, **parsley**,
and **thyme** or **marjoram**

———

½ pound **mushrooms** (any variety), sliced and fried in **butter**
with **thyme** and **dry mustard**

———

½ cup chopped roasted **red pepper**, 1 cup sliced marinated
artichoke hearts, and ¼ cup pitted **black olives**

———

Several chopped or whole sautéed **garlic scapes**,
1½ cups chopped sautéed **broccoli raab**, ribboned **basil**,
and a pinch of dried **red pepper flakes**

———

1½ cups lightly steamed **broccoli florets** tossed with a squeeze
of **lemon**, with **tarragon** and **dill**

EASY COQ AU VIN *with* BUTTERMILK SPAETZLE

Coq au Vin traditionally involves soaking a rooster in wine and then cooking it for hours in your French country kitchen. This recipe requires neither rooster nor French country kitchen but the house will smell like heaven, and the result is one of the most comforting dinners you can make. I love this with spaetzle, a German pasta similar to scrambled eggs in shape, but more like fresh egg noodles in flavor. If you have a spaetzle maker, by all means use it here, but I find that any large slotted spoon does the job. If you need to get dinner out quickly with minimal stress, skip the spaetzle and make pasta or polenta instead.

FOR THE CHICKEN	2 cups chicken stock	FOR THE BUTTERMILK SPAETZLE
5 ounces bacon, diced	1 cup diced carrots (2 to 3 carrots)	3 cups (360 g) all-purpose flour
½ cup all-purpose flour	½ cup chopped celery (2 ribs)	¼ teaspoon freshly grated nutmeg
1½ teaspoons kosher salt	1 tablespoon fresh thyme or 1 teaspoon dried	6 large eggs
3 pounds bone-in, skin-on chicken thighs (7 or 8 thighs)	Freshly ground pepper	½ cup (120 ml) buttermilk (for homemade, see page 34), plus additional if needed
1 to 2 tablespoons olive oil, as needed	1 cup chopped fresh, roasted (see page 23), or canned tomatoes	Kosher salt
2 tablespoons minced shallot (about 1 shallot)	1 tablespoon minced garlic (2 to 3 cloves)	2 tablespoons unsalted butter
2 medium onions, cut into wedges	2 cups red wine	1 tablespoon finely chopped shallot (about ½ shallot)
1 cup coarsely chopped white button or cremini mushrooms	¼ cup coarsely chopped fresh flat-leaf parsley	Freshly ground pepper

1 **Cook the chicken:** Heat a large cast-iron skillet or Dutch oven over medium-high heat. Add the bacon and cook, stirring often, until crispy, 5 to 7 minutes. Remove the bacon, let the fat remain in the pan, and set the bacon aside.

2 Meanwhile, combine the flour and 1 teaspoon of the salt in a medium mixing bowl. Dredge each thigh in the flour mixture and set on a plate.

3 Add the chicken thighs to the hot pan, a few at a time. Cook in batches until each side is golden but the chicken is not cooked through, 3 to 4 minutes per side. If the pan seems dry at any point, add a tablespoon of olive oil. Transfer the chicken to a clean plate and set aside.

4 Reduce the heat to medium and add the shallot and onions to the pan. Cook, stirring occasionally, until soft, 3 to 5 minutes. Add the mushrooms and continue to cook until they shrink, about 5 minutes. If the pan dries out, add ¼ cup of the stock. Add the carrots, celery, thyme, several grinds of pepper, and the remaining ½ teaspoon salt. Cook, stirring often, until the carrots and celery are soft, 5 to 7 minutes. Add the tomatoes and garlic, raise the heat to medium high, and add the wine and remaining stock, scraping any brown bits from the bottom of the pan into the sauce as it comes to a boil. Return the chicken and bacon to the pan and adjust the heat so the liquid gently bubbles. Cover and simmer until the chicken is cooked through, 20 to 25 minutes.

5 Make the spaetzle while the chicken is cooking. Combine the flour and nutmeg in a large mixing bowl. Make a well in the center and add the eggs. Use a wooden spoon to incorporate the eggs into the flour from the center out. When you have a stiff batter, add the buttermilk and stir with all your strength to incorporate the buttermilk until you have a batter similar to cake batter. It's okay if there are a few lumps. If the batter is very stiff, add more buttermilk one tablespoon at a time. Put the bowl in the refrigerator for at least 20 minutes.

6 Set a large pot of salted water over high heat, and cover until it comes to a boil. Set two large bowls on the counter; fill one with ice water and set a colander inside the second. When the water boils, take the batter out of the refrigerator. Scoop about ¼ cup batter onto a large slotted spoon, then use a smaller spoon to stir and press the batter through the slotted spoon over the pot of boiling water. Bits of batter will drop through the slotted spoon into the water. Work quickly to cook about a quarter of the batter at a time. When the spaetzle drift to the top of the water, allow them to cook there for another minute, then fish them out with a strainer and transfer to the ice water. Once cool, the spaetzle can go into the colander. Repeat with the remaining batter.

7 Set a large saucepan or frying pan over medium-high heat. Add the butter and heat until it foams. Add the spaetzle in a single layer and let them sit undisturbed until they brown, 3 to 4 minutes. Add the shallot and pepper, shuffle, and continue to cook, stirring often, for another few minutes. Divide among individual bowls, spoon the chicken over the spaetzle, and top with parsley.

STORAGE NOTES ✦ Freeze coq au vin in an airtight container for up to 4 months.

CONGEE *with* CHICKEN *and* GREENS

SERVES 4 TO 5 (AND DOUBLES FLAWLESSLY)

If I come home from a hard day and there's a little box of dinner sitting on my counter, it's probably from Janet. It's almost as if she has an alarm in her house that dings when a friend is in distress. I'll call her, near tears with gratitude over my delivered dinner, and I can hear her shrug over the phone.

"It was nothing—I just skimmed a little off the top of our dinner. One less thing you have to think about, right?"

Janet has shown me what an amazing gift it is to drop off a meal. Once, I was just home from a long day with one of the girls at the doctor. Everything was okay, but it was a day of tests and nurses, and I was exhausted. Janet had known about the appointment, and when we got home, there were a few warm containers on the counter: eight corn tortillas, warmed and wrapped in foil, a little container of pulled pork, and one perfect avocado, ready for guacamole. It was that simple, and I've never felt so taken care of.

This congee is signature Janet. She learned it from her friend Millie Chan, who she claims has been the source of congee rivers flowing to all sorts of people who have needed it. Congee is a smooth rice porridge, and it's really all about the toppings. Even in its plainest form, however, it's wonderful. Top with hot sesame oil, Kimchi (page 108), scallions, soy sauce, sesame seeds, cilantro, or anything else that calls to you.

1 cup white rice 10 cups water, stock, or whey 1 tablespoon kosher salt	2 boneless, skinless single chicken breasts (4 to 6 ounces each), partially frozen for easy slicing	1½ cups tender greens, cut into thin ribbons (spinach, tatsoi, or any other green you have on hand)

1 Combine the rice and water in a large pot. Bring to a boil, lower the heat to medium low, and cover. Cook for 1½ hours, stirring every so often. It will seem like there is too much liquid and not enough rice, but it will thicken. When it does, add 2 teaspoons of the salt.

2 Rub the remaining teaspoon of salt over the chicken breasts. Using a sharp knife, cut the chicken into thin slices, about ½ inch. Add them to the pot, stirring the chicken into the hot rice. Stir in the greens. Continue to cook until the chicken turns white and the greens are soft, about 5 minutes.

VARIATIONS

• For a coconut congee, replace 2 cups of the liquid with a can of coconut milk.

• Replace the chicken with sliced pork tenderloin or tofu.

STORAGE NOTES ✦ Congee freezes well: consider storing in single-size portions in airtight containers for up to 4 months.

DO THE
WORK

We weren't talking about bread—at least, not at first.

I was visiting a friend who'd had a hard couple of weeks. There was a sick kid, some challenges at work, and he was exhausted. "You know how you can tell that things have been hard?" he asked me. "Look in the bread box. Pepperidge Farm. I haven't made bread in weeks."

I'd never thought about it that way until then, but I knew exactly what he meant. Homemade bread is the indicator that everything is where he wants it to be in his life.

Bread, like so many other staples, is one of those foods that we imagine to be more of a project than it really is. In fact, there are dozens of easy ways to make bread at home, and you probably already have everything you need in your kitchen to make a great loaf. Many appliances can do most of the work for us. There are no-knead and five-minutes-a-day loaves that have turned millions of people into bread bakers. Most recipes require very little active time from the baker—if anything, the biggest challenge is just to remember there is dough rising on the counter.

Many people ask me if it counts if they use a bread machine. That always makes me laugh! Whatever works for you—it all counts. People have been making bread for thousands of years, and their methods and recipes have changed with their circumstances. Your bread is your bread. Of course, any of these methods are wonderful, if that's what inspires you. But if you have a loaf of bread you like on your counter at the end of the day, I say you're a bread maker.

> Bread, like so many other staples, is one of those foods that we imagine to be more of a project than it really is.

Bread occupies one-third of what I've come to recognize as the trinity of foods that set the tone for my week: bread, yogurt, and granola. Of course, many weeks include other recipes that come and go with the season or needs of my family. But if those three foods are made, I know everything is okay on a basic level. Both the presence of these foods—the homemade yogurt in the fridge, the gallon jar full of granola, and the loaf in the bread box—and the process of creating them in the first place set the tone for the week.

I have three favorite loaves in weekly rotation: a sweet honey oat, a perfectly sliceable rye, and a cinnamon swirl bread. Although any of these recipes will lead you to a good loaf the very first time, with practice and patience, you'll have the ability to make fantastic bread on a schedule that will work for you. Even more, this is a process that naturally becomes habit, and before you know it, you'll just use the ratios and work without a recipe. I make my dough in the stand mixer and let it knead the dough while I wash the breakfast dishes. It rises all morning, and by the afternoon, I have fresh bread ready to go. Bread freezes well, so I'll often use one loaf fresh and slice the other loaf for freezing. When we need a piece of toast, the bread goes right from the freezer to the toaster.

Depending on the make and model of your stand mixer, the first time you knead bread with the machine could be slightly alarming. No matter how it complains, your mixer should be up to the job. If you have a bowl-lift style mixer (if it's a KitchenAid, this will be in the professional series), then your mixer will be secure enough that you can leave the room while it kneads. If, however, you have a tilt-head style mixer, the machine may wobble and move a bit as it kneads. This is totally okay, but you'll want to stay close by. I once walked away from a kneading tilt-head mixer, and when I came back it had waddled right into the sink.

Bread dough will vary with subtleties in the weather, which you might not even think of, but the good news is that it's very forgiving. These recipes do make wet doughs, but if a dough is entirely too wet to handle, add a few extra tablespoons of bread flour as you mix. The main tense moment for me comes with knowing when it really is time to bake the bread. If you don't let it rise enough, the bread may be a bit denser than you want, but if you let it rise too much, the loaves will collapse in the center and be downright square (although entirely edible). I suggest that you trust your instincts, and the moment you think the final rise is almost done, preheat the oven. Poke your loaves, and if they hold a firm indent, that's one more sign they're ready. You'll learn the way your bread behaves, and after a few loaves, your instincts will get stronger, smarter, and more likely to lead you in the direction of perfect bread.

⟩⟩⟩⟩⟩⟩⟩ HONEY WHEAT BREAD ⟨⟨⟨⟨⟨⟨⟨

MAKES TWO 8½ X 4½-INCH LOAVES

This is a great all-purpose bread, as perfect for sandwiches as it is for toast. Feel free to play around with different kinds of flour here—just keep the flour to liquid ratio the same.

2¼ cups (540 ml) warm water

3 tablespoons honey

2 teaspoons active dry yeast

4 tablespoons (½ stick/56 g) unsalted butter, melted and slightly cooled

4 cups (480 g) white bread flour, plus more for shaping the dough

2½ cups (280 g) spelt or whole-wheat flour

½ cup (50 g) rolled oats

1 tablespoon kosher salt

Oil for greasing the bowl and pans

1 Combine the warm water and honey in the bowl of a stand mixer and stir to dissolve the honey. Sprinkle the yeast over the surface of the liquid and let it sit for 10 minutes. Add the butter to the bowl and stir gently to combine.

2 Add the bread flour, spelt flour, oats, and salt to the yeast mixture. Stir with a wooden spoon until you have a loose, shaggy dough. Let rest for 5 minutes. Fit the stand mixer with the dough hook and knead on medium-low speed for 9 minutes. Transfer the dough to a greased bowl, cover with a clean dish towel, and let rise at room temperature until puffed and increased by about half of its original size. The timing of this will vary depending on the temperature in your kitchen, from 1 hour in a hot summer kitchen to 2½ hours in a colder kitchen.

3 After the first rise, lightly flour the counter and your hands. Turn the dough out onto the counter and use a bench knife or large kitchen knife to cut it in half. Use one hand to shape the first ball of dough into a round, turning it clockwise on the counter like a dial. Gently lift the dough off the counter and tuck any ragged edges underneath it, creating a dome-like shape. Repeat with the second ball of dough, and let them rest together on the counter for about 15 minutes.

4 Grease 2 standard 8½ × 4½-inch loaf pans. Now shape the loaves. The domes will have flattened out a bit. Fold one side in toward the center, and then the other side over it. Starting at the top, roll the dough tightly into a log. Transfer it seam side down to the prepared pan. (Don't worry if the ends of the log don't meet the ends of the pan.) Repeat with the other ball of dough and cover the pans with the dish towel. Let the dough rise again until it's about an inch above the pan rims and it holds a firm indent when you poke it, 1½ to 3 hours. Again, your timing will vary depending on the temperature in your kitchen.

5 Preheat the oven to 450°F. Bake the bread in the middle of the oven until the tops are golden brown, 25 to 27 minutes. Set the pans on a wire rack and let cool for 30 minutes, then gently release the bread from the pans to finish cooling.

STORAGE NOTES ✦ Slice bread before freezing. Freeze in freezer bags and toast directly from the freezer.

RYE BREAD

This is my favorite bread to have in the breadbox, as I have a major weakness for rye toast with salty butter. The pickle juice might seem like a crazy addition, but it's the secret magic ingredient. It creates a soft and fragrant bread with just the right amount of sour.

2 cups (480 ml) warm water	¼ cup (60 ml) pickle juice (from fridge pickles, page 29, or any vinegar dill pickle)	2 cups (200 g) rye flour
2 tablespoons sugar		1 tablespoon kosher salt
2 teaspoons active dry yeast	5 cups (600 g) white bread flour, plus more for shaping the dough	2 tablespoons caraway seeds
½ cup (120 ml) safflower or other neutral oil, plus more for greasing the bowl and pans		Oil for greasing the bowl and pans

1 Combine the warm water and sugar in the bowl of your stand mixer and stir to dissolve the sugar. Sprinkle the yeast over the surface of the liquid and let it sit for 10 minutes. Add the oil and pickle juice to the bowl and stir gently to combine.

2 Add the bread flour, rye flour, salt, and caraway seeds to the yeast mixture. Stir with a wooden spoon until you have a thick, shaggy dough. Fit the stand mixer with the dough hook and knead on medium-low speed for 10 minutes. The dough will be wet and sticky. Transfer the dough to a large, greased bowl. Cover with a clean, damp dish towel and let rise until puffed and increased by about half of its original size. The timing will vary depending on the temperature in your kitchen, from 1 hour in a hot summer kitchen to 2½ hours in a colder kitchen.

3 From here on, the process is the same as Honey Wheat Bread (page 208). Follow steps 3 through 5.

CINNAMON SWIRL BREAD

MAKES TWO 8½ X 4½-INCH LOAVES

This bread is so sweet and buttery, it almost passes as dessert. And of course it makes the best French toast.

2¼ cups (540 ml) warm water

3 tablespoons maple syrup

2 teaspoons active dry yeast

4 tablespoons (½ stick/56 g) unsalted butter, melted and slightly cooled

7 cups (840 g) white bread flour, plus more for shaping the dough

1 tablespoon kosher salt

Oil for greasing the bowl and pans

1 large egg, beaten with 1 tablespoon water

¼ cup (50 g) sugar

1 tablespoon ground cinnamon

1 Combine the water and maple syrup in the bowl of a stand mixer. Sprinkle the yeast over the liquid and let it sit for 10 minutes.

2 Add the butter, flour, and salt to the yeast mixture. Stir until you have a shaggy dough. Let rest for 5 minutes. Fit the stand mixer with the dough hook and knead on medium-low speed for 9 minutes. Transfer the dough to a greased bowl, cover with a dish towel, and let rise until increased by half, 1 to 2½ hours.

3 Turn the dough out onto a lightly floured counter and cut it in half. Shape the first ball of dough into a round, turning it clockwise on the counter. Repeat with the second ball of dough and let them rest on the counter for 15 minutes.

4 Grease 2 standard 8½ x 4½-inch loaf pans. Put the egg wash nearby, and combine the sugar and cinnamon in a small bowl. Use a rolling pin to roll the first ball of dough roughly 10 inches square. Paint with egg wash, then sprinkle half the sugar mixture over the entire square. Starting at the bottom of the square, roll the dough into a log, giving each end a press to seal in the cinnamon as you transfer the log to the prepared pan. Repeat with the second ball of dough, cover the loaf pans with a dish towel, and let rise again until the dough is about an inch above the rim of the pan and it holds a firm indent when you poke it, 1½ to 2 hours. Save the remaining egg wash for the next step.

5 Preheat the oven to 450°F. Paint the top of each loaf with egg wash. Bake in the middle of the oven until the tops are golden, 25 to 27 minutes. Let cool for 30 minutes, then release the bread from the pans to finish cooling.

SEEDED BAGELS

I love a good New York bagel, but there's such a swagger around them! Give me a Montreal bagel instead. Watch those guys in the back of St. Viateur shape, roll, and slide their small, dense bagels into the fire. They've got nothing to prove. That's the bagel I've tried to re-create here.

Great bagels are surprisingly easy to make. Bakers at St. Viateur roll out their dough in one long rope that gets segmented and turned into rounds; I go for the less traditional but much easier thumb-poke method. If someone tells you you're doing it wrong, just hand them a homemade bagel. That will shut them right up.

FOR THE DOUGH

1½ cups (300 ml) warm water

2 tablespoons honey

2 teaspoons active dry yeast

4 cups (480 g) white bread flour, plus more for shaping the dough

½ cup (58 g) whole-wheat flour

2 teaspoons kosher salt

Oil for greasing the bowl

FOR THE BOIL

3 quarts (3 L) water

2 tablespoons honey

FOR THE TOPPINGS

1¼ cups (180 g) sesame seeds or poppy seeds, or a mix of the two

Optional: ½ teaspoon finishing salt

1 Combine the warm water and honey in the bowl of a stand mixer and stir to dissolve the honey. Sprinkle the yeast over the liquid and let sit for 10 minutes.

2 Measure the flours and salt into the bowl and mix with a wooden spoon until you have a loose, shaggy dough. Let sit for 5 minutes. Grease a large mixing bowl and set aside. Fit the mixer with the dough hook and run the mixer on medium-low speed for 10 minutes. The dough should be smooth, slightly tacky, and just sticking to the bottom of the bowl. Transfer the dough to the large bowl and cover with a damp dish towel. Let the dough rise until puffed and nearly doubled in bulk. This will take about 1 hour in a warm kitchen and closer to 2 hours in a colder kitchen.

3 Turn the dough out onto a lightly floured board or counter. Divide the dough in half, then each piece in half again, then those pieces into thirds, for a total of 12 pieces of dough, each roughly 2½ ounces. Shape each piece into a ball by rolling it gently once or twice on the counter. You'll feel some lightness come into each ball. Cover the balls of dough with a damp dish towel and let them rest on the counter for 30 minutes.

4 Line 2 baking sheets with parchment paper. After the full resting time, pick up 1 ball of dough. Push your thumb through the center and gently shape into a ring by pulling the hole wider, to about 1½ inches. Place the bagel on the prepared baking sheet and repeat with the remaining balls of dough. You can fit all 12 bagels on one pan at this point, but you'll need the second baking sheet for the boiled bagels. Cover the bagels with a damp dish towel and let them rest while you prepare the boil.

5 Preheat the oven to 500°F. Combine the water and honey for the boil in a large, wide pot and bring to a boil. Combine the seeds and salt, if using, in a wide bowl. Pick up 1 bagel by its hole and slip it gently into the water. Add 2 more bagels to the water and boil for 1½ minutes. Use a slotted spoon or tongs to flip each bagel and boil for 1 minute more. Remove the bagels from the water, carefully (they're hot!) dunking each bagel in seeds on its way back to the baking sheet. In the end, you'll have 2 trays of 6 boiled, seeded bagels each. Bake until golden, about 25 minutes, rotating pans between upper and lower racks halfway through baking.

VARIATIONS

- **For plain bagels** (and every other variation), omit the seeds.

- **For cinnamon raisin bagels,** add 1 tablespoon cinnamon to the flour and ¾ cup raisins in the last few seconds of kneading.

- **For garlic bagels,** combine 1 tablespoon finely minced garlic with 3 tablespoons olive oil. Brush the garlic mixture over the bagels for the last 2 minutes of baking time.

TENSE MOMENTS ✦ Any time I bake something at such a high temperature, my smoke alarm tends to goes off. Keep an eye on your oven, run your oven fan if you're lucky enough to have one, and open a window.

STORAGE NOTES ✦ To freeze your bagels, slice them in half and freeze in freezer bags. That way they can be toasted right out of the freezer.

FLAVORED CREAM CHEESE

YOU CAN MAKE YOUR OWN FLAVORED CREAM CHEESE with either store-bought or homemade cream cheese. To make your own cream cheese, follow the process for Chèvre (page 99), substituting 2 cups heavy cream and 2 cups whole milk for the ½ gallon goat milk. Even though you have half the liquid, still use the entire quantity of culture. Reduce the culture time to 12 hours, and strain through a cheesecloth-lined strainer for 8 hours.

Use a wooden spoon and a strong arm to churn in chopped chives, scallions, smoked salmon, fresh herbs, capers, or anything else you can dream up. Taste, and add a little salt if needed. On the sweet side, stir in some jam (see page 24), walnuts and honey, or cinnamon and brown sugar.

THE KITCHEN IN THE MORNING

My family has learned that if they stay in bed on the weekends and pretend to sleep, they have a much better chance of getting baked goods for breakfast.

The windows in my kitchen face west, so the room never sees the sun rise. Instead, the light slides in gently, almost scooping under the counters with a clear blue that seems left over from the moon itself, which often shares the sky with the rising sun as I preheat the oven.

I preheat the oven without knowing what's for breakfast; 350°F or 375°F is usually a safe bet, and with the press of the button, I'm already baking.

Whatever needs baking is what gets baked. Mushy bananas mean banana chocolate muffins. Sad and spotty pears, usually sent in lunch boxes and rejected, are revitalized, chopped into something to fold with hazelnuts into batter. The last cup of frozen blueberries that was left out and then refrozen—time for blueberry almond muffins. This is how I most love to be in the kitchen.

My first baking job fell to me because someone at the coffee shop where I worked had to make the muffins, and I was willing to try. I was unhappy and young and stuck in my hometown. But every morning, I'd roll out of bed and pull on clothes to the earliest part of NPR. I'd walk across the street from my apartment to the restaurant kitchen we borrowed for morning baking, unlock the door, turn on the lights, and preheat the gas oven. There was often some remnant of last night's service, a streak on the stainless counter, a water glass left with its final sip. That quiet kitchen, growing lighter as the muffins puffed and grew from batter to breakfast, filling the kitchen—it was as if my mind took on those very qualities, quiet just for that time. I would never have called myself a baker, but I was. I couldn't roll a piecrust or recall a perfect chocolate chip cookie recipe from memory, but the hum of the preheating oven calmed me, and I've since learned that it's emotion that pulls you closer to being a baker or a cook. Which form of heat makes your skin tingle as you roll up your sleeves in the kitchen? A pot of boiling water? A grill or open fire? A wood-fired bread oven? For me it's the early-morning oven, humming and rattling to build heat for whatever will go inside.

▶▶▶▶▶▶▶▶ MUFFINS ◀◀◀◀◀◀◀◀

MAKES 12 LARGE MUFFINS

For years, I looked for a basic muffin recipe that achieved the shape I wanted. So often, homemade muffins are compact rounds, tight and withholding when compared to the sprawling tops of good diner muffins. In the end, the answer was simply to increase the amount of batter. Because of the added batter, these muffins require more time in the oven than what you might be used to, and there's a slight risk of the batter migrating all the way across the tin and actually dripping off. If that starts to happen or if you're worried about it, just put a big baking sheet on the lowest oven rack. Or if your tin is a bit smaller than average and you feel like you have far too much batter, start a second tin and fill the empty cups halfway with water to help the adjacent muffins bake evenly.

8 tablespoons (1 stick/ 115 g) unsalted butter, melted, plus additional for greasing the tin

3 cups (360 g) all-purpose flour

½ teaspoon baking soda

1 tablespoon baking powder

¾ teaspoon kosher salt

2 large eggs

1 cup (200 g) sugar

1 cup (240 ml) whole milk

1 cup (225 g) plain whole-milk yogurt (for homemade, see page 34)

1 tablespoon vanilla extract

2½ cups berries or 2 cups other coarsely chopped fruit, fresh or thawed

Optional: ½ cup coarsely chopped or sliced nuts

1 Preheat the oven to 350°F. Grease the cups and top of a standard 12-cup muffin tin. Alternately, you can use muffin liners, but still grease the top of the tin.

2 Whisk together the flour, baking soda, baking powder, and salt in a large mixing bowl. Set aside. In a medium bowl, lightly beat the eggs just enough to incorporate the yolk in the white. Add the sugar, butter, milk, yogurt, and vanilla to the eggs and whisk thoroughly to combine. Pour the egg mixture into the flour mixture. Use a wooden spoon to combine the two with a few swift strokes, making sure the dry ingredients are just barely incorporated into the wet.

3 Add the fruit and again, with just a few strokes, fold it into the batter. Use a large spoon or an ice cream scoop to evenly divide the batter between the cups. The cups should be filled to overflowing. If you're using nuts, sprinkle them over each muffin. Bake until the muffins are golden and the center muffin is cooked all the way through, 40 to 50 minutes, rotating the pan halfway through baking. Allow to cool in the pan for about 20 minutes, then turn the pan upside down, gently coax the muffins out of their cups, and let them cool upside down until you're ready to eat them.

- For a bit of whole grain, replace 1 cup all-purpose flour with 1 cup spelt or whole-wheat pastry flour.

- You can also make this recipe as a quick bread. Divide the batter between 2 standard loaf pans, and bake for 1 to 1¼ hours.

- For a streusel topping, combine ⅓ cup all-purpose flour, 1½ tablespoons cold, grated butter, and 1½ teaspoons cinnamon. Sprinkle over the muffins just before baking.

STORAGE NOTES ◆ Muffin batter can be stored in a covered container in the refrigerator for up to 1 day. To freeze muffins, cool completely and freeze on a baking sheet. Transfer to freezer bags and freeze for up to 4 months. Thaw at room temperature and refresh in a 325°F oven for 10 to 15 minutes if needed.

some of MY FAVORITE FLAVOR combinations

Blueberry and Lemon Zest: 2½ cups blueberries + 1 teaspoon lemon zest

Pear Chocolate Hazelnut: 2 cups peeled and coarsely chopped Bosc pears + ¾ cup bittersweet chocolate chips + ¾ cup toasted, skinned, coarsely chopped hazelnuts

Raspberry Almond: 2½ cups raspberries + ½ teaspoon almond extract; scatter ½ cup sliced almonds over the muffins

Apple Pecan: 2 cups peeled and coarsely chopped apples + ¾ cup toasted, coarsely chopped pecans; top with streusel (see variation above)

Ginger Peach: 2 cups peeled and coarsely chopped peaches + 1 teaspoon ground ginger + 1 tablespoon coarsely chopped crystallized ginger + ½ teaspoon grated nutmeg

THE LIVING FINISHES

I have come to believe that it is a mistake to feel like a kitchen should serve us. Instead, I think this room above all others requires our participation, our commitment, even our love.

My kitchen has been through many different phases. When I was pregnant with Rosie, we bought a little ranch house with my parents. The plan was that we'd move in right away, and eventually we'd renovate and create enough space for all of us. The original kitchen was tiny, designed around the centerpiece of the microwave. The sink was smaller than an average pot, the old electric stove heated to temperatures different from the dial reading, and the cabinet doors were a sharp and shiny metal that once, when left open, collided with my head and sent me to the emergency room with what I assume was the first kitchen-cabinet-induced concussion the doctors had seen in a while. Despite its failings, I loved the kitchen. I chopped late into the night in the dull flickering light. I learned how to can jam as the tiny windows refused to bring in any breath of August breeze. I bounced back and forth in the three feet between counters, plating the courses for my first dinner party. When it was finally time to renovate the house to make it large enough for my parents and my sister to move in, I used all the goodness in that kitchen to inspire the new design, happy for the chance to let go of the not-so-good rest of it.

The metal cabinets became wide-open wooden shelving. We put in better lighting and a bigger sink, and tried to create enough space to actually allow seven people to move at once. Sometimes, we were one family, but more often we were two families who lived differently.

We tried to find new systems. We created dish schedules and personalized water glasses and napkin rings. We each had different nights when we were responsible for the family meal. There was an entire rack in the kitchen devoted to lunch boxes. Sadie would set the table. My sister, Maia, then a freshman in high school, would clear the table. Most of the time, there was dinner. Much of the time, we'd sit at the table after our plates were scraped clean, laughing about something or other. But then, more and more, it didn't work.

The priority was to keep living together, and if we wanted that, we'd need two kitchens. We saved up and built a smaller second kitchen perfectly suited to my parents' needs. We built a wall with a door that's open most of the time. We flow through the door, and the kids especially claim the whole house as their own, poking into each kitchen to see who's making the better dinner. And it's still work, but it's working.

Somewhere in the middle of the kitchen transition, my friend Adam came to replace the temporary plywood countertops with something more permanent. He pieced together a combination of recycled chalkboard and butcher block with one little piece of marble for rolling piecrust. As he set each piece into its place, he'd rub oil into the wood and the slate. He said it was a "living finish," and that it would grow and change and get more beautiful as it was used. We just have to pay attention, he said, to season and rub oil into the surfaces and to understand that they need care.

This kitchen really is the heart of this house, right smack in the center. It's almost as if the room itself is a living finish. Not slate or wood or cast iron, but a whole space that requires our attention, love, and care. And like tung oil on butcher block or lard on cast iron, it might just be the act of eating that seasons a kitchen. Cooking, spilling of wine, laughing, breaking of dishes, feeding with grace, accepting with gratitude, washing of dishes as if they were your own baby. Quiet snacks on the counter late at night, with only a tiny light on to see. Children learning how to caramelize onions, how to whisk an egg. Hollering over the island, accepting that it's hard. We work again, and harder, and we promise to pay attention. And we oil and season and care for the kitchen and all of its surfaces so that we can work together with that space in the task of feeding those who live within it.

SPOON BUTTER

MAKES ABOUT 1 CUP

There are few kitchen jobs I love as much as treating my spoons and cutting boards with spoon butter. Every so often, I pull out all the woodens, and I buff every surface with the soft, sweet-smelling oil. The smell of beeswax fills the room, the spoons and counters shine, and I feel like I've done something truly wonderful for my kitchen. I rub any excess into my hands, and my skin gets a little love, too. My friend Christina Davis introduced me to the wonder of spoon butter, and both my woodens and I owe her lots of gratitude.

| ¾ cup mineral oil or walnut oil | 1 ounce beeswax |

1   Combine the oil and beeswax in a wide-mouth pint jar and place the jar in a heavy-bottomed saucepan. Heat water in a kettle and fill the pan with boiling water to come about halfway up the jar. Set the pot over low heat and let it sit, stirring occasionally, until the beeswax is melted and the oil and wax have come together as one golden liquid. Remove the pot from heat, carefully take the jar out of the pan, and allow to cool. The spoon butter will solidify as it cools.

2   To give your woodens a treat, scoop a bit of oil out of the jar with a clean cloth. Rub it into the wood and let it sit for a few hours. Buff off any excess with your cloth. Keep your spoon oil in a covered jar at room temperature, and give your woodens a polish whenever they seem a little dry or dull.

STORAGE NOTES ✦ If you make it with walnut oil, your spoon butter will keep in a covered jar at room temperature for up to 6 months. If you make it with mineral oil, it will keep indefinitely.

When I need to create time, I walk out the door and try to find it in the yard.

Just a year or two after we moved into our house, I planted the orchard out front. It was a big decision, due to the cost of the little trees, necessary compost, and a year or two later, a fence. My neighbors were curious, and then some of them got upset, whether about the fence or the whole growing-food-in-the-yard thing, I never could quite discern. Over the years, I've heard fewer complaints and more compliments, and I've sweetened the deal by putting a sign on the fence when the plum trees go into overdrive.

Too many plums! Come help yourself!

There are also apples, a few pear trees that haven't quite born fruit, and a sour cherry that at this point is just a gift to the birds. The trees give me fruit, but they also give me blossoms and shade, and a sense of slow progress that I drink like cold wine in August. (Even better when I drink cold rosé in August under the trees.)

> Time moves differently in an orchard.

Most of all time moves differently in an orchard.

It happens every time we go to any pick-your-own orchard: plums, peaches, cherries, and of course, apples. We go to pick for an hour, and before we know it, we're all lost in the branches, off on our own quest for the perfect fruit. When we moved into our house and planted our tiny orchard, I dreamed of the far-off future of our fruit grove where I could slow time whenever I wanted. After a decade of growing, the dream is real, and now I slip out for ten minutes here and there on summer days. I'll go out with the intention to pick a few plums and run back into the kitchen. But then I stand with the branches all around me, listening to the fruit grow. I could stay in that orchard forever, and lucky for me, ten minutes can slow down and stretch out under the branches of my nine little trees.

Sometimes the time is hiding on the back porch, where our laundry line hangs from one end of the house to the other. When it's full, it stretches across the back porch, shielding the kitchen from the hot sun and flying like mismatched prayer flags of little underwear and collared work shirts and cloth napkins. There's a pulley system between the two ends, so we can stand on the bench of our picnic table and pin up one item at a tune before sending it down the line. On any sunny day between May and November, I try to forgo the dryer and make use of the line.

It takes ages to get everything up there. Because I work at home, I'm often the one hanging the laundry, and I'll walk away from my desk with the thought that I'll just throw it up on the line real quick. But twenty minutes later I'm still up there, perched on the bench with the honeybees buzzing around me and the sun on my back. There's nothing else I can do while I hang the laundry. I've got both arms over my head, I'm fiddling with clothespins, and once I've started the task, there's nowhere to go but through it. And there, just like that, those twenty minutes become a gift in my day, a pocket of quiet and sun that I never could consciously put there. And that, secretly, is why I love my clothesline.

There are other opportunities to slow down the day, and I've learned to seek them out, especially when I feel there's just not enough time.

Taking a few minutes to sit and enjoy my coffee, setting out a little "tea time" for us all before we jump into the chaos of homework and dinner prep, or heading out for a walk no matter how much work I still have to do—each of these decisions seems to create time rather than take it away. And maybe my favorite of all, the tiny walks I take around the perimeter of the yard, looking for something, anything I can put in a vase for the table. Daffodils, wild phlox, or geranium, or for those few wonderful weeks of the year, lilacs, deep and fragrant. And with the flowers comes the slowness of the walk that brought them in, and it's almost as if those few wandering minutes also sit in the jar with the more tangible blooms, together continuing to slow time right there at the center of the table.

APPLE CHIPS

MAKES 3 BAKING SHEETS FULL OF APPLE CHIPS (ABOUT 10 DOZEN CHIPS)

Apple chips are irresistible, and they seem to inspire a certain snacking mania in anyone who comes in contact with the tray. I've learned that these are one of the few snacks I have to hide and bring out a tiny jar at a time. Many thanks to Aimee Wimbush-Bourque and her blog *Simple Bites* for introducing me to the wonder of the apple chip. I use granulated maple sugar in this recipe because it sweetens without adding moisture, but if you don't have any, just leave it out.

2½ pounds (1.2 kg) small apples (6 to 8)	1 teaspoon ground cinnamon	Optional: 1 tablespoon maple sugar

1 Preheat the oven to 250°F. Line 3 baking sheets with parchment paper. If your oven has only a 2-tray capacity, you can cut the recipe in half.

2 Core the apples, but do not peel them. If you don't have a corer, just cut the sides away from the cores in pieces that are as large as possible. Slice the apples between ⅙ and ⅛ inch with the slicing blade of a food processor, a mandoline, or a knife. I prefer the food processor for this job, as it gives me just the right thickness. And if your apples are small enough, they should be able to fit into the feeding chute of the food processor.

3 Lay the apple slices in a single layer on the baking sheets. Combine the cinnamon and maple sugar, if using, in a small bowl and sprinkle over the apples.

4 Bake until the chips have just a touch of chew to them but mostly crunch, between 2½ and 4 hours, flipping the apples after the first hour. The timing really depends on the apples. They will continue to crisp up as they cool.

STORAGE NOTES ✦ Apple chips keep well in an airtight container at room temperature for up to 1 month.

TENSE MOMENTS ✦ I'm not going to gloss it over. This recipe requires many hours in the oven for a small amount of food. The apples need to be in one layer to crisp up, and the end result will disappear faster than you want it to. If only you had three ovens to fill, then we could call this preservation. But. BUT, those apple chips! They are wonderful, and the prep is minimal enough that it really is an easy recipe.

THE RITUAL

I was nineteen when I quit smoking, and I was working at a coffee shop at the time. In my first cigarette-free months, I became keenly aware of some injustice at work. At various moments in my shift, my coworkers would plead addiction and head out the back door for a cigarette when they needed it. There was a certain respect for these breaks, as we all knew that anyone who needed a cigarette and didn't get one would become a bear to work with within ten minutes.

I knew the joy of these little breaks. I had loved sitting out by the back fire escape, staring into space (this was also the late nineties, pre-smartphone) and using the cigarette to remind me to breathe in, and breathe out. After a few minutes of smoking-induced meditation, I was always ready to head back into the throng of crazy New Yorkers demanding their lattes just so. I missed those breaks, probably more than I missed the cigarettes themselves.

So I did something radical. I started bringing oranges to work. I told my coworkers I needed an orange break, and then I'd go out by the fire escape, space out, and breathe deeply (just regular air this time) while I peeled and ate my orange. I took to making myself really great coffees for these breaks too—perfectly steamed lattes or gently sweetened iced coffees. In the few minutes it took me to peel the orange and drink a bit of my coffee, I was able to clear my mind, slow down, and reset. It was even better than a cigarette.

What fuels our national obsession for fancy coffee shop coffees? We may need the caffeine (I know I do), but I think we need the ritual of it all just as much. And although we drink coffee to fuel us through our busy-ness, I think we also use it to slow down, zone out, and reset.

My weakness for coffee shops hits its peak in the summer, when I crave really good iced coffee. I still indulge when I can, but since I learned how to make great cold brew concentrate, I can get my fancy-coffee fix at home. Now I take my breaks on my back porch, and I get to slow down and zone out on the field beyond. Sometimes, I even take an orange with me for good measure. It still works.

COLD BREW CONCENTRATE

Cold brew concentrate is ideal for iced coffee, as it keeps well in the fridge and lacks the bitterness of regular brewed coffee. It's also great for flavoring desserts like Ricotta Mousse (see page 301) or ice cream (see page 291).

There are differing opinions out there about the best grind for cold brew coffee. When I've experimented with different grinds, I've found very little difference in the end product. When it comes to the quality of the coffee, I've found that cheap coffee works well, so I buy whatever pre-ground coffee is on sale.

| 2 cups ground coffee | 6 cups water

1   Combine the coffee and water in a ½-gallon Mason jar. Cover the jar and let it sit at room temperature for 24 hours. Give the jar a stir, then carefully strain the mixture through a cheesecloth or paper-towel-lined strainer into a second jar and refrigerate.

2   To make iced coffee, pour ½ cup coffee concentrate over ice. Dilute to your taste with milk, water, or both.

VARIATIONS

+ My favorite addition to iced coffee is mint simple syrup. It's not overly minty, but rather just makes iced coffee more refreshing. To make the syrup, combine 1 cup sugar with 1 cup water in a small saucepan. Heat until the sugar dissolves, then remove from heat. Add 10 fresh mint leaves, cover, and steep for 15 minutes. Strain and refrigerate for up to 2 weeks.

+ Make an iced mocha with ½ cup coffee concentrate, a hefty squeeze of Chocolate Syrup (page 297), and ¼ cup milk. Combine in a quart jar along with a handful of ice cubes. Screw the lid on and shake hard.

+ For a frappe, combine ½ cup coffee concentrate with a handful of ice cubes, 2 tablespoons honey or maple syrup, ¼ cup milk, and, if you like, 1 tablespoon coconut oil in a blender. Blend until smooth.

STORAGE NOTES ✦ Refrigerate concentrate for up to 10 days. You can also freeze concentrate in ice cube trays or an airtight container, for up to 4 months.

RHUBARB SNACKING CAKE

MAKES ONE 9 × 9-INCH CAKE

Although I'm a fifty-fifty mix of old British stock and European Jew, I was raised 100 percent by the Jewish side, with only a few stories of my British heritage to fill in the holes. Still I blame my hidden British side for my love of British cookbooks, gooseberries, and most of all, tea time.

Somewhere between three and four in the afternoon, the day can start to break me. The hopeful optimism of the morning is over, and now the clock is ticking and the to-do list feels way too long. This is when tea and cake come to the rescue. It creates a break, a remedy for the frantic searching through the fridge for peanut butter (that's Joey), the immediate post-school "I'm hungry!" and the hungry panic that gets dinner prep started on the wrong foot.

This is not-so-sweet teacake, simple and easy to make. I love it with rhubarb but it works with any seasonal berry or stone fruit. Top with whipped cream or ice cream and it's great for dessert, too.

8 tablespoons (1 stick / 115 g) unsalted butter, at room temperature, cut into chunks, plus more for the pan	3 large eggs	¾ cup (180 ml) buttermilk (for homemade, see page 34)
¼ cup (50 g) granulated sugar	2 teaspoons vanilla extract	2½ cups ¼-inch sliced rhubarb (2 to 3 stalks)
¼ cup (55 g) packed light brown sugar	2 cups (240 g) all-purpose flour	1 tablespoon turbinado or other coarse sugar
	1 tablespoon baking powder	
	½ teaspoon kosher salt	

1 Preheat the oven to 375°F. Grease a 9-inch square baking pan with butter.

2 Combine the butter, granulated sugar, and brown sugar in the bowl of a stand mixer fit with the paddle attachment and beat until fluffy, about 3 minutes. Scrape down the sides of the bowl, add the eggs and vanilla, and beat again until combined.

3 Whisk together the flour, baking powder, and salt in a medium mixing bowl. Add the dry mix and the buttermilk to the stand mixer bowl and beat just until the ingredients are incorporated, scraping down the sides of the bowl if necessary. The batter will be lumpy, but that's okay.

4 Fold the rhubarb into the batter and transfer it all to the prepared pan. Sprinkle with the turbinado sugar and bake until the cake starts to pull away from the sides of the pan and is slightly golden on top, about 40 minutes. Cool for 20 minutes before serving from the pan.

SADIE'S DINNER NIGHT

When Sadie turned nine, she asked for a weekly cooking night. Thursday nights became Sadie's, and I knew we'd work out the details as we went.

These weekly dinners have been extraordinary. In the midst of what you would expect—the extra time it takes to cook, me breathing deeply to stop from taking over a difficult step—the meals have been full of pride, enthusiasm, and great food. But the piece I didn't expect is how much these few hours each week have changed Sadie. Watching her, I see more clearly that feeding people is as nurturing for the cook as it is for those who sit around the table. And although many will extol the benefits of bringing children into the kitchen to cook by your side—they, peeling potatoes and you, chopping them, together in familial bliss—I will not. Over the years, my advice to parents who want their kids in the kitchen is to set them up with a cookbook and a stool, and back away slowly. They have to own the process. The best way you can help is by carving out the space for them to do it.

We tend to strive toward speed in the kitchen, but when it comes to kids' cooking, I think that needs to go. The time it can take for a child to think through a recipe, prepare their *mise en place*, even just chop a carrot—it can be torture to watch when our goal is dinner at 6:00. Our solution is to treat dinner night more like an afterschool activity. Dinner prep starts just after school, and although I'm around to help if needed, I keep my distance.

I can see Sadie learning her own way through time management and efficiency. We eat whenever she decides dinner is ready. And I know that these skills—how to chop and steam and roast—will follow Sadie through her life. I love to imagine the decades ahead with my idealistic mother's hopes: late-night teenage dinner parties where Sadie is the one who knows how to make the perfect garlic bread to go with spaghetti and meatballs. I think of the day she'll cook for her first love, whisking the roux for the chicken potpie that she learned long ago would win over anyone. I don't know what she'll grow up to become, and I can't protect her from the wide and messy world. But she'll always be able to roast a chicken or layer a lasagna, and those meals will fuel her through whatever comes, as will the empowerment she feels when she creates exactly what she wants to eat. She's learning how to put love into a tangible thing that she can give to others so they can take it in and make that love part of their own fiber.

ONE-DISH CHOCOLATE CAKE

When Sadie plans her dinner menu, she always includes dessert. This is her favorite chocolate cake, adapted from a recipe in one of the first books she took into the kitchen, Mollie Katzen's *Honest Pretzels*. It's somewhere between a cake and a brownie, a great treat for weeknights and birthdays alike. Top with ice cream (page 291) to make it even more special.

½ cup (40 g) unsweetened cocoa powder

1 cup (120 g) all-purpose flour

¾ cup (150 g) granulated sugar

½ teaspoon kosher salt

½ teaspoon baking soda

¼ teaspoon baking powder

1 cup (240 ml) water

⅓ cup (75 ml) safflower or other neutral-tasting oil

1 teaspoon cider vinegar

Optional: Powdered sugar, for dusting

1 Preheat the oven to 350°F. Whisk together the cocoa powder, flour, granulated sugar, salt, baking soda, and baking powder in a 9-inch square cake pan.

2 Add the water, oil, and vinegar to the pan, stirring gently to blend the wet ingredients into the dry. Scrape down the sides with a silicone spatula and bake until a cake tester inserted in the center comes out clean, about 30 minutes. Cool for 30 minutes before serving. Serve plain or dusted with powdered sugar.

TURKISH BREAKFAST

In 2010, my friend Lissa and I went to Istanbul. We were visiting our friends Molly and Aurel, and, after a fourteen-hour flight, we climbed up the cobblestone street we hoped was our destination, already lost in a country that would continue to baffle us in a wonderful way for the next eight days.

"Allo!" Aurel poked his head out of the third-story window of one of the crammed-together apartment buildings. "I have breakfast for you!"

That was my very first Turkish breakfast, but it wouldn't be my last. That week alone, I experienced different versions of the same formula, and by the end of the trip, Turkish breakfast was the only kind of breakfast I wanted to eat forever. What I love most about it is the care put into each piece and the artistry involved in creating each plate. It feels so luxurious both to create and to eat it, and it's a daily luxury that I can have any time I need it. You can arrange all the ingredients on a single platter, or you can craft a separate plate for each person.

4 large eggs, boiled to your preference (see page 18)	12 dates (Medjool and Deglet are my favorites)	Optional: Muhammara (page 79), sliced tomatoes, sliced fruit, or any wonderful little thing you have in your fridge
4 small cucumbers, sliced	4 slices bread	
½ cup kalamata olives	Honey	
About 4 ounces feta (for homemade, see page 113), cut into thick slices	1 small bunch flat-leaf parsley	

Arrange your plate, or plates, in any way that pleases you. Eggs can go into egg cups. Cucumbers, olives, feta, dates, and bread can go right onto the platter. Pour honey and any other spreads into ramekins for dipping or spreading. Add parsley sprigs, both for extra color and for freshening the breath after the meal.

PLOUGHMAN'S SNACK

"You'll ruin your appetite!"

This is one of those phrases I have decided to abandon. I find myself warning Joey or the girls about this mysterious "ruining" without thinking about what I'm actually saying, just because I want to say "no" to something. Often, dinner isn't getting out as fast as I'd hoped, and I'm both frustrated with myself and hungry, but holding back from snacking as I cook because I'm desperately holding on to the illusion that dinner really will be ready in five minutes, just like I've been saying for the last half an hour. If I take a moment to stop and listen to myself, I'll remember that, first, there is absolutely nothing that can ruin Joey's appetite. (I mean it. I've seen him down a 5 Guys burger and fries and then have first, second, and third helpings of lasagna.) Second, if I put out before-dinner bites for us all to munch on before dinner's ready, then we're all still eating good, homemade food, we're less grumpy, and I have a much better time cooking. If less actually gets eaten at the dinner table, it's totally okay. It just means more leftovers for lunch, and more time and space for me when I'm getting dinner ready.

Of course, putting out a few starters also adds a bit of fancy to the meal, especially if you shout "Hors d'oeuvres!" from the kitchen. And for those of us who like small bites of this and that, a few little plates put together on the table can be the perfect dinner, too.

Years ago, Joey and I ate a perfect "ploughman's snack" at a bar, and we've been calling our predinner snacks by that name ever since. We might not be plowing the fields all day, but by dinnertime, we've usually all done enough hard work to feel like it, and a little assortment of snacks helps us all out. We make our plate with whatever's on hand, but in an ideal world, my perfect ploughman's snack includes the following elements:

PLOUGHMAN'S SNACK

THE PICKLE

Any quick-pickled vegetable (see page 29)

Sliced cucumbers tossed in rice vinegar and salt, left to marinate for a few minutes

THE PROTEIN

A few slices of cured meat (saucisson, prosciutto, or ham)

A scoop of cooked, salted chickpeas (better yet, dry them, toss with paprika, lemon zest, salt, and a drop of oil, and roast in a 425°F oven for 25 to 30 minutes)

THE CHEESE

Sliced Feta Cheese (page 113), soft Chèvre (page 99), or a hunk of the good stuff you've been saving just for this moment

THE FRESH

Sliced fresh vegetables and fruit: radishes, cucumbers, snap peas, tomatoes, apples, pears

THE NUTS

Any nut, toasted, or to fancy it up, combine 1 tablespoon melted butter, ½ teaspoon chili powder, 1 teaspoon maple syrup, 1 teaspoon salt, and 1 teaspoon chopped fresh rosemary or dill. Toss 2 cups mixed nuts in the mixture and roast on a greased baking sheet in a 300°F oven for 25 to 30 minutes, shuffling midway through the baking time.

THE CRUNCH

A few crackers or bagel or tortilla chips (see page 132)

THE SPREAD

Muhammara (page 79), Preserved Lemon Hummus (page 97), or any simple pesto (see page 44)

⫸⫸⫸⫸⫸⫸ BRAISED LAMB SHANKS ⫸⫸⫸⫸⫸⫸

SERVES 2 TO 4, DEPENDING ON THE SIZE OF THE SHANKS

Joey and I take dates whenever we can get them. They're rarely classic hire-a-babysitter-and-go-out-for-dinner affairs. More often, a "date" is a walk down to the grocery store in which we take the long way or a second dinner after the girls are in bed. This is one of my favorite home-date-night meals. I brown the shanks when I have a moment, tuck them into the oven to braise through the afternoon, then pull the pan out of the oven just as the girls are brushing their teeth. Shanks are often small when you buy them directly from a farmer, and larger if you buy them from the supermarket. Either size will work but I created this recipe with small shanks. If your shanks are larger, just increase the other ingredients as well.

1½ cups red wine (Pinot Noir is a good choice here)	1 fresh rosemary sprig or a pinch of dried rosemary	1 medium onion, cut into wedges
2 tablespoons red or white wine vinegar	2 bay leaves	2 medium carrots, cut into 1-inch lengths
3 unpeeled garlic cloves, smashed	10 peppercorns	3 medium red or Yukon Gold potatoes, peeled and cut into large bites
3 fresh thyme sprigs or ½ teaspoon dried thyme	2 lamb shanks	
	1 tablespoon safflower or sunflower oil	Kosher salt and freshly ground pepper

1   Combine the wine, vinegar, garlic, thyme, rosemary, bay leaves, peppercorns, and lamb shanks in a shallow dish. Cover and marinate at room temperature for 30 minutes.

2   Preheat the oven to 325°F. Heat the oil over medium-high heat in an oven-proof skillet or roasting pan. Remove the shanks from the marinade and reserve the marinade. Pat the shanks dry with a paper towel, and lightly brown them in the oil. Transfer the shanks to a plate, add a touch more oil if the pan seems dry, and lower the heat to medium.

3   Add the onion and carrots and cook, stirring often, until the carrots are tender, 10 to 15 minutes. Add the potatoes and shanks. Pour in the marinade. The liquid should reach halfway up the sides of the meat, but you can add water if the liquid level is low. Heat liquid until barely steaming, then cover the pot, transfer to the oven, and braise until the meat is tender and falls off the bone, 3 to 4 hours. Taste, and add salt and pepper as needed. Serve the shanks along with the vegetables and sauce over polenta, rice, or just on their own.

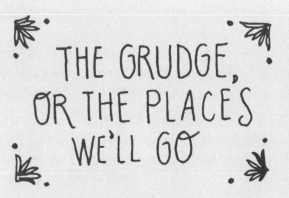

THE GRUDGE, OR THE PLACES WE'LL GO

Someday, Joey and I are going to walk from the southern end of Berkshire County to the north. We want to walk the roads we drive every day, so we can see all the details we miss as we speed by with only the destination in mind.

We're always talking about trips we hope we'll take someday. We have countless little tins and boxes secreted away in our bedroom, each with a few dollars we shoved in there and gave to the other with a promise.

"This is for Morocco."

"This is for England."

But of all the trips, this is the one we talk about most. That week when the kids are taken care of and we can set off? That's a plan for the future. But the destinations are all around us, and even the planning helps us see that we're already there.

I love to travel, and I dream of new places. But especially in the moments when far-away travel feels out of reach, long walks with Joey calm my wanderlust. "We're training," we say, and we walk through the entire winter afternoon until the sun starts to set and it's time to make dinner. We walk down a new dirt road we've never taken before, or we head out on foot to the grocery store, walking the two miles down the railroad tracks and through the sweeping and beautiful cemetery instead of the more-traveled sidewalk. We take a thermos of something sweet and hot, and with every walk, a new little bit of our home reveals itself.

I think sometimes the best remedy for wanting to leave a place might just be to go deeper into it.

We often take a thermos cocktail for those long, cold winter walks. My favorite recipe comes from Jenny Claster, a friend of my friend Sarah. She calls it "The Grudge," and so do we, although if anything, it's a drink to inspire letting go of grudges and whatever else might be weighing you down. Better to be lighter and free as you set out for a good walk.

THE GRUDGE

MAKES JUST UNDER A QUART

3 cups apple cider	3 tablespoons fresh lemon juice (about 1 lemon)	Optional, for serving: cinnamon stick, a twist of lemon
¼ to ½ cup Scotch		

1 Heat the cider in a medium saucepan until it steams. Add ¼ cup Scotch and the lemon juice, and stir to combine. Taste, and add more Scotch if you like. Transfer to a thermos.

2 If you're not on a walk and not drinking out of a thermos, serve with a cinnamon stick and a twist of lemon.

Mile 10.5. Mile 14. Mile 31.75. These are just some of the numbers I've scribbled in my notebook during the hundreds of trips we've taken across the state on the Massachusetts Turnpike.

Joey can tell when I get a certain look in my eye as I stare out the window. "You're right," he says. "It's a good one. Write it down."

These numbers are the miles (starting at my house) of the perfect picnic spots on the Massachusetts Turnpike, and believe me, there are a lot of them. The only problem is the near-impossibility of safely pulling over on the highway, but I like to dream. I have a weakness for roadside picnics.

It's the possibilities of a picnic that whet my optimistic appetite. Rushed sandwiches in the car to a family gathering? Sometimes a necessity, I know. But what if we stop the car instead? What if we look for a patch of suitable grass and dig through the trunk for that blanket we put there with this very moment in mind? If we do that, then a rushed gobbling of sandwiches in the car turns into . . . a roadside picnic. It's quite a transformation, and it takes us from necessity to all-out celebration. Even when I'm alone, I try to practice roadside picnicking whenever possible. There are days when the supermarket parking lot is filled at lunchtime, each vehicle with someone in the driver's seat in their own private world, eating lunch "alone." But when I open the car door and bring my lunch outside, both the moment and the food itself transform into something much better.

Everything just tastes better outside.

As soon as the snow melts, we start moving outside for every meal we can. From morning coffee on the back porch to full-fledged picnics in the woods, everything just tastes better outside. We have an old picnic table Joey wrapped up in oilcloth, and it migrates around the yard for dinner parties. Once the kids are done, they can go romp through the field, and we get to sit until it gets dark, with only the candles and fireflies to light the table.

LENTILS TO GO *with* BEER

Novare Res Bier Café is one of my favorite places in Portland, Maine. It's just an earthy cellar that leads out to a collection of sunny picnic tables and everyone calls it the Beer Garden. Totally unpretentious, welcoming, and family friendly, it's one of those rare locations that helps us sit for a while, slow down, and enjoy an afternoon of being together. The beer list goes on forever, but I always go for one of the new beers the owners found on their last trip to Montreal, or the classic Portland Allegash white. The food menu always features five or six little plates that are perfect with beer, and this lentil salad is a staple. If you're making it ahead of time, omit the arugula and tomatoes and add them just before serving.

1 cup French green or brown lentils, rinsed and picked over for stones	3 tablespoons red wine or champagne vinegar	3 cups loosely packed baby arugula
1 bay leaf	Kosher salt	1 cup cherry tomatoes, halved or quartered
4 slices bacon (about 4 ounces)	Freshly ground pepper	½ cup finely chopped fresh flat-leaf parsley
1½ tablespoons finely chopped shallot (about 1 shallot)	¼ cup extra-virgin olive oil	½ lemon
	1 tablespoon whole-grain mustard or Dijon mustard	

1 Preheat the oven to 425°F. Combine the lentils and bay leaf in a medium pot and cover with water by at least 2 inches. Bring to a boil, lower the heat to a simmer, and cover. Cook until the lentils are tender, about 20 minutes. Remove from heat and drain. Discard bay leaf.

2 Meanwhile, lay the bacon on a rimmed baking sheet and bake until crispy, 15 to 20 minutes, flipping the slices midway through. Transfer the bacon to a paper-towel-lined plate.

3 While the bacon cooks, make the dressing. Combine the shallot and vinegar in a medium serving bowl. Add a hefty pinch of salt, several grinds of pepper, and let sit for a few minutes. Then whisk in the olive oil and mustard, just a bit at a time, until the dressing emulsifies. Add the warm lentils, arugula, cherry tomatoes, and parsley, and gently turn the whole mixture over in the dressing. Crumble the bacon over the bowl, give the mixture one more gentle stir, and squeeze the lemon over the top. Add salt and pepper to taste.

PESTO EGG SALAD

I had the perfect pesto deviled egg in my head, and I just couldn't make it happen. Over and over my imagined recipe would fall apart, or the eggs wouldn't peel cleanly and I'd give up again. But in the process, I ended up making the best egg salad I'd ever had. I finally got to the deviled egg of my dreams, and not only was it fussy (the sad reality of deviled eggs), but it just didn't beat my pesto egg salad. So in the spirit of picnics and all the good simplicity they carry, I decided that a piping bag had no place in my picnic chapter. Instead, I offer you a wonderful egg salad—simple, unfussy, and delicious.

1 large egg yolk

1 teaspoon water

1 tablespoon whole-grain mustard

½ cup grapeseed oil

6 large eggs, hardish-boiled (see page 19)

¼ cup finely minced fresh basil leaves

1 tablespoon minced shallot (about 1 small shallot)

¼ cup finely minced fresh flat-leaf parsley

1 tablespoon capers, coarsely chopped

Kosher salt and freshly ground pepper

1   First, make the mustard mayonnaise dressing: Whisk the yolk, water, and mustard together in a medium bowl. Using a measuring cup with a pouring spout, pour the oil into the yolk mixture a few drops at a time, whisking constantly. As the mixture thickens and emulsifies, you can add the oil a bit faster, but keep whisking until you have a thick mayonnaise.

2   Gently mash the eggs into the mayonnaise. Add the basil, shallot, parsley, and capers to the egg mixture. Add salt and pepper to taste.

VARIATION

Any roastable vegetable will stand in for the asparagus. Green beans, garlic scapes, and carrots are all good choices.

ROASTED POTATO SALAD

Potato salad can be one of the most delicious dishes there is. That's why the bowl is often empty at every picnic. We all scoop with abandon, hoping it will be as good as we want it to be. Either it wins, and everybody raves, or it's gloppy, and we walk away dreaming of the next potato salad, the one that *will* be delicious.

This recipe makes the cut in spades. The roasted potatoes hold their shape, texture, and sweetness, and the vinaigrette makes all the flavors in the bowl shine instead of hiding them in mayonnaise.

FOR THE SALAD

1½ pounds red or Yukon Gold potatoes, cut into large bite-sized pieces

4 teaspoons olive oil

¾ teaspoon kosher salt

4 ounces asparagus, cut to 1½-inch lengths

4 large eggs, hardish-boiled (see page 19) and coarsely chopped

FOR THE DRESSING

3 tablespoons red wine vinegar

1 tablespoon finely chopped shallot

1½ teaspoons whole-grain mustard

¼ cup olive oil

1 tablespoon capers, coarsely chopped

1½ tablespoons coarsely chopped pickles

¼ cup coarsely chopped fresh flat-leaf parsley

2 tablespoons coarsely chopped fresh dill

Kosher salt and freshly ground pepper

1 **Make the salad:** Preheat the oven to 450°F. Toss the potatoes with 1 table-spoon of the olive oil and ½ teaspoon of the salt in a mixing bowl. Transfer the potatoes to a baking sheet and roast until brown and crispy, 30 to 40 minutes. Toss the asparagus in the same bowl with the remaining teaspoon of olive oil and ¼ teaspoon salt. Transfer to a second baking sheet and set aside. When the potatoes are brown and crispy, remove them from the oven and slide in the asparagus. Roast the asparagus until tender, about 5 minutes.

2 **Meanwhile, make the dressing:** Combine the vinegar and shallot in a medium serving bowl, and let the shallot pickle for a few minutes. Whisk in the mustard and olive oil, using a few strong strokes to emulsify the dressing. Add the capers, pickles, parsley, and dill, stirring to combine. Scrape the warm potatoes and asparagus into the bowl, along with the eggs. Gently stir, folding the vegetables and eggs into the dressing. Add salt and pepper to taste. Serve warm, at room temperature, or cold.

HOW TO FANCY IT UP

If there were a tournament of picnic spreads, it would be held at Tanglewood.

From June through August, the Boston Symphony Orchestra takes up residence in its summer home at Tanglewood, in Lenox, Massachusetts. The sweeping estate was given to the BSO in 1936, and every year since, it's been one of the primary institutions of summer life in the Berkshires. When I was a child, my grandparents would take me a few times a summer, and I'd stay up way past my bedtime, wrapped in a blanket with my eyes on the stars as I learned to love Aaron Copland's "Appalachian Spring" and Tchaikovsky's *1812 Overture*. Every Tanglewood outing was a holiday, and my grandmother would spend all day packing up cold salads to fill the special cart she kept just for this occasion. I thought it was the fanciest place, and I'd go wandering through the vast lawn beyond the music shed, hopping from one tiny green patch to another, checking out everyone's picnics. It seemed that each blanket tried to outdo the next, and some people had carts they built especially for the season. The carts would convert to huge tables, and each guest would bring a tiny folding chair. Once the table was set up, there was always a tablecloth, candles, and wineglasses set for a full dinner.

When I first took Joey to Tanglewood, I didn't know what to expect. I wasn't sure if I'd half made up those picnics, or if they just seemed so grand and wonderful because I'd been so small. But sure enough, the green lawn was dotted with white tablecloths, and the candles flickered as far as I could see. We sat on our wool picnic blanket, drinking beer and eating roast chicken, taking in the splendor of all the feasts around us. We were happy for our little picnic, but we swore we'd fancy it up next time.

Over the years I've developed a few standards for those nicer Tanglewood picnics. They're all quick and easy, but with a few touches that make them feel just special enough.

COLD BUTTERMILK BORSCHT

This is a great summer soup. It travels well for picnics and is nourishing and refreshing. Transport it in single-serving Mason jars and top with yogurt, feta, or crème fraîche and extra herbs just before serving.

1 tablespoon olive oil

2 cups chopped leeks (1 to 2 leeks, using all of the white and half the green)

Kosher salt

3 to 5 red beets (about 1½ pounds), roasted (see page 22), skinned, and quartered

4 cups water or stock

1½ cups buttermilk (for homemade, see page 34)

3 tablespoons fresh lemon juice (about 1 lemon), plus more if needed

½ cup coarsely chopped fresh dill

¼ cup finely chopped fresh mint leaves

¼ cup finely chopped fresh basil leaves

Freshly ground pepper

Optional: yogurt (for homemade, see page 34) or crème fraîche (for homemade, see page 34), extra herbs, chopped cucumbers, feta cheese (for homemade, see page 113), for serving

1 Warm the olive oil in a small skillet over medium heat. When it starts to shimmer, add the leeks and 1 teaspoon salt. Cook, stirring occasionally, until the leeks are soft, about 5 minutes. Remove from heat and allow to cool for a few minutes.

2 Combine the beets, leeks (along with any pan juices), water, buttermilk, lemon, dill, mint, basil, and several grinds of pepper in a blender. Depending on the size of the blender, you might have to do this in batches. Alternatively, you can combine the ingredients in a large upright pot and blend with an immersion blender. Blend until entirely smooth and transfer to the refrigerator. Taste when the soup is cold, and add salt or lemon if necessary. Serve cold, with extra pepper and the toppings of your choice.

CHICKEN SALAD *with* GRAPES

SERVES 6 TO 8

This salad is equally wonderful in sandwiches or on greens for a summer dinner. If you're roasting a chicken (see page 33), roast an extra and plan on chicken salad later in the week. Don't leave out the grapes—they really make this special.

5 cups cubed cooked chicken (1 small chicken)	2 tablespoons plain whole-milk yogurt (for homemade, see page 34)	¾ cup seedless grapes, halved
1 teaspoon fresh lemon juice	1 teaspoon kosher salt	1 cup finely chopped celery (3 to 4 ribs)
1 large egg yolk	½ cup coarsely chopped fresh flat-leaf parsley	½ cup pecans, toasted and chopped
1 teaspoon water	2 tablespoons finely chopped fresh tarragon	Freshly ground pepper
1 teaspoon Dijon mustard or whole-grain mustard	4 or 5 chives, finely snipped with scissors	Lettuce, microgreens, or pea shoots, for serving
½ cup grapeseed oil		
½ cup olive oil		

1 Toss the chicken and lemon together in a bowl. Let it rest in the refrigerator while you make the dressing.

2 Whisk the yolk, water, and mustard together in a medium bowl. Combine the grapeseed oil and olive oil in a measuring cup with a pouring spout and, whisking constantly, pour it into the yolk mixture a few drops at a time. As the mixture thickens and emulsifies, you can add the oil a bit faster, but keep whisking. When you have a bowl of homemade mayonnaise (that's right, you just made mayonnaise!), whisk in the yogurt and salt.

3 Remove the chicken from the refrigerator and add it to the bowl with the mayonnaise. Add the parsley, tarragon, chives, grapes, celery, and pecans, gently folding them into the dressing until it coats everything. Add several grinds of pepper, and taste for salt. Cover and chill until you're ready to eat.

4 Lay the lettuce out on a serving platter and mound the chicken salad on top of the lettuce.

CORN SALAD *with* NECTARINES *and* BASIL

SERVES 4

This is, hands down, my favorite salad to bring to potluck picnics. It takes only a few minutes to pull together and seems to wow everyone who tastes it. And during that hot, hot span of summer when corn and nectarines are at their peak, I can eat this every single night. Don't be put off by the thought of raw corn—it's juicy and sweet and an ideal partner to ripe nectarines. Double, triple, or multiply it by ten for summer parties—it will come out perfect, and there will never be enough.

4 or 5 ears of corn

2 ripe nectarines, pitted and cut into 1-inch pieces

¼ cup thinly sliced scallions (using all the white and half the green)

¼ cup fresh basil leaves, cut into ribbons

½ teaspoon kosher salt

Freshly ground pepper

2 tablespoons fresh lime juice (1 lime)

1 Husk the corn, then cut the kernels off right into a serving bowl. There's a simple tool that does this without slicing the kernels. I keep it around just for corn season, but you can also use a knife, taking care not to cut directly through all the kernels. Even with this gadget, you'll end up with a fair amount of corn juice—another reason to cut directly into the bowl.

2 Add the nectarines, scallions, basil, salt, and pepper to the bowl with the corn. Squeeze the lime over the salad, and stir gently to combine.

VARIATIONS

- If you're a cilantro lover, you can swap the basil for cilantro.

- Peaches will do fine for the nectarines, but peel them first, as the fuzzy skin doesn't work as well with the corn.

- Add a finely chopped (seeded) jalapeño pepper for heat.

SESAME NOODLES

I've waitressed at a few different noodle joints, and I've always been secretly in it for the staff meals. In broth, hot, cold, fried—I could eat Asian noodles every day and be happy. One of the restaurants had a dish called ramen (pronounced *ray-men*), a sweet and salty noodle dish that slid off your chopsticks if you weren't perfectly attentive. It was served cold, and there was nothing so wonderful as a container of leftover ramen after work on a hot day. It was, the owner claimed, a traditional Korean dish. The only problem with it was the name—no matter how much we said, "Not Rah-men. RAY-men!" everyone thought we were serving a glorified cup o' noodles. This bowl of sweet and salty noodles comes from my memory of that dish, but for clarity's sake, I'll call it sesame noodles. My friend Jess Fechtor shared the basis for the sauce, and it captures all the cold sweetness and saltiness I loved about that ramen. If you've never been a fan of peanut buttery "sesame" noodles (or even if you have), give this one a try.

1 pound firm tofu (for homemade, see page 158)

2 tablespoons sunflower or safflower oil

6 tablespoons tamari or soy sauce

2 cups thinly sliced purple cabbage (about ½ small cabbage)

1 large carrot, cut into thin matchsticks or shaved with a vegetable peeler

1 sweet red pepper, seeded and cut into thin matchsticks

Kosher salt

1 pound store-bought spaghetti or linguine or 1¼ pounds homemade (page 46)

¼ cup sesame seeds

1 tablespoon finely minced shallot or garlic

1 tablespoon grated fresh ginger

2 tablespoons sugar

6 tablespoons rice vinegar

2 tablespoons toasted sesame oil

¼ cup chopped scallions (white and green parts)

Optional, for serving: Hot sauce, dried red pepper flakes, sesame chile oil, toasted peanuts, microgreens

1 First, press the tofu. Place the block of tofu on a rimmed plate or wide bowl, set a plate on top of it, and put a jar or similar weight on top of the plate. Let it sit for 20 minutes, pouring off the water as it drains out of the tofu. Cut the tofu into 1-inch cubes.

2 Heat 1 tablespoon of the sunflower oil in a large skillet over medium-high heat. Add the tofu and cook undisturbed until it begins to brown, about 5 minutes. Shuffle the tofu and cook, stirring occasionally, for 5 more minutes. Add 1 tablespoon of the tamari and continue to cook until the tofu is dry and crispy,

another 3 to 5 minutes. Transfer the tofu to a plate and wipe out the pan. Heat the remaining tablespoon of sunflower oil. Add the cabbage and carrot and cook, stirring constantly, until slightly tender, about 3 minutes. Add the red pepper and cook for another 3 minutes. Remove from heat.

3 Meanwhile, make the pasta. Bring a large pot of salted water to boil and cook the pasta until tender, 7 to 10 minutes for dried or 2 minutes for fresh. Drain and rinse the pasta, then transfer it to a large bowl. Add the tofu and vegetables to the pasta.

4 Toast the sesame seeds in a small frying pan over medium heat, stirring frequently, until the seeds darken, about 2 minutes. Remove from heat.

5 To make the sauce, combine the shallot, ginger, sugar, rice vinegar, remaining 5 tablespoons tamari, and sesame oil in a small saucepan. Bring to a low boil, then lower the heat to medium and simmer for 3 minutes. Pour the sauce over the pasta and vegetables, and top with the toasted sesame seeds and chopped scallions. Serve warm, at room temperature, or cold with additional toppings of your choice.

VARIATIONS

- Replace the tofu with shredded grilled or broiled chicken.

- Use soba or udon in place of the spaghetti.

- Use whatever vegetables you have on hand in place of the vegetables in the recipe. Asparagus, green beans, kale, and broccoli are all great options.

TENSE MOMENTS ✦ Frying tofu can be a little tense. Pressing your tofu before you cook it creates a drier product that's easier to brown. Still, depending on your pan, it might stick a bit. Keep an eye on the tofu as it browns, and if it looks like it's sticking, add a bit more oil and shuffle it earlier.

ICE POPS

Oh, the homemade Popsicle problem! I'd pour juice into the molds and freeze them. Then we'd sit on the back porch and slurp all the juice out of the ice so that all that was left was a Popsicle-shaped ice cube. No one complained, as anything cold and sweet outside in the middle of the summer does the job. But then I had the opportunity to help out with the photo shoot for a perfect little book from a pop-making trio in New York called *People's Pops*. We shot the pops in an apartment in Brooklyn on a 100-degree day with only a window fan to keep us cool (which it did not). The downside was that all the pops melted as fast as we could photograph them; the upside was that all the pops melted and had to be eaten right away. That day, I learned the secret of those wonderful pops, and a year later when the book came out, the rest of the world did, too.

It turned out that I'd been going about it all wrong. Juice seems like the right idea, but the key to a good homemade pop is to decrease the water content and pack it full of good, fresh fruit sweetened with simple syrup. Now we make People's Pops at home, and the method has banished pop-shaped ice cubes from our back porch forever. You can make these in any shaped mold, but my favorite is the classic rectangular shape that fits into a metal tray. If you don't have a mold, paper cups and Popsicle sticks work just fine.

This recipe makes roughly enough to fill a classic ten-pop rectangular mold, but if you have some mix left over, just freeze it and shave it like a granita. This formula works for most fruits, but the quantities and flavor will vary by fruit and ripeness. If you end up with leftover simple syrup, store it in the fridge and use it in cocktails.

½ cup sugar ½ cup water	1 to 1¼ pounds berries or stone fruit, pitted and chopped as appropriate	Optional: a few stems of fresh herbs, fresh ginger, or other flavors; heavy cream, yogurt, or buttermilk

1 Make the simple syrup: Combine the sugar and water in a small saucepan. Bring to a simmer, stirring to dissolve the sugar. Remove from heat and allow to cool. If you're using herbs, add them to the syrup and cover for about 15 minutes as it cools.

2 Make the pops: Combine the fruit, dairy, if using, and ¾ cup of the syrup in a blender. Blend until smooth, taste, and add more syrup if you want a sweeter pop. Pour the fruit mixture into pop molds and freeze for at least 6 hours.

STORAGE NOTES ✦ Remove pops from their molds and store in a freezer bag for up to 2 weeks.

some of MY FAVORITE FLAVOR combinations

Feel free to use these as a guideline, and experiment with what you have. Always taste your unfrozen mix, as a good mix will make a good pop.

Blueberry Buttermilk Lavender: Infuse your simple syrup with 3 tablespoons dried lavender for 30 minutes. Start with ½ cup of the lavender syrup, and add ½ cup buttermilk.

———

Raspberry Basil: Infuse your simple syrup with ¼ cup basil leaves for 15 minutes. Use 1¼ pounds raspberries, and start with ¾ cup simple syrup.

———

Plum and Ginger: Infuse your simple syrup with 2 tablespoons coarsely chopped (unpeeled) fresh ginger. Start with ½ cup simple syrup.

———

Peach Cinnamon Yogurt: Replace the simple syrup with ⅓ cup honey. Add 1 cup plain yogurt, 2 teaspoons ground cinnamon, and a squeeze of lemon.

INVITE PEOPLE OVER

Every Tuesday, we all meet for dinner.

My friend Alejandro, who started "Social Tuesday," originally chose the day because it was a day no one ever seemed to have anything to do. So he asked a few friends if they would commit to a standing Tuesday group date. And that's how we came to hold Tuesdays sacred on the calendar.

This is how it works: Every Tuesday, one family hosts. They decide on a theme, which might be based around a food (taco night), a country (Vietnam), or something more conceptual like a color or even an emotion. Everyone brings a dish, and we eat together. It sounds like a standard potluck, but there are a few elements that make it different, and that is what makes Social Tuesday extraordinary.

The first is the food. I always say that I think the best food in any community probably happens in people's home kitchens, and some of my favorite meals have been on Tuesday nights. I'd take a Social Tuesday meal over a good restaurant meal any day.

> Even if the house isn't sparkling clean, or if we worry that the table won't be big enough, we host anyway.

The second element that makes Social Tuesday so special is our commitment. There's a general understanding that unless we have a serious reason not to come, we'll show up. It's easy to decide to stay home on a cold night in February, but the commitment gets us out into the night, and we're always happy it does. We also know that we'll be hosting on a pretty regular basis. Even if the house isn't sparkling clean, or if we worry that the table won't be big enough, we host anyway. Especially those who might not be used to inviting people over learn quickly that their house is enough. *They* are enough. Everyone's just happy to have a place to sit down together. It's enough.

SWISS CHARD TACOS *with* FRESH CHEESE *and* A FRIED EGG

Taco night is one of my standards when it's our turn to host. Everyone else in the group brings salads, homemade pickles, hot sauces—anything that can go on a taco. I love to serve these alongside Pork Tacos (page 270) on one platter. Between the green of the chard and the bright yellow of the eggs, the food is enough to decorate the table.

3 tablespoons olive oil, plus additional if needed

2 bunches Swiss chard, leaves cut into thin ribbons, stems coarsely chopped

½ cup water

1 tablespoon chopped garlic (2 to 3 cloves)

Kosher salt

Freshly ground pepper

12 large eggs

12 corn tortillas, warmed in the oven or on the stovetop

6 ounces queso fresco, crumbled feta cheese, or chèvre (for homemade, see pages 113, 99)

Optional: Hot sauce, for serving

1 Heat 1 tablespoon of the oil over medium heat in your largest pot. Add the chard stems and cook for about 2 minutes, stirring frequently. Add the leaves, water, garlic, ½ teaspoon salt, and pepper. Cover the pot and cook, stirring occasionally, for about 3 minutes. Remove from heat and set aside.

2 Heat another tablespoon of oil in your largest frying pan over medium heat. Crack 4 eggs directly into the pan and reduce the heat to medium-low. Cover the pan and cook the eggs, undisturbed, until the edges of the whites are crispy and a faint layer of white surrounds the circumference of the yolks, about 3 minutes. Transfer the eggs to a plate and repeat with the remaining eggs.

3 Lay the tortillas on a cutting board or large platter. Use tongs to arrange about ½ cup cooked greens on each tortilla. Gently set 1 egg on top of the chard and top with cheese crumbles, a sprinkle of salt, and a few more grinds of pepper. Top with hot sauce if you like.

TENSE MOMENTS ✦ You want to assemble these just before serving; otherwise, the tortillas will get soggy. So be sure to cook the eggs right at the last minute, and assemble the tacos as each batch of eggs is done.

PORK TACOS

MAKES 12 TACOS (WITH A BIT OF LEFTOVER MEAT FOR TOMORROW'S LUNCH)

All three of the toppings do well with an hour or two of resting time in the refrigerator, so make your toppings just after you put the pork in the oven.

1 dried chile de arbol	1 tablespoon kosher salt	1 bay leaf
2 dried ancho chiles	1 teaspoon whole cumin seed	12 corn tortillas, warmed in the oven or on the stovetop
2 teaspoons garlic powder (for homemade, see page 75)	3 pounds boneless pork butt	Radish Salad, Quick Pickled Cabbage, and Spicy Crème Fraîche, for serving (recipes follow)
1 tablespoon dried oregano	1½ to 3 cups chicken stock, warm but not steaming	

1 Combine the chiles, garlic powder, oregano, salt, and cumin seed in a spice grinder or mortar and pestle and grind until you break up the chiles into tiny pieces. Place the pork in a wide dish and massage the rub over its entire surface. Cover the dish and refrigerate for 8 to 24 hours.

2 Preheat the oven to 300°F. Remove the pork from the refrigerator and transfer to a Dutch oven or roasting pan with a cover. Pour enough stock into the pan to come about halfway up the meat. Add the bay leaf and cover the pot. Braise until the meat falls apart, 3 to 3½ hours. Alternatively, you can cook the pork in a slow cooker, starting out on the high setting for 2 hours, then reducing the heat to low for an additional 5 to 6 hours. Let the meat cool until it's comfortable to touch, then use your hands or a fork to shred the meat. Transfer it to a plate, removing any large chunks of fat as you go. Skim the fat off the braising liquid and strain the remaining liquid through a fine-meshed strainer. Return 1½ cups of the strained liquid to the pot along with the shredded pork. (At this point, you can refrigerate the whole thing if it's not yet dinnertime.) Heat the liquid and pork together over medium heat until the liquid thickens and the meat is hot, 5 to 10 minutes. Serve on tortillas topped with Radish Salad, Quick Pickled Cabbage, and Spicy Crème Fraîche.

RADISH SALAD

MAKES ABOUT 1 CUP

1 bunch (5 to 7) radishes, sliced paper-thin	1 tablespoon fresh lime juice	¼ cup coarsely chopped fresh flat-leaf parsley
1 teaspoon kosher salt		

Toss the radishes and salt and let sit for 15 minutes. Drain off any liquid that the radishes release and give them a quick rinse in cold water. Add the lime and parsley and toss to combine.

QUICK PICKLED CABBAGE

MAKES 2 CUPS

3 cups finely sliced cabbage (½ small cabbage)	¾ teaspoon kosher salt	1½ tablespoons red wine vinegar
	¼ teaspoon whole cumin seed	

Toss the cabbage with the salt and cumin seed in a medium bowl. Use your hands to massage the cabbage, breaking it down so it releases its juice. Pack the cabbage and its juices into a quart jar and pour the vinegar over it. Refrigerate for at least an hour. Give the jar a shake to distribute the vinegar just before serving.

SPICY CRÈME FRAÎCHE

MAKES 1 CUP

1 cup crème fraîche (for homemade, see page 34)	1 teaspoon fresh lime juice	¼ teaspoon kosher salt
	2 teaspoons hot sauce, or more to taste	

Combine the crème fraîche, lime, hot sauce, and salt in a small bowl or jar. Stir, taste, and add more hot sauce if needed.

JAMBALAYA

SERVES 6 TO 8

Jambalaya always feels like party food. This version is not quite traditional, but it's especially timely at midsummer. All the vegetables and herbs are right there in the garden, and it's just perfect for an easy dinner at the table in the yard.

1 pound boneless, skinless chicken thighs, cut into 2-inch pieces

1 tablespoon smoked paprika

1 teaspoon kosher salt

6 ounces chopped bacon

Optional: 2 tablespoons olive oil

3 cups halved and sliced leeks (2 to 3 leeks)

¾ cup finely chopped onion (1 small onion)

3 cups coarsely chopped sweet red peppers (2 large peppers)

1 jalapeño pepper, seeded and minced

2 tablespoons finely chopped garlic (4 to 5 cloves)

1 cup diced summer squash

3 cups hot chicken stock

2 bay leaves

1½ cups uncooked white rice

12 ounces cooked andouille sausage, cut into ½-inch rounds

Optional: 1 pound shrimp, cleaned and deveined

¼ cup chopped scallions

¼ cup finely chopped fresh flat-leaf parsley

1 Toss the chicken with the paprika and salt and set aside. Heat a large, heavy-bottomed pot over medium heat. Add the bacon and cook, stirring often, until crispy, about 10 minutes. Transfer the bacon to a large bowl, leaving the bacon fat in the pot. Cook the chicken in the fat, stirring occasionally, until brown, about 5 minutes. Remove the chicken from the pot and add it to the bacon bowl. Add enough oil to cover the bottom of the pot, if needed.

2 Add the leeks and onion to the pot and cook, stirring often, until soft, about 5 minutes. Add the red peppers, jalapeño, garlic, and zucchini and cook over medium heat, stirring occasionally, until the whole mixture is reduced, slightly browned, and smells wonderful, about 20 minutes. If it seems likely to burn, reduce the heat and add a few tablespoons of the stock.

3 Add the bay leaves, rice, and sausage and continue to cook, stirring occasionally, for 5 minutes. Add the stock as well as the reserved bacon and chicken, bring to a boil, lower the heat, and cover the pot. Cook undisturbed until the rice is tender and the stock is absorbed, about 30 minutes. If you're using the shrimp, add it to the pot for the last 5 minutes of cooking. Remove bay leaf, top with scallions and parsley and serve immediately.

GARDEN PIE, OR WORK PARTY

When our friend Kelly first told us about work party, we couldn't imagine how we could contribute to such a utopian idea. It was simple: five families met five times over the warmer months of the year, with each meeting at one family's home. The host family would put the rest of the members to work on any task that needed doing, and the result was one day a year for each household when they had enough people to help do the work on their house or garden they'd been putting off. We knew all the families (some just couples then) a little bit, but the group was heavy on carpenters and farmers. We joked that Joey could be the official mix-tape maker, and I could be the one who always organized everyone's kitchen drawers. Nearly a decade later, I have certainly organized my fair share of kitchen drawers at work parties. But I've also stretched way beyond my comfort zone, and I've put up greenhouses, laid flooring, and learned how to identify every invasive plant species in Massachusetts. Each work party is an education in itself, and through each job, our work builds the places we love, the gardens we grow, and our own sense of possibility. Can I run a wood splitter? Okay! Build a root cellar? There must be a book somewhere!

We've been working with this group for nine years. Nine full seasons of gardens, wood piles, houses built, houses sold, and new houses built again. We've had work parties that have doubled as celebrations, and we've had them in moments after loss, when there's no chatter. Only work. But each of us in our own time has the chance to invite people in and ask for help. We open up our messy basements and our weedy garden beds. We show off the parts of our houses that we don't usually let people see. We let our friends in, and we do the work together.

Every work party ends in a meal, and I'm usually scrambling to make something good the night before. Garden pie is one of my common contributions to work party. It makes use of whatever greens I have in my fridge and it is even more delicious on day two. I can best describe it as a marriage between spanakopita and a quiche, with all the best qualities of both. Deeply green, packed with herbs and feta—I have to give out the recipe every time I make it for friends.

GARDEN PIE

If you're working with a high-speed blender or large-capacity food processor (more than 11 cups), you can blend the ingredients in one go, but if your machine is smaller, blend in batches.

1 small head of cauliflower (about 600 g), cored and cut into small florets

2 tablespoons olive oil, plus additional for greasing the pans

Kosher salt

1 recipe Piecrust (page 41), following the guidelines for whole-grain crusts

4 cups (350 g) sliced leeks (2 to 4 leeks, using all the white and most of the green)

10 cups (about 385 g) packed coarsely chopped greens (2 large bunches of Swiss chard; de-stemmed kale; or the greens from broccoli, turnips, or kohlrabi)

¼ cup water

¼ teaspoon freshly ground pepper

½ cup (25 g) coarsely chopped fresh dill

½ cup (55 g) walnuts or pecans, toasted

8 ounces (225 g) feta cheese (for homemade, see page 113)

3 large eggs

1 Preheat the oven to 425°F. In a large bowl, toss the cauliflower with 1 table-spoon of the olive oil and ½ teaspoon salt. Spread on a baking sheet and roast until golden, 25 to 30 minutes. Remove from the oven and reduce the oven temperature to 375°F.

2 Grease two 9-inch pie pans. Roll out the piecrusts and lay them in the pans. Put the crusts in the freezer.

3 Heat the remaining tablespoon of oil over medium heat in a large soup pot. Add the leeks and cook until soft, about 5 minutes. Add the greens and water. Cover and reduce the heat to medium low. Cook, stirring occasionally, until the greens are wilted, 3 to 7 minutes, depending on the green. Drain the liquid and add ½ teaspoon salt and pepper. Remove from heat and let cool for a few minutes.

4 Combine the greens mixture, cauliflower, dill, nuts, and feta in a blender or food processor and process until you have a rough puree. Taste, add salt if necessary, add the eggs, and process again.

5 Remove the piecrusts from the freezer and divide the filling equally between them. Bake until the crust is golden and the center is firm, 35 to 40 minutes. Allow to cool for 30 minutes before slicing.

MAKI ROLLS

"Once upon a time, not so long ago, giving a dinner party was a snap. A filet of beef, a leg of lamb, roast duck." So begins Laurie Colwin's 1992 essay "The Once and Future Dinner Party." "Nowadays," she continues, "a menu like that makes some people envision little skulls and crossbones of the sort that used to be put on poison." She laments the extinction of the "group of people who will sit down and eat what you feed them without problem," trying, in inimitable Colwin fashion, to address the question that now is more frustrating than ever: "How will we ever manage when half one's pals are on diets, the other half have food allergies, and the third half, so to speak, simply will not and cannot bear to eat that way anymore?"

How, indeed. I threw a dinner party once where I ended up putting little sticky notes on all the plates in the kitchen, just so I could remember who got what. *Gluten-free. Vegan and grain-free. Dairy-free, but can have eggs and butter. Allergic to nightshades. Paleo. Or was it Paleo, gluten-free?*

Colwin thought it was bad then. My best solution now is to create a meal with endless variation, and then let my guests make it themselves. Tacos (pages 268–270), spring rolls, and even Congee (page 202) are all good candidates. I fill the table with little bowls of toppings and sauces, and let them get into it. It makes for a beautiful table, everyone's happy with their meal, and the casual nature of reaching and passing breaks the ice at the table right away.

Maki rolls are a perfect make-your-own dinner party option. They're easier to roll than you might think, and even kids love to roll their own.

8 sheets nori 6 cups cooked and prepared sushi rice (from 2 cups dried; see page 37)	Fillings: peeled cucumbers cut into long, thin strips; thinly sliced avocado; toasted sesame seeds; sushi-grade fish, sliced long and thin; pickled radish or daikon; scallions . . .	For serving: soy sauce or tamari, wasabi, pickled ginger

Have a small bowl of water nearby. Lay a sheet of nori on a cutting board. Dip your hands in the water, and use wet hands to grab a small handful of rice and press it into a flat layer on the nori, covering the center of the sheet but leaving a few open inches at the top and bottom of the square. The rice layer should be no thicker than ½ inch. Place a line of fillings across the rice in a horizontal line just below the center of the square, extending so they hang just a bit over the edge of the nori on both sides. Then, again with wet hands, starting from the side closest to you, roll the nori around the rice and the fillings, pulling it tighter as you go. When you have a roll, seal the edge with a few dabs of water. Finally, use a sharp, wet knife to cut the roll into 6 to 8 equal pieces. Set them up on a serving dish, and repeat with the remaining sheets of nori.

NEW YEAR'S CHILI, *and*
ENOUGH CORN BREAD TO GO *with* IT

SERVES 12 TO 15

The first year, there were just a few of us. Sadie was still a baby, and I was seven months' pregnant with Rosie, so there was no way we were going *out* for New Year's Eve. We invited a few other expectant (and therefore, early to bed) friends over and had a little party. I made chili, as I'd heard it brought good luck for the New Year. Joey found a live stream of a British radio station, five hours ahead of us. He marked a line on the floor, and at seven, we all jumped over the line, traveling from home to England. We cheered and celebrated the New Year with England, and by eight, we were done.

Be careful. You never know when you might be creating a tradition.

Each year, it grew bigger. Word spread of a family-friendly New Year's party, and friends of friends, cousins of friends, and total strangers showed up at our door. One year, the party seemed to peak to extraordinary numbers, and the next day, Sadie and Rosie sat with a pad and paper, trying to remember everyone we had actually fit into our little house. In the end, the count was 110. That broke down into an exact split: 55 adults and *55 children*. Somehow, we still all managed to fit on one side of the line that Joey had taped to the floor. I think there was less of a jump over the line at seven, and more a herding of cows, but still, we all got there.

Every year, I still make chili and a big flat of corn bread. Guests bring salads and sweets and lots of bubbly drinks, and everyone gets fed. This recipe doesn't quite feed a hundred, but if you stretch it, it should be close. (If you are feeding a horde, just scale this up and use all of your biggest pots!) I like to use dried ancho chile powder, which is just the chiles. It's available in most supermarkets and at any Latin grocer. Chili powder is a mix of chiles and a few other spices, so if you must substitute, add sparingly and taste as you go. If you're not having crowds of people over, no need to downsize—this recipe freezes beautifully. I use dried beans because they taste better and are a big money saver, but if you don't have all day, use canned beans.

2 tablespoons sunflower or safflower oil, plus additional if needed

2 pounds ground beef, or a mix of ground beef and pork

4 cups diced onions (about 3 onions)

3 cups diced sweet red peppers (2 large red peppers)

2 to 3 jalapeño peppers (or other hot peppers), seeded and minced

¼ cup dried ancho chile powder

1 tablespoon ground cumin

1½ tablespoons dried oregano

Kosher salt

¼ cup finely minced garlic (about 1 head)

2 28-ounce cans whole tomatoes or 7 to 8 cups roasted tomatoes (see page 23)

1 pound dried black beans, pinto beans, or a mix of the two, rinsed

6 cups water, or more as needed

For serving: grated cheese, hot sauce, pickled jalapeños (see page 29), sliced black olives, sour cream or creme fraîche (for homemade, see page 34), lime wedges, sliced avocado, Tomato Salsa (page 192) . . .

1 Heat the oil in your largest pot over medium-high heat. (I use a 9-quart Dutch oven.) Add the beef and cook, stirring often, until all the liquid from the beef has evaporated, about 10 minutes. Add a bit of extra oil if the pot gets dry during this time. Lower the heat to medium low and add the onions, sweet peppers, jalapeños, chile powder, cumin, oregano, and 2 tablespoons salt. Continue to cook, stirring often, until the whole mixture softens and shrinks, about 20 minutes. Add the garlic and cook, stirring often, for another 5 minutes.

2 Add the tomatoes and all their liquid to the pot, crushing the tomatoes with your hands as you go. Stir in the beans and water, and bring the mixture to a boil. Cover the pot, reduce the heat to maintain a low simmer, and cook, stirring occasionally and checking to see if more water is needed, until the beans are tender and the ingredients have melded together, 4 to 5 hours. Taste, and adjust the salt if needed.

VARIATIONS

+ For a vegetarian chili, omit the meat and increase the beans to 1½ pounds. Add 2 sliced zucchini and 4 chopped carrots just after the peppers. Soak 1 cup bulgur in 1 cup water for 30 minutes and add it along with the beans.

+ For a quicker version, use canned beans. Substitute 5 or 6 15-ounce cans of beans and their liquid for the dried. Omit the water, and cook for 45 minutes after adding the beans.

TENSE MOMENTS + The cooking time for beans varies depending on their age, which of course you usually can't detect when you start the recipe. There's no harm in cooking chili longer (it just gets better with time), but an undercooked bean will make everyone grumpy. I prefer the texture of unsoaked beans, but if you prefer to soak, that will speed the cooking along a bit.

▸▸▸▸▸▸▸▸▸ CORN BREAD FOR A CROWD ◂◂◂◂◂◂◂◂◂

SERVES 12 TO 15

1½ sticks (170 g) unsalted butter, melted and slightly cooled, plus additional for the pan

3 cups (360 g) all-purpose flour

3 cups (415 g) yellow cornmeal

3 tablespoons (45 g) baking powder

1 tablespoon kosher salt

6 large eggs

3 cups (720 ml) buttermilk (for homemade, see page 34)

½ cup (120 ml) maple syrup

1 Preheat the oven to 400°F. Grease a 13 × 18-inch rimmed baking sheet with butter.

2 Whisk together the flour, cornmeal, baking powder, and salt in a large mixing bowl.

3 Break the eggs into a separate large bowl and whisk to break up the yolks. Add the buttermilk, maple syrup, and melted butter to the eggs and whisk until combined. Add the wet mixture to the dry ingredients and stir just until incorporated, taking care not to overmix. Pour the batter into the prepared baking sheet and bake until a cake tester comes out clean when inserted in the center, 20 to 25 minutes. Allow to cool for 20 minutes before serving.

STORAGE NOTES ◆ Freeze any leftover corn bread in a freezer bag to use as future stuffing.

DON'T BE afraid OF FOOD

I have spent a fair amount of time living and eating alongside the fantasy of a future body.

In those moments, I eat dinner, and I am me, sitting alongside future me, skinnier or fatter depending on what's on the menu.

I do this less than I used to. I'm more comfortable in my own skin and more confident in the goodness of my own body as I get older. Still, the future me shows up every so often. And when I do eat with the thought of some differently shaped me, the food tastes different than it does when I rest in the deliciousness of the meal, when my focus is on enjoying my food. In fact, I don't really taste it at all. Instead, I feel afraid of my food.

That future me sits down at the table and pushes the moment aside. The sheer enjoyment of baked macaroni and cheese, the reward for having made it myself, is interrupted by second-guessing. *All that cheese, so much butter! So many empty carbohydrates! Next time, you should use whole-grain noodles. You should carve noodles out of parsnips!* By the time the future me is done scolding, I've finished my dinner and I don't even remember what it tasted like.

Of course, the future body isn't just heavier or lighter. Sometimes it's glowy, it's less achy, or it looks younger. The future body will never get cancer or heart disease. All these are fine aspirations in themselves, and what we eat certainly has an impact on how we feel. But I think enjoyment might just be a nutrient in itself—in fact, it might be the most important one of all.

Enjoyment might just be a nutrient in itself—in fact, it might be the most important one of all.

I can't keep up with the news of what I should or shouldn't eat. The list of "good" foods and "bad" foods varies by the day, and although there are plenty of books claiming to have the one true way to the perfect future body, I have yet to find a diet that beats the one I already follow: the eat-what-I-love diet. The truth is that when I eat what I really want, it tastes good, it feels good, and I know I'm eating the right thing. That holds as true for a well-timed bowl of steamed greens or miso soup as it does an ice cream cone or a slice of warm gingerbread. And when it's time for dessert, I want to be right there at the table; the present me, spoon in hand.

⟫⟫⟫⟫⟫⟫⟫ POUND CAKE ⟪⟪⟪⟪⟪⟪

MAKES TWO 8½ X 4½-INCH LOAF CAKES

My grandmother was a baker, and a low-sugar, whole-grain one at that. People loved her baked goods, but I had very little interest in her dense whole-wheat zucchini breads or date nut cakes. It was for this reason that I could never believe my luck when I'd come upon a small stack of Entenmann's pound cakes stashed away in her freezer.

I can only imagine my grandmother had a weakness for Entenmann's left from her suburban New Jersey, pre-whole-wheat-flour days. But she was a smart woman, and she always liked to pack as much enjoyment into each bite as possible. I'd say that if she was going to make an exception to her austerity, pound cake was an excellent choice.

Pound cake is incredibly versatile, and, as I learned from my grandmother, it does well in the freezer. My favorite way to use pound cake is in a trifle (see page 287). Most pound cakes are variations on the same theme (lots of butter, sugar, and eggs), but this recipe is adapted from one of my favorite baking bibles, *The King Arthur Flour Baker's Companion*. It makes two loaves, so you can keep your freezer well stocked.

4 sticks (1 pound/450 g) unsalted butter, at room temperature, plus additional for the pans	1 teaspoon kosher salt	3½ cups (420 g) all-purpose flour
	2 tablespoons vanilla extract	8 large eggs
	2 teaspoons baking powder	
1½ cups (300 g) sugar		

1   Preheat the oven to 350°F. Lightly butter 2 standard loaf pans.

2   Combine the butter, sugar, salt, vanilla, and baking powder in the bowl of a stand mixer fit with the paddle attachment. Beat until fluffy, about 2 minutes. Add the flour and beat until the batter becomes very thick, about 20 seconds. Beat in the eggs 2 at a time, scraping down the sides of the bowl between each addition. Continue to beat for another 10 seconds. The batter will be dense. (Alternatively, you can beat the batter in a mixing bowl with a handheld mixer.)

3   Scrape the batter into the prepared pans, smoothing the top with a wet silicone spatula. Bake until a cake tester inserted into the center of each cake comes out clean, 45 to 50 minutes. Cool for 15 minutes in the pans, then turn the cakes out onto a cooling rack. Cool completely before slicing.

STORAGE NOTES ✦ To freeze, let the cakes cool completely. Wrap them tightly in plastic, then in a freezer bag. Thaw at room temperature.

SUMMER TRIFLE

Trifles are often made with sponge cake, but I love the rich, buttery texture of pound cake here in my favorite summer picnic dessert. The cake soaks up all the flavors around it, while still maintaining its own identity. If you're using more than one kind of fruit, you can either layer them separately or mix them all in together.

4 to 5 cups blueberries, sliced strawberries, raspberries, sliced peaches, or a combination 2 tablespoons sugar	¼ teaspoon balsamic vinegar 1 Pound Cake (page 285), 1 to 2 days old, cut into 1-inch cubes	⅓ cup (75 ml) cream sherry 4 cups Pastry Cream (recipe follows) Optional: Whipped Cream (page 294), for serving

1 Pick out the most perfect fruit for decoration and set aside. Combine the rest of the fruit with the sugar and balsamic vinegar and stir gently to combine. Let the mixture sit for 10 minutes.

2 Set aside a handful of pound cake cubes for the top of the trifle. Then, lay a third of the remaining pound cake on the bottom of a trifle dish or large glass bowl. Sprinkle a third of the sherry over the cake. Spoon a third of the fruit mixture over the cake, and top with a third of the pastry cream. Repeat the process, for a total of three layers of cake, fruit, and cream. Wrap tightly and refrigerate until ready to serve. Just before serving, top with the reserved fruit and pound cake and the whipped cream, if using.

PASTRY CREAM: Combine 2½ cups whole milk, ⅓ cup sugar, ¼ teaspoon kosher salt, and the seeds and pod of a vanilla bean in a saucepan. Bring to a low boil, then remove from heat and take the pod out of the mixture. While the milk mixture heats, whisk 4 egg yolks and 3 tablespoons cornstarch into another ½ cup milk. Whisk a hefty glug of the hot milk mixture into the egg mixture—then pour the whole egg mixture back into the hot milk and return the pot to heat. Bring to a boil and stir constantly until the mixture thickens into a creamy pudding, 1 to 2 minutes. Transfer to a covered container in the refrigerator to cool. Makes about 4 cups.

THE STAYCATION

There are advantages to living in a vacation destination. Whereas others have to travel and pay loads of money and find hotel reservations to enjoy our lakes and rivers and cultural attractions, we're already here. We're already on vacation. *All the time.*

Except, of course, we're not. Growing up in the Berkshires, I always saw the humor in the great numbers of people who seemed to think that the entire town disappeared when they went back home to the city.

"Does the town shut down entirely in March and April? Are there schools? What does anyone actually do for work? Is there cell service here?"

The truth is that we do what everyone does where they live: we work; we take our kids to school; we go out for a beer every so often; we have friends over for dinner. But sometimes, the reality of not vacationing in such a good place to vacation gets to us. And that's where the staycation comes in.

Sometimes it's just a day or two, when all normal work goes out the window. Instead, it's all river swimming or homemade muffins and a picnic blanket at some cultural event packed with New Yorkers. Or it might be a whole summer, when work continues as usual, but we find a way to bring a little bit of vacation into every day. There's an ice cream parlor in town that opens its doors to create space for the line that can stretch down the block as soon as winter ends (that's May, if anyone's counting). Then, it's almost as if a little alarm goes off in the girls. Every single day on the way home from school, they crane their necks toward Railroad Street and ask, "Ice cream? Just today?"

It will not be just today. For as long as school runs into the summer and beyond, every town drive-by will inspire this question. And that is why we created a box that contains a certain number of ice cream tokens, each round piece of hand-cut cardboard good for one family ice cream date. We all agree on the number of tokens for the summer, and that's how many times we'll go for ice cream that summer. And as soon as the girls agree to use a token, we head down the hill and wait on line with the rest of the tourists, and vacation has begun.

When we're out of ice cream tokens, or for the days in between, there's homemade ice cream. We can make it with all the fixings without paying an arm and a leg, and I think sitting on the back porch beats waiting in line at the ice cream parlor any day. Even more, the list of homemade flavors is limited only by our imaginations.

ICE CREAM

MAKES ABOUT 1 QUART

This is my favorite easy ice cream base. It's egg-free, so there's no fussy custarding involved, and it transforms seamlessly into any flavor you can dream of. The range of sugar and whole milk needed for the recipe varies depending on your choice of flavoring, so I've included a chart (page 292) as a guideline.

2 cups heavy cream	¼ teaspoon kosher salt	½ to 1 cup whole milk
⅓ to ½ cup sugar	Flavors and additions (chart follows)	

1 Combine 1 cup of the heavy cream, the sugar, and the salt in a medium saucepan. Warm over medium heat, stirring to dissolve the sugar.

2 Now add any flavors you want to your ice cream (see chart). Remove from heat and add the milk (see chart for quantity) and remaining 1 cup cream to the pan. Stir to combine, then cover and refrigerate for at least 2 hours and as long as 2 days.

3 Churn the mixture according to your ice cream maker's instructions. Transfer the soft ice cream to the freezer for at least 2 hours before serving.

STORAGE NOTES: Homemade ice cream freezes hard, and it gets icy in the fridge after a few days. Try to eat it within a day or two after it's made, and let it soften on the counter for a few minutes before scooping.

VANILLA

Additions: 1 vanilla bean

Method: Use ½ cup sugar and 1 cup whole milk. Cut the vanilla bean in half lengthwise and scrape the sticky seeds into the cream mixture with a paring knife. Drop the bean into the cream mixture. Remove the bean before churning.

CHOCOLATE

Additions: ½ cup Chocolate Syrup (page 297)

Method: Use ⅓ cup sugar and ⅔ cup whole milk. Stir the chocolate syrup into the hot cream mixture.

COFFEE

Additions: ½ cup Cold Brew Concentrate (page 233)

Method: Use ½ cup sugar and ½ cup whole milk. Stir the coffee concentrate into the hot cream mixture.

STRAWBERRY

Additions: 3 cups strawberries, mashed

Method: Use ⅓ cup sugar and ½ cup whole milk. Stir the mashed berries into the hot cream mixture.

MINT

Additions: 1 cup loosely packed fresh mint leaves

Method: Use ⅓ cup sugar and 1 cup whole milk. Add the mint leaves to the hot cream mixture. Cover the pot, let it infuse for 1 hour, then strain. Add the milk and remaining cream and refrigerate.

MAPLE

See page 308.

EASY CARAMEL SAUCE

MAKES 1 CUP

½ cup packed light brown sugar	4 tablespoons unsalted butter, cut into pieces	½ cup heavy cream
		¼ teaspoon kosher salt

Stir together the sugar and butter in a heavy medium saucepan over medium heat until the butter melts. Let it sit undisturbed until it begins to bubble, 2 to 3 minutes. Add the cream (it will bubble and spurt), and stir to combine. Again let the mixture cook undisturbed, this time until the color of the caramel darkens just a bit, about 3 minutes. Remove from heat, stir in the salt, and let the mixture cool slightly before serving.

STORAGE NOTES ✦ Store caramel sauce in the refrigerator. To reheat, put the jar in a bowl of near-boiling water. Stir until the caramel is loose and warm.

WHIPPED CREAM

MAKES 2 CUPS

1 cup heavy cream	1 tablespoon maple syrup or sugar	1 teaspoon vanilla extract

Combine the cream, maple syrup, and vanilla in the bowl of a stand mixer fit with the wire whip attachment. Beat until the cream holds stiff peaks, 3 to 4 minutes.

CHOCOLATE SHELL

MAKES 1 CUP

| 4 ounces bittersweet or semisweet chocolate, coarsely chopped | 3 tablespoons coconut oil | 1 tablespoon maple syrup |

Combine the chocolate, coconut oil, and maple syrup in a double boiler. Stir over medium-low heat until smooth, 3 to 5 minutes. Allow to cool slightly, then pour over ice cream. Chocolate shell will harden as soon as it comes in contact with ice cream.

STORAGE NOTES ✦ Store Chocolate Shell in the refrigerator. Reheat in a double boiler.

MAKES ABOUT 2 CUPS

This is my all-purpose chocolate syrup, and it's as great for chocolate milk and homemade mochas as it is a dessert topping. I even use it to make Chocolate Ice Cream (page 292). This makes a chocolate milk to rival that found in the ubiquitous squeeze bottle, but with only three ingredients. Although this recipe is most cost-effective with sugar, I love it with maple syrup, too. Just use an equivalent amount.

| 1 cup unsweetened cocoa powder | ½ cup packed light brown sugar | 1½ cups near-boiling water |

1 Combine the cocoa powder and sugar in a medium saucepan. Whisk in the hot water until the mixture is smooth. Cook over medium-high heat, whisking constantly, until the mixture comes to a low boil. Reduce the heat to medium and continue to whisk until the syrup thickens slightly, about 30 seconds. Let the syrup cool, then transfer to a jar or squeeze bottle.

2 To make chocolate milk, add 1 to 2 tablespoons syrup per cup of milk.

STORAGE NOTES ✦ Chocolate syrup keeps in the refrigerator for 2 weeks.

PLUM TART

My two plum trees are the heroes of my little front-yard orchard every year. One of the varieties is called Alderman, and if we wait till they're ripe, the big, juicy fruit come clean away from their center stones. These are my favorite plums for tarts and cakes, and as plum season comes to an end, we freeze hundreds of plums in freezer bags, so we can have plum tarts all winter.

This recipe is adapted from a wonderful tart made by Marianti Asymyadis for the Istanbul Organic Market. She was kind enough to share her recipe with me, and it's been helping me through every plum season since. I prefer to use smaller plums for this tart, as they cook quickly. If you're using larger or off-season plums, expect the tart to bake a little longer.

8 tablespoons (1 stick/ 115 g) cold butter, cubed, plus additional for greasing the pan

2 cups (240 g) all-purpose flour, plus additional for rolling the dough

⅓ cup (65 g) granulated sugar

1 teaspoon baking powder

1 large egg

3 to 5 tablespoons ice water

8 to 12 ripe plums (depending on their size), halved and pitted

¼ cup (23 g) sliced, blanched almonds

1 tablespoon turbinado or other coarse sugar

1 Preheat the oven to 375°F. Grease a 9- or 10-inch tart pan.

2 Combine the flour, butter, granulated sugar, and baking powder in the bowl of a food processor and pulse until the mixture resembles pea-sized crumbs. Add the egg and pulse one more time. Then, pulsing after each addition, add 1 tablespoon of ice water at a time, stopping when the dough is smooth and just a bit sticky. It will be wetter than what you'd expect from a piecrust. Gather the dough up into a ball and wrap it in plastic. Let it rest in the refrigerator for at least 30 minutes, and as long as 2 days.

3 Roll out the dough on a floured surface until it's ⅓ to ½ inch thick. Transfer to the prepared pan, trimming off any excess. (If you have enough extra crust and you have a mini-tart pan, make a smaller tartlet as well.) Lay the plums flesh side down on the crust in a single layer. Top with the blanched almonds and turbinado sugar. Bake on a rimmed baking sheet until the crust starts to brown and the plums begin to collapse and release juice, 30 to 40 minutes. The top will be filled with juice when you take it out of the oven. Let the tart sit on the counter for at least 30 minutes before you lift the tart away from the sides of the pan and cut into it. The plums will reabsorb their juice during this time.

THE RICOTTA MOUSSE TRICK

I like to have a few tricks in my back pocket to make sure I can always turn dinner into something guest-worthy. When it comes to dessert, ricotta mousse is my trick, and I'd be lost without it. My favorite time of any dinner, whether it's the four of us or a dinner party, is the last little bit, when the plates are clear, dinner was good, and we're all leaning in toward the candles that, we hope, have at least another half hour in them. It's dessert that keeps us there around the table, and there's no way I'm letting go of that.

This recipe is far too good to be as easy as it is. It takes ten minutes (five if you're speedy), pleases everyone, and chills in the fridge, so it's ready to pull out when the dishes are clear. It's also endlessly customizable, and although chocolate is a classic winner, it lends itself to all sorts of variations.

This is how it works: Put 1 pound of ricotta cheese in your food processor. It can be whole milk or part skim, store-bought or homemade (page 35). Add a pinch of salt along with something delicious to the ricotta. This could be 4 ounces of melted and slightly cooled dark chocolate mixed with a few spoonfuls of Cold Brew Concentrate (page 233), or just ¼ to ½ cup coffee concentrate with a bit of sugar or maple syrup. It could be ½ cup Lemon Curd (page 305) or strawberry jam, or ¼ cup maple syrup. Blend in the food processor until silky and smooth, about 30 seconds. Taste, and add a tablespoon of honey, maple syrup, or sugar if you think it needs a bit more sweetener. Divide among little juice glasses or ramekins, and refrigerate. Serve with whipped cream (page 294), shaved chocolate, or nothing at all.

PEAR GINGERBREAD

MAKES ONE 9 × 9-INCH CAKE

I dreamed of this cake before I ever figured out how to make it.

For an entire fall, I made every pear ginger upside-down cake and classic gingerbread with pears. Each recipe made a delicious gingerbread that just wasn't mine.

I confessed my search to a friend, who picked up the book on my table.

"And this isn't it?" She waved the little paperback book in the air. "Because Laurie Colwin's got two, and they're both perfect."

I should have known the secret was on my shelf all along. Laurie Colwin's Damp Gingerbread provided the inspiration for this cake. Serve with Whipped Cream (page 294), Crème Fraîche (page 34), Easy Caramel Sauce (page 294), or just on its own.

8 tablespoons (1 stick/ 115 g) unsalted butter, plus additional for the pan	2 cups (240 g) all-purpose flour	¼ teaspoon grated nutmeg
	½ teaspoon kosher salt	1 large egg
½ cup (120 ml) Lyle's Golden Syrup or honey	1 teaspoon baking soda	1 cup (225 g) plain whole-milk yogurt (for homemade, see page 34)
½ cup (110 g) packed light brown sugar	2 tablespoons ground ginger	
	½ teaspoon ground cloves	2 Bosc pears, peeled and cut into ¼-inch slices
	1 teaspoon ground cinnamon	

1 Preheat the oven to 350°F. Grease a 9-inch square or equivalent pan.

2 In a small saucepan, melt together the butter, syrup, and brown sugar over low heat. Gently stir to combine as the mixture melts. Set aside.

3 In a medium mixing bowl, whisk together the flour, salt, baking soda, ginger, cloves, cinnamon, and nutmeg. Pour the butter mixture into the flour mixture and combine with a few strokes of a wooden spoon, taking care not to overmix.

4 In a small bowl, whisk together the egg and yogurt. Add the egg mixture to the batter, and gently combine. Transfer the batter to the prepared pan.

5 Lay the pears on top of the batter in a pinwheel shape. Bake until a toothpick or cake tester comes out clean when inserted into the cake, 30 to 35 minutes.

STORAGE NOTES ✦ Store tightly wrapped at room temperature. This cake gets better on the second and even third day.

THE LOST CAUSE

For years, I hovered over the lemon trees my local nursery kept in their greenhouse. They were spindly and delicate, as if clearly pissed off to be in New England. I would say the trees called to me, but it was more of a challenge.

"You just try, you silly locavore. You try to keep me alive. Move to Florida if you want a lemon tree."

But still, I wanted to eat real, fresh lemons that didn't smell like an old refrigerator. So Joey bought me a lemon tree for my birthday.

Immediately, the tree erupted in blooms, and my house smelled of life and sweetness and hope. I showed off my tree to every guest as if it had a little routine to perform.

"Bloom!" I commanded. "Isn't it doing such a good job blooming?"

The smell would intensify at certain moments, and the air in the kitchen would make me drunk. The tree stood handsomely in its faux terra cotta pot, and I built barriers around it when toddlers came over. What if they plucked its precious leaves? Every time someone would open the door, I'd shout, "Close the door! The tree is getting chilled."

The blooms transformed into tiny green lemons. They grew, slowly, and I moved the tree around as the sun moved through the house. The lemons became marbled, green mixed with yellow, and I knew they were almost there. The leaves also turned yellow, and then brown. My friend Lisa, who also has a lemon tree, said that I shouldn't worry.

"This is what happens! You think it's dead, but it's just resting. It will all be fine."

I believed her. I was blinded by love, and I had ten of the most expensive, loved, and local lemons in New England. I picked each lemon, and I lined them up on the counter. I zested every fruit, and I squeezed each perfect hemisphere until every bit of juice filled my measuring cup. I used eggs from my neighbor's chickens, and I whisked up nearly a full quart jar of lemon curd. It was nothing less than sweetened, buttery sunshine, and I felt its glow every time I opened the refrigerator. We ate it on everything: in yogurt, on toast, on a spoon. And as the jar emptied, and I declared the lemon experiment a great success, my tree dropped its very last leaf, and, in fact, died.

Still, that was the best lemon curd I've ever had.

LEMON CURD

If you can get organic lemons, do, as you'll be using lots of the zest. The flavor of the eggs comes through too, so if you have access to fresh eggs, this is a good place for them.

¾ cup (180 ml) lemon juice, from 4 to 5 room-temperature lemons	8 tablespoons (1 stick/ 115 g) unsalted butter, cut into chunks	1¼ cups (250 g) sugar
Grated zest of 4 lemons		5 large eggs, beaten

1 Combine the lemon juice, zest, butter, and sugar in the bowl of a double boiler over medium-low heat and stir just until the butter melts.

2 Add the eggs to the bowl, pouring them through a fine-meshed sieve. Whisk to combine, and rinse out your sieve for the next step.

3 Stir, scraping down the sides of the bowl as you go, until the mixture thickens and gets creamy, 5 to 8 minutes. Pour through your sieve into a jar.

STORAGE NOTES ✦ Lemon curd stays good in the refrigerator for up to 2 weeks. It also freezes well for up to 6 months.

LEMON CURD *with* YOGURT *and* TOASTED ALMONDS

This is a simple dessert, perfect for those nights when we need the ritual of dessert.

2 cups plain whole-milk yogurt (for homemade, see page 34)	½ cup Lemon Curd (recipe above)	½ cup sliced almonds, toasted

Divide the yogurt among 4 to 6 juice glasses or ramekins. Add a hefty dollop of lemon curd and top with toasted almonds.

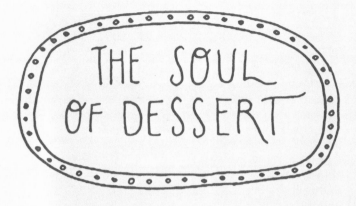
THE SOUL OF DESSERT

It's a Wednesday in October, and I'm making baked apples. It's just an ordinary Wednesday. No one's coming over; there's no birthday or special accomplishment to celebrate. But still, I'm making dessert.

"What's that smell?" Rosie pops into the kitchen. "Are you making dessert?"

If you've ever smelled a baked apple, you know exactly what she means. The combination of cinnamon and fruit and the apple as it caramelizes—there's nothing like it.

"I am." There's no use trying to keep a secret when a smell like that is coming out of the oven.

Her eyebrows pop up, and she hops to give herself a little boost as she throws herself back down the hall. "SADIE! MOM IS MAKING DESSERT!"

And with that, an ordinary Wednesday becomes something else entirely. It's hard to see how a few apples and a little brown sugar can have so much power, but they do. The little bit of sweetness, that specialness, and most of all, the above-and-beyond quality of that extra last course transforms moods, creates an occasion out of anything, and changes the whole night. It doesn't have to be anything fancy. It can be just a little fruit and cream, or a simple plate of dried fruit, chocolate, and a few nuts. But the soul of dessert, and all it holds, creates a celebration of the moment, however ordinary it may be. What are we celebrating? Take your pick. Anything. Anything at all.

SERVES 4

This is probably my favorite way to use apples in the kitchen. the recipe is simple enough to make on a weekday, fancy enough to end a dinner party, and loved by kids and adults alike.

An apple corer is a great tool to have for this recipe (it also comes in handy for Apple Chips page 230). Make sure the hole in the center of each apple is over an inch wide. That way, you'll have lots of room for filling and the apples will cook evenly.

1 vanilla bean

2 tablespoons packed light brown sugar

3 tablespoons dried currants

¼ cup chopped almonds, toasted

½ teaspoon ground cardamom

½ teaspoon ground cinnamon

¼ teaspoon kosher salt

4 large apples, cored

½ to 2 cups apple cider (depending on the size of your vessel)

5 cardamom pods

1 teaspoon fresh lemon juice

1 tablespoon maple syrup

2 tablespoons unsalted butter, cut into 4 pieces

Maple Ice Cream (page 308)

1 Preheat the oven to 350°F. Use a small paring knife to open up the vanilla bean lengthwise. Then, use the tip of the knife to scrape the sticky inner seeds into a small bowl. (Save the pod for the next step.) Add the brown sugar, currants, almonds, cardamom, cinnamon, and salt to the bowl and stir to combine.

2 Set the apples in a baking dish or roasting pan with the holes facing up. Stuff the holes to overflowing with the fruit/nut mixture. Pour the apple cider into the pan so that it comes about an inch up the apples. Throw the vanilla bean pod into the liquid, along with the cardamom pods, lemon juice, and maple syrup. Distribute the pieces of butter throughout the liquid.

3 Bake the apples, uncovered, until they are soft and bursting, about an hour. Cool slightly, then remove the cardamom pods and vanilla bean pod from the liquid. Serve with lots of the baking liquid, topped with maple ice cream.

MAPLE ICE CREAM

MAKES 1 QUART

When I was a kid, one of the highlights of the sugaring season was maple tea, a thrown-together combination of maple sap, heavy cream, and Lipton tea. My mother worked at a farm, and I'd stop by the sugar shack whenever I could in the hopes of a warm cup of the sweet creamy tea. This simple ice cream is the taste of that memory, and it's become my very favorite one to make at home. There's no whisking of eggs or stirring over the stove, so the base comes together in just a moment. If you can get grade B maple syrup, use it here. The deeper the maple flavor, the better the ice cream.

2 cups heavy cream ¾ cup whole milk	½ cup maple syrup (grade B is best for this, if you have a choice)	¼ teaspoon kosher salt

1 Combine the cream, milk, maple syrup, and salt in a quart jar. Screw on the lid and give it a good shake to combine the ingredients.

2 Pour the maple mixture into your ice cream maker and churn according to the manufacturer's instructions. Transfer to a freezer-safe container and freeze for 2 hours before serving.

ACKNOWLEDGMENTS

Thank you.

To my agent and my hero, Rob Weisbach.

To Jennifer May, for inviting me a second time into the gorgeous world she sees through her camera lens. I couldn't ask for a better partner in all of this.

To Lissa McGovern, recipe tester, dishwasher, proofreader, and friend. It's a more wonderful world with you in it.

To Erin McDowell, who can make a piecrust beautiful enough to bring on tears of joy.

To my editor, Doris Cooper, for always being kind, thoughtful, and most of all, right.

To Marysarah Quinn and Stephanie Huntwork, for saving the day and showing me how beautiful a page really can be.

To Emily Takoudes, for her support through the first stages of this book.

To everyone at Clarkson Potter: Jane Treuhaft, Lauren Monchik, Ada Yonenaka, Kim Tyner, Kate Tyler, Anna Mintz, Carly Gorga, Aaron Wehner, and Michael Nagin.

To those who helped me through the tense moments, tested and inspired recipes, gave me quiet corners to write, let me borrow their favorite dishes, and popped in to inspire me when I needed it most: Kari Chapin, Eric Nixon, Janet Reich Elsbach, Jess Fechtor, Megan Gordon, Cheryl Sternman Rule, Morgan Smith, Jane Kasden, Christina Davis, Emily Kasden, Molly de St. Andre, Carrie Bachman, Courtney Maum, Isabella Califano Erlich, Dani Shapiro, Andrew Smith, Megan Sielken, Ben Ransford, Teresa Lee, Mollie Katzen, Lisa Landry, Hedley Stone, Mistral Louw, Aimée Wimbush Bourque, Marisa McClellan, John McCarthy and Juan Manzo, Jean-François and Helen Bizalion, Carol Nash, Sarah Yanni and Jefferson Navicky, and Maria Leigh.

To Sascha Woolfe, who thought she was just labeling my spice jars, but really was creating the typography of my homemade kitchen.

To Abby Webster of One Mercantile in Great Barrington, Massachusetts, who let me fill the book with all her beautiful things.

To everyone at Hammertown in Great Barrington, Massachusetts, for their kindness, generosity, and classy stuff.

To Janna Lufkin at Raw Materials for making my very favorite aprons.

To those who contributed their gorgeous work to this book: Daniel Bellow of Daniel Bellow Porcelain and Arla Bascom of Wheel and Loom.

To the Tuesday night crew, for always being up for a dinner party.

To the farmers who created food for the photos in this book: Elizabeth Keen and Al Thorpe of Indian Line Farm, Jen and Pete Salinetti of Woven Roots Farm, and Sean Stanton of North Plain Farm.

To Gordon and Mary at Strawberry Hill for sharing their raspberries, and to Echo, for helping Joey pick them.

To the readers of *Eating from the Ground Up*, who keep me sane, honest, and writing.

To the memory of Lenny Chernila, for teaching me that the celebration is the revolution.

To my sister, Maia, the best berry picker in the Berkshires.

To my parents, Jamie and Chris Vlcek, for being there for me, unconditionally.

To Sadie, for constant inspiration and honest reports on every bite.

To Rosie, for filling my days with love.

And to Joey, the cream in my coffee, the fancy salt on my egg, the butter on my bread. With you, life is always so good.

BIBLIOGRAPHY

The following books were particularly helpful to me during the writing of this book, whether for their recipes, instruction, power of inspiration, or a combination of the three.

Carroll, Ricki. *Home Cheese Making*. North Adams, MA: Storey, 2002.

Chang, Joanne. *Flour: Spectacular Recipes from Boston's Flour Bakery + Café*. San Francisco: Chronicle Books, 2010.

Colwin, Laurie. *Home Cooking: A Writer in the Kitchen*. New York: Vintage, 1988.

———. *More Home Cooking: A Writer Returns to the Kitchen*. New York: Vintage, 1993.

Corbin, Pam. *The River Cottage Preserves Handbook*. Berkeley: Ten Speed Press, 2010.

Gray, Patience. *Honey from a Weed: Fasting and Feasting in Catalonia, the Cyclades, and Apulia*. New York: Harpercollins, 1987.

Henry, Diana. *Salt Sugar Smoke*. Chicago: Mitchell Beazley, 2012.

Jordi, Natalie, et. al. *People's Pops*. Berkeley: Ten Speed Press, 2012.

Karlin, Mary. *Mastering Fermentation*. Berkeley: Ten Speed Press, 2013.

Kasper, Lynne Rossetto. *The Splendid Table: Recipes from Emilia-Romagna, the Heartland of Northern Italian Food*. New York: William Morrow, 1992.

Katz, Sandor. *Wild Fermentation*. White River Junction, VT: Chelsea Green, 2003.

———. *The Art of Fermentation*. White River Junction, VT: Chelsea Green, 2012.

Katzen, Mollie. *Moosewood Cookbook*. Berkeley: Ten Speed Press, 1977.

———. *The Enchanted Broccoli Forest*. Berkeley: Ten Speed Press, 1982.

———. *Honest Pretzels*. Berkeley: Tricycle Press, 2009.

King Arthur Flour. *The King Arthur Flour Baker's Companion*. Woodstock, VT: Countryman Press, 2003.

Madison, Deborah. *Local Flavors: Cooking and Eating from America's Farmers' Markets*. Berkeley: Ten Speed Press, 2008.

Nguyen, Andrea. *Asian Tofu: Discover the Best, Make Your Own, and Cook It at Home*. Berkeley: Ten Speed Press, 2012.

Sass, Lorna. *Whole Grains Every Day, Every Way*. New York: Clarkson Potter, 2006.

Waters, Alice. *The Art of Simple Food*. New York: Clarkson Potter, 2007.

INDEX